"Syd Field is the preeminent analyzer in the study of American screenplays. Incredibly, he manages to remain idealistic while rendering practical 'how to' books."

—James L. Brooks,
Scriptwriter, *The Mary Tyler Moore Show*,
Terms of Endearment, Broadcast News

"An informative, engaging look at the inside of the dream factory. This is a terrific aid for screenwriters who are trying to gain insight into the Hollywood system."

—David Kirkpatrick,
President, Touchstone Pictures

"A wonderful book that should be in every filmmaker's library."

—Howard Kazanjian,
Executive Producer, *Raiders of the Lost Ark;*
Producer, *Return of the Jedi, The Rookie,*
More American Graffiti

"If I ever decide to do something crazy, like try to sell a screenplay, this is the book I'll stuff in my back pocket when I go to market."

—Steven Bochco,
Producer, *Hill Street Blues, L.A. Law, Civil Wars*

FIND OUT HOW THESE INNOVATIVE, SUCCESSFUL
SCREENWRITERS MADE THEIR SCREENPLAYS
INTO TODAY'S BEST FILMS

OLIVER STONE

Midnight Express, Scarface, Platoon, Wall Street

DAN PETRIE, JR.

Beverly Hills Cop, The Big Easy, Shoot to Kill

ALVIN SARGENT

The Sterile Cuckoo, Paper Moon, Julia, Ordinary People

JAMES L. BROOKS

The Mary Tyler Moore Show, Terms of Endearment, Broadcast News

ANNA HAMILTON PHELAN

Mask, Gorillas in the Mist

DOUGLAS DAY STEWART

An Officer and a Gentleman, The Boy in the Plastic Bubble, Blue Lagoon

WILLIAM KELLEY/EARL WALLACE

Witness

Books by Syd Field:

The Screenwriter's Workbook

Screenplay: The Foundations of Screenwriting

Selling a Screenplay: The Screenwriter's Guide to Hollywood

Four Screenplays

The Screenwriter's Problem Solver:

How to recognize, identify, and define screenwriting

problems

Selling a Screenplay

The Screenwriter's Guide to Hollywood

Syd Field

A DELL TRADE PAPERBACK

A DELL TRADE PAPERBACK
Published by
Dell Publishing
a division of
Bantam Doubleday Dell Publishing Group, Inc.
1540 Broadway
New York, New York 10036

ISBN: 0-440-50244-6

Printed in the United States of America

Published simultaneously in Canada

December 1989

20 19 18 17 16 15 14

BVG

Contents

"Hollywood is the only place where you can die from encouragement."

Dorothy Parker

To Gurumayi

and all the Siddha masters who have walked the path

ACKNOWLEDGMENTS

Special thanks to all those who shared themselves so openly for the benefit of screenwriters everywhere. . . .

And to Margie, who waded through hours and hours of transcribing tapes burdened with the noise and clatter of restaurants. . . .

And to Dan, Gabrielle, Hugh, and Carolyn of the Writer's Computer Store in West Los Angeles, who were always there when I needed them.

Preface

At the 1987 Academy Awards, Steven Spielberg was presented with the Irving Thalberg Award, given to an individual filmmaker whose body of work reflects a consistently high quality of creative motion picture production.

"I'm told Irving Thalberg worshiped writers," he said in his acceptance speech, "and that's where it all begins. We are first and foremost storytellers, and without, as he called it, the photoplay, everybody is simply improvising. He also knew that a script is more than just a blueprint. That the whole idea of movie magic is that interweave of powerful image, dialogue, performance, and music that can never be separated—and when it's working right, can never be duplicated or ever forgotten.

"I've grown up most of my life sitting in the dark, looking at movies. Movies have been the literature of my life. The literature of Irving Thalberg's generation was books and plays. They read the great words of great minds. In our romance with technology and our excitement at exploring all the possibilities of film and video, I think we've partially lost something that we now have to reclaim. I think it is time to renew our romance with the word . . . for only a generation of readers will spawn a generation of writers."

Introduction: On the Road to Find Out

"When you try to second-guess Hollywood, you only end up in heart-break." That's what one film executive told me when I interviewed her, and it's true.

Everybody tries to second-guess Hollywood. People in and out of the industry think they know what the public likes and what the public wants, what will sell, what will not sell. But the truth is nobody really knows.

Why then are more people than ever before writing screenplays? In 1988 more than 40,000 scripts were registered at the Writers Guild of America West and East. The two most popular courses on college campuses today are business and film, and the "great American novel" has been replaced by the "great American screenplay."

Today America is a *visual* society: we get our news on television, we *see* our music on MTV, our books are presold to movies or television, and our children are learning to use computers in grade school. Everything is visual, and it's going to be more so in the future.

The movie business is *big* business, and the prices movie companies are willing to pay for screenplays can be astronomical. Six-figure sales prices have become common, and a few writers are paid a million dollars or more a script.

If you've written a screenplay and spent months, perhaps years, writing and rewriting, what do you have to do to sell it? Are there any set, prescribed rules to follow? What are they? Do you need an agent? How do you go about getting one? What does he or she look for in a screenplay?

Or if you're thinking about writing a screenplay, what are you going to write about? Is there any way you can "scope out" the market to see if there *is* a market for what you want to write?

When I first started writing this book, I wasn't really clear on the specifics of what I wanted to say. All I knew was that this was going to be a book about selling a screenplay.

My original idea was to interview people in Hollywood whose job it is to buy and sell screenplays, but as I began my interviews, I started to focus on what producers and executives look for in a screenplay. When I interviewed Don Simpson and Jerry Bruckheimer, two of the most successful producers in Hollywood, I realized their success is due to their unique ability to create material; you don't make films like *Flashdance, Beverly Hills Cop, Beverly Hills Cop II,* and *Top Gun* without knowing what you're doing.

When I interviewed producer Peter Guber, perhaps the most creative entrepreneur in Hollywood, I learned the process he goes through in terms of isolating and defining the "success factors" in making movies, building a package, or marketing a project.

It was at this point that I began to realize this book was to be about more than just selling a screenplay and was turning out to be an inside look at the process a film executive goes through in order to make a movie.

Success in Hollywood is getting the movie made, whether you're an agent, producer, or executive, and I learned very quickly that everybody in Hollywood is both a buyer and a seller. If an executive says "Yes, I love this script and want to buy it," it means that he has to turn around and *sell* it to his boss, whether that person be the head of production, the CEO, or the chairman of the board.

In most cases the reason anybody buys a script in Hollywood is that they *believe* in the material. The biggest selling tool someone has at their disposal is their belief in the project, and they must communicate that belief with passion and persuasion. That's why there's so much hype in the film business.

Hype will take you only so far, however. The truth is, if you want to sell something, you've got to have something to sell. That "something" can be an idea or a concept, and it may exist initially in the form of a script, book, play, magazine article, or even personal experience. In other words, it can be *anything* that can be turned into a screenplay.

So what started out as a text on how to sell a screenplay has evolved into a book about the inside workings of Hollywood, as seen from the point of view and perspective of the people who are the writers, buyers, sellers, and moviemakers.

Part One
Buyers and Sellers

The Market

The market potential for the screenwriter is enormous. But what *is* the market? How do you describe it, define it, articulate it?

That was a question I kept asking myself over and over again. In my screenwriting experience, I had never explored the market, had never taken the time to find out what the parameters were and how they effected the writer.

I had some notions about the market, yes, but nothing else. The only thing I had, really, was the question, What is the market for the screenwriter today?

The market is a vague and nebulous term. You can talk to ten different people and get ten different answers. A producer views a script differently than an agent; an agent views it differently than a studio executive; a studio executive views it differently than a reader; the reader views it differently than an independent producer; an independent producer views it differently than a marketing executive; a marketing executive views it differently than a person in development. And so on.

So I went to a friend of mine, Stan Corwin, an independent producer and publisher, who with his partner found a novel titled ". . . *And Ladies of the Club*" and through sheer marketing strategy catapulted it onto the *New York Times* best-seller list as the number-one best seller for over a year. If anyone knows what the market is, I thought to myself, it would be Stan, now president of Tudor Communications, a national paperback and film development company.

So, we sat down and talked, and during the course of the conversation I slipped in *The Question:* What is the market?

"For what?" he replied.

I looked at him, taken aback. "An original screenplay," I replied.

He looked at me for a moment. Then, "What kind of screenplay?" he asked guardedly.

I took a deep breath and shifted into my most confident, optimistic attitude. I didn't know what to say. What kind of screenplay would I like to write, I wondered, and immediately thought of *The Last Emperor*. "A period action-adventure," I said.

"That's a tough one."

"Why?"

He explained that in today's movie market a big-budget, period screenplay is a very difficult sale. What about a contemporary script, a comedy, or action-adventure? I asked. The first thing you have to do, he said, is see if there are any buyers interested in the material.

"Who are the buyers?"

He then gave me a thumbnail sketch of the marketplace for film and television. Most feature films, he told me, are produced or distributed by the eight major studios: Twentieth Century Fox, Disney, Paramount, Universal, MGM, UA, and Columbia (which has since merged with Tri-Star). Then there are the many independent production companies that supply the studio with product: Amblin, David Geffen, Weintraub Entertainment, Don Simpson/Jerry Bruckheimer Productions, Carolco, Cannon, Hemdale, Kings Road, Lorimar, Guber-Peters, and many, many more. These are some of the buyers and the producers of films.

In television, the buyers are the three networks, ABC, CBS, NBC, now joined by Fox Broadcasting, and the Public Broadcasting Service (PBS). At the present time the market is proliferating, and cable TV is emerging as a major market; video companies like Vestron, HBO, Showtime, Lorimar, and Prism are becoming the suppliers of product, and they are starting to initiate their own projects rather than buying or renting them from the studios.

Today, to intelligently discuss the marketplace, you've got to understand that there are many different combinations that can get a movie made. You can create your own, just like creating your own omelet in a restaurant. For example, a producer could buy or option a screenplay, and then generate a combination of financing from Paramount, a studio, Hemdale, an independent production company, and Vestron, a cable TV company; then he could presell the project in Europe so that by the first day of principal photography the production costs of the film are covered. That's the way they did *Platoon*.

In other words the market is a living, breathing entity that reflects the time and economic conditions of the industry and, of course, the country. It changes constantly. The market is not just one thing, it's many things, and if you're looking to expand your awareness of what the market is, you can't be limited by what you don't know.

At the present time the marketplace is more sophisticated than it ever was. You can walk into an agent's office, whether it be the William Morris Agency, ICM, CAA, or Triad, and the tables and shelves are lined from floor to ceiling with screenplays, galleys, and books from New York publishers.

That's what you're competing against if you're trying to sell the screenplay you hold in your hand. Last year, remember, more than 40,000 screenplays were registered at the Writers Guild of America and less than 120 movies were made.

How do you deal with that? How do you go about trying to get your screenplay read, either by an agent for representation, or by a studio or a producer, to get it made? Everybody in Hollywood, I began to see, was a buyer and a seller.

I thought about that for a while. Then I remembered something I'd read in a Kurt Vonnegut novel: when you're trying to find the answer to a question, the answer is in the question.

Is that true? If the answer is found in the question, how does it relate to the market and the selling of the screenplay? And then one day, while riding my bike, it dawned on me that when you write a script you create the marketplace. Who you present your material to, and how you present it, is almost as important as the screenplay itself.

That would certainly explain why so many terrible movies get made.

When you have a script you want to put into the marketplace you've got to have some kind of a plan, a strategy; your primary goal is to get somebody to respond to your material. Don't just write a letter and start sending your script all over town and hope that somebody's going to be interested. It doesn't work that way.

To get somebody to read your script with any degree of interest or enthusiasm, you've got to find out who might be interested in what you've written. Here's an exercise that may possibly define a market for your screenplay. Take a sheet of paper and make four columns. The first column is for agents you want to represent your work. That's assuming, of course, that you don't have an agent. The second column is for casting the major roles. Who's the best actor or actress for the part? Write it down. Who else? Write it down. Do as many as you can. The third column is a list of possible directors or filmmakers you think would do this kind of material. The fourth column is a list of people you know in the industry.

Everybody knows somebody. When you start thinking about who you know in the industry start jotting down names, and before you know it, you'll find somebody—a friend, relative, lover—who knows somebody who knows somebody. You'll end up with twenty or thirty names of people who might be interested in your screenplay.

If you want to get an agent to represent your work, make a list of the agents. You can get a complete list from the Writers Guild of America West, Inc., 8955 Beverly Boulevard, Los Angeles, CA 90048, (213) 501-2000. They'll send you a list of authorized agents, some of whom, as indicated, are willing to read unsolicited screenplays. Make a list of ten agents, then call or write, telling them you've written a screenplay and asking if they would be interested in reading it. If you write, you might include a one- or two-sentence story line, but no more. I would recommend calling and talking to the secretary. A secretary can be your best friend. If the agent is not interested in reading your material, ask if they can recommend anybody. This is how you start compiling your list of agents.

Most of them will say no. Keep trying.

When you find an agent who is willing to read your script, submit it and then wait four to six weeks. If you do not get a reply by then, call and ask if they received the screenplay. If they have, ask if there's a good time for you to call, say in a couple of weeks. Call in a couple of weeks. Agents, like other people, respond to passion and persistence, but not to annoyance.

You can send the screenplay to as many agents as you like. You should be so lucky that they all like your material.

People sometimes talk about the mystique of the agent. There is no mystique. An agent should serve you the same way your stockbroker, real estate agent, or insurance agent serves you.

One of my students, after writing a screenplay in my screenwriting workshop, spent five months trying to find an agent to represent it. Seventeen agents said no before she found one to say yes. That agent sold the script within six weeks—for $250,000.

Sometimes it's easier to get a response from a producer or production company than it is from an agent. Most companies require you to sign a release, stating you are submitting this material and that you release the company from all liability if a movie similar in story and theme ever gets made. Some companies, like Steven Spielberg's Amblin Entertainment, will not read any unsolicited material with or without a release.

Determine the parameters of your market and make your screenplay submission an event. I remember a conversation I had with Tony Bill, coproducer of *The Sting* (David Ward) and *Taxi Driver* (Paul Schrader), director of *My Bodyguard* (Alan Ormsby) and *Five Corners* (John Patrick Shanley), and a well-known actor. He told me about a man who sent him a screenplay. Tony was in his office one day when he was called to the front lobby. When he arrived he found an elegantly attired chauffeur waiting for him holding a large gift-wrapped box. He gave it to Tony, then left. When he opened the box, he found another box inside. He opened that one, and inside was a note on a silver tray: "It arrives on Thursday."

This was on a Monday.

On Tuesday the chauffeur arrived with another gift-wrapped box, and the note inside read "Thursday's the day."

On Wednesday the same thing happened.

Thursday arrived. By this time everybody in the office was curious. Around noon an armored car pulled up and the chauffeur stepped out, picked up a package, and walked inside. When he arrived, he placed on an embroidered maroon pillow a ten-by-thirteen envelope and presented it to Tony, who took it and opened it.

Guess what was inside? A script, of course. A covering letter proclaimed that this screenplay was exactly what the movie industry was looking for, a story that would appeal to a massive audience, and that Tony was absolutely the perfect filmmaker for it. Tony Bill couldn't say no. He had to read the screenplay. You can't ask for more than that.

The script either stands or falls on its own. In this case the script wasn't very good; the script was a C, the delivery an A+. But what imagination and ingenuity the writer had in presenting his material! That's class.

To get a broader perspective, I decided to interview a number of industry professionals whose job it is to know the market. I talked to a studio executive, an independent producer, an executive for an independent production company, a screenwriter who used to be an agent, a director of marketing, and a reader.

I really didn't know what I was looking for, or what I was going to find out; all I knew is that I wanted to ask a basic question: what is the market for the screenwriter today?

"Anything an audience wants to see," says Sidney Ganis, now president of production at Paramount Pictures, and formerly head of worldwide marketing for George Lucas. In other words, there's a market for everything. Ganis, responsible for the marketing of *Raiders of the Lost Ark, The Empire Strikes Back, Return of the Jedi*, and more, is in my opinion the sharpest marketing expert in the business. Since he's been at Paramount, he's worked on the marketing campaigns of such movies as *Beverly Hills Cop II* (Larry Fergason and Warren Skaaren), *Top Gun* (Jim Cash and Jack Epps, Jr.), and *Fatal Attraction.*

Everybody's looking for product. You'll find old TV shows, live comedy, sporting events, anything that's ever been filmed to be a potential subject. It's almost like the book business was fifty years ago.

Everybody I interviewed agreed on one thing: before the writer even attempts to write a screenplay, he or she must research the market to find out if anybody is doing anything similar, or if anybody has any scripts in development along the same lines. Many of my students spend more than six months writing a screenplay only to learn that a movie with a similar idea is just about to be released. Doing some simple research before you sit down to write makes all the sense in the world. Why spend six months to a year writing a screenplay that has no chance of being sold because something just like it is in the works?

Take responsibility for defining the market. You've got to know who's doing what for which studio. You can find that out very simply, by reading the trade papers, *Variety* and *The Hollywood Reporter*. Every Tuesday a production chart lists all films currently before the cameras. If you need to know what the story line is, try calling the production office at the studio. Talk to anyone who will talk to you; as mentioned, secretaries are wonderful. They won't necessarily tell you the story line or answer all your questions, but you could tell them you're thinking of writing a story about such and such and ask if it is close to what they're doing.

Before you begin, you must determine the market for yourself.

A student of mine—an actress who came to me to write a mystery thriller—completed a first words-on-paper draft and the rewrite during the course of three workshop sessions. She's a good writer; the story was well constructed and rich in character. When it was complete, I sent the material to a production executive I thought might be interested. She liked it but had to pass, as the star she worked for had just finished a detective story.

My student then asked if I could help her get an agent. So I called a few, who read it and agreed it was good, well-written material that showed a lot of potential. But they passed. That's show biz.

Now my student calls and wants me to tell her what to do. I don't have the time anymore. I did what I could. Rather than determine the market for herself, she wants me to guide her.

She's got to read the trades, call the agents, call the production companies, call the agents of the actors she thinks are right for the parts, call the people she knows in the industry; in other words, she's got to determine if there's a market for her script.

It only takes one person to like it. Just one.

Right now is a wonderful time for the writer of the original screen-play. Everybody's dying for good material. Independent producers and major production companies are springing up every day, and they're willing to pay a lot of money for a screenplay they like and think is commercial.

Dennis Shryack is a marvelous example of a screenwriter in Hollywood. Working with a partner, Shryack wrote such films as *Pale Rider, Gauntlet, Flashpoint, The Good Guys and Bad Guys*, and *The Car*. He started out in the shipping department at Universal Studios, worked on the old *General Electric Theater,* then became a literary agent. He worked first at the Sindell Agency, where I first met him, then moved to Eisenback-Greene-Duchow. He stayed there several years, then started writing original screenplays. When his screenplay for *The Good Guys and the Bad Guys* was sold, written with Ron Cohen, he left the agency and became a full-time writer.

"When I was an agent, I was always on top of things," he says. "I knew exactly what every producer was looking for. I went out every day and talked to them. You have to understand that when you go out with an original screenplay to sell, you have no package, no star, no director. The script has to stand or fall on its own.

"Your script has to get past all those initial readers to the head of the studio who reads it and sees nothing but dollar signs. Their job is to pass, so you can't give them a reason to say no. And the bottom line is money. They've got to read it and know if they buy this script (a) they can cast it, and (b) even if they can't get a big name for it, the picture itself, the idea, the action, or whatever else is in it, is going to sell it.

"On the other hand they've got to feel free to go to the marketing people and say 'What do you guys think? Can we sell it in Europe? Will it play Japan?' The marketing guys are the number-two guys at the studio now, and they're very important."

Sidney Ganis explains the process. "If the studio is thinking of buying a script, this is what happens most of the time: 'What do you think of this story?' the production executive asks. 'What is it that you think is marketable? What happens if we put Robert De Niro in it? What happens if we put Charles Grodin in it, and not De Niro? In your marketing opinion what elements are going to make this idea work?'

"We have a script right now in production," he continues, "that is about a kid committing suicide (*Permanent Record,* written by Jarre

Fees, Alice Liddle, and Larry Ketron). A very serious subject matter. And this story is about what happens to his friends. How this has changed their lives forever. We have two marketable lines. We can possibly market it directly to a seventeen–eighteen-year-old audience, to whom the subject matter is extremely important. So we can use suicide as an element to sell the movie.

"The other thing we can talk about is the exact opposite of that, that is, what happens to the group of friends? How do they come together, and how do they decide to live their lives after this has happened? What good, uplifting connection is made between the tragedy and moving on with their own lives?

"One of the ways we figure this out is by isolating the elements and creating story concepts and then testing those concepts through market research. We feature different elements of the story in each of the different concepts. We'll write three separate and distinct ways to position the story and send those concepts into the world, via our research machinery. One concept would likely be about teenage suicide, another would be about 'renewal,' and a third would be about the cast of highly talented young newcomers in a story set in contemporary teenage times. As we sample potential audiences, you'd be amazed at how clear people are about what's going to turn them on to see a movie. It's a good technique and gives us a sense of how we might position our advertising. I say 'might' only because you can never count on research to tell you what to do. As long as we're in this business, it's going to be our own instincts plus whatever other intelligence we can gather to finally lead us in an appropriate direction."

This is standard marketing procedure within the industry. Using insight and basic marketing skills, the marketing people isolate and select those few elements that can sell a picture. Just look at *Fatal Attraction* (James Dearden). The emotional ingredients of a brief extramarital encounter are carried to their logical extreme. It is, as advertised, a "terrifying love story." Sometimes the consequences of an emotionally charged moment can be very high.

There are certain elements in a screenplay that evoke an interesting response from the reader, and that's what marketing people look for. Fanny Couturie, staff reader for the David Geffen Company, argues that "there will always be movies that cater to the most basic audience interests. But in the last couple of years, mainstream audiences have become more interested in movies that are less obvious, less flagrantly commercial. They seem to be ready for something more thought-provoking or unusual. Movies like *Amadeus* (Peter Shaffer), *Stand by Me* (Raynold Gideon and Bruce Evans), *Platoon* (Oliver Stone), *Blue Velvet* (David Lynch), and *Beetlejuice* (Michael McDowell and Warren Skaaren) might not have been produced five years ago and are reaching a much bigger audience than they would have then. We're on the edge of the culture in this business, so the scripts I recommend change with the times. It's only natural, and I have to say I'm delighted with this particular change.

"When you work as a reader," she continues, "the executives you work for are bound to disagree with your decisions from time to time. So I'm analytical. I don't just give my opinion. I try to explain why I think a script works or doesn't work, why I think it will play well or fall flat for an audience. When executives can understand how I think about a script, I feel they're in a better position to form their own opinions and to improve a script even if they disagree with my recommendations."

Anyone who evaluates the market—reader, head of marketing, or studio executive—has to know what elements seem to be the most salable ingredients of the individual screenplay.

"What astounds me," says one studio executive, "is that writers go off and spend months of their lives writing a screenplay before they go to the trouble to find out what pictures are being made, and what pictures the studios are about to make. There've been too many occasions where a script, or a story, or an idea that someone comes up with is very similar to Steven Spielberg's next movie, and how the hell are you going to sell that?

"I think selling a script," he continues, "is the same thing as getting a job. The talents of getting a job in the movie business are the same talents that are required to become and stay successful. They are initiative, exploration, original thinking, and innovative ideas.

"Many writers—and I read more than five hundred scripts a year—do not realize that a screenplay is a selling document. When they're writing a screenplay, they're not writing a movie. They're writing a script, material that's going to be read, not seen. And it's the reading experience that will determine whether the movie gets made or not.

"For example, we read a script about three brothers. They all grew up in the backwoods, hillbilly country. Two of them moved away to the city, and one stayed behind. In the city one of the brothers goes crooked, the other becomes a cop. The script opens with one of the brothers being killed, and the hillbilly brother comes to the city for the first time to link up with his city brother and help solve the murder.

"What's appealing about the script is the wonderful fish-out-of-water elements; someone who is out of their familiar environment and the clash of cultures between the city boy and the country boy. There's a lot of richness in this story, and it has some definite marketable elements, but the script was poorly written, and we passed. UA picked it up and bought it, I think, for $600,000."

Not bad. A fish-out-of-water story has many marketable features. Just look at *Short Circuit* (Steve Wilson and Grant Maddock), *Splash* (Lowell Ganz, Bobaloo Mandel, and Bruce J. Friedman, from a story by Friedman and Brian Grazer) *E.T.* (Melissa Mathison), or *Three Men and a Baby* (James Orr and Jim Cruickshank, based on Coline Serreau's French Comedy *Three Men and a Cradle*) to name a few. The elements found in these screenplays are salable; the situation can be expressed in a few sentences.

It's important to remember that most of the people in Hollywood only "see" what's on the written page. "If it ain't on the page, it ain't on the stage" is the old Hollywood saying. When I was reading at Cinemobile and Cine Artists I sometimes would recommend how something could be fixed, and I would get no response at all; simply a blank stare. The executives had no visual understanding of what I was trying to say about the material. They just checked out. It's no different today. Nobody can "see" anything. If the script does not appear to be marketable at the present time, nobody's interested in how it could be fixed or made better.

So people pass.

"You can't give people a reason to say no," emphasizes Dennis Shryack. "People in Hollywood only get in trouble when they say yes.

As long as they keep saying no they keep getting promoted and one day may run a studio.''

The elements that make your story attractive, salable, commercial, *marketable,* whatever, need to be executed on the page. Readers have to be able to "see" it.

Not many people in this town buy a screenplay or a treatment for the idea, because then they have to find a writer to write or rewrite it. It's too costly a process, and Hollywood spends too much money as it is.

"It's the most expensive art form there is," says Larry Jackson, now vice president of production at Orion Pictures, formerly vice president of production at the Samuel Goldwyn Company. "That makes us one of the most conservative industries in the country. Because it takes so much money to mount an individual project. There's no way you can do a prototype for a few bucks to test it with the consumer. You've got to spend millions of dollars to do something. That's the nature of the movie business. Therefore, the financing is always precarious, so there's a tendency for people to take a very conservative approach. Everybody thinks that when they finance something, it should be 'safe,', which means doing something that's already been proven successful.

"The whole aura of the movie business that's been built up over the last ninety years has been about fantasy. It's been about selling sizzle to the audience. The biggest danger we have is when we start to believe the fantasy ourselves, and then people on the creative side and the business side start to sell each other the fantasy and the sizzle, hustling each other. That's where you start to lose control. Fantasy and sizzle is what we should be selling to the audience. When we start to lose sight of that reality, we start making the wrong pictures.

"I get calls from producers all the time saying they're looking for scripts with sizzle, something like a cross between *Star Wars* and *Annie Hall*. The truth is that these producers don't have any kind of singular vision or point of view. They don't understand that there is no such thing as a Woody Allen movie. There are Woody Allen movies and other movies. You don't make a 'Woody Allen movie'; Woody Allen makes Woody Allen movies.

"People don't get it. It's so simple that they don't see it. Most studio executives don't really look at what the audience responds to in a movie.

They only see the result, not the cause, like a doctor treating the symptom, not the cause, of the illness.

"So the schlockmeisters of Hollywood," Jackson continues, "look out there, see the box office results of *Star Wars,* for example, and declare that what the KIDZ really want is a science fiction Western with robots that look like overhauled Electrolux vacuum cleaners. 'I've got one of those in the attic,' they say.

"At one point I went through a list of the hundred top-grossing films of all time in *Variety* and calculated that essentially sixty of them were original to the audience at the time they appeared. That's not to say that nobody had ever made a movie like it before, nobody ever made a success story like *Rocky* before, but they were not following an established trend at the time they appeared. They created the trend, they didn't follow it. It wasn't a stab in the dark; it was the recognition of emerging tastes and myths."

Research the market before you begin. See whether your idea is in sync with what the market is today. Then you can sit down and spend six months to a year writing your screenplay. Forget trends, they don't work. Forget commercial, because commercial is what sells, not what you *think* will sell.

Not too long ago I had an experience that illustrates this. I received a letter from an elderly man in Texas who stated he had a screenplay that would ultimately be more successful than *Star Wars, Beverly Hills Cop,* or *E.T.* He went on to explain that it was the kind of script that would attract everyone, young and old, rich and poor, student and nonstudent. Then he started talking about the Bible and the power and influence of Jesus. Then he pitched me: "This is a story about Jesus and his dog," he wrote. And he went on to explain that nowhere in the Bible does it say that Jesus had a dog, but nowhere in the Bible does it say *he didn't!*

Well, there it is.

There is a moral to that story. When you sit down to prepare your screenplay, part of your preparation should be devoted to researching the market. Bible films are not being made today, regardless of how good or bad the screenplay is. You might point your finger and say: "What about *King David* (Andrew Birkin and James Costigan) with Richard Gere? And I say look at the cost of that film and look at the return: it cost 20

million to make and never broke into profit. (A film has to gross 2½ times its negative cost to break even.) It didn't do well at all. There's not much difference between that script and the man's script from Texas about Jesus and his dog. *King David* is obviously better written, with more of a story and commercial appeal, but the bottom line is whether there is a market for your material.

What kind of scripts offer the greatest marketability?

"I don't think anyone can go wrong writing action," Dennis Shryack states. "It doesn't have to be action from cover to cover, but basically it should be a story that moves fast and has some action in it.

"The studio wants to make about fifteen movies a year. Of those, they're looking for a Woody Allen movie, something like *Turning Point*, and a *Terms of Endearment*. Plus four or five comedies. The rest are going to be action-oriented pictures, a *Robocop*, *Lethal Weapon*, or a romance thriller like *Fatal Attraction*. So if you write action, you've got half of their scheduled budget to aim for. And the odds increase that you can sell one.

"Action films always play Europe well. The studio knows they can make their money back from them. When I was at the Cannes Film Festival with *Pale Rider*, the most common question I heard was 'Will it play Japan?' In other words, does this picture need a lot of subtitles to explain what's going on, or can it be understood on its own, without anything? Is the subject something that only the American mentality can understand, or can it be understood by everyone, of any culture?

"An action picture plays well anywhere. It doesn't need a lot of subtitles to explain what's going on. Most of the number-one box-office stars in the world are action stars. Almost everyone. Why is that? Because these pictures play well in Japan.

"Most new writers don't want to hear that. But, that's the bottom line."

It's something to think about. When I'm traveling, I always watch the in-flight movie without earphones. If I don't understand what the film's about, then I know the film wasn't very successful. I remember watching *Maxie*, and I couldn't understand anything. I first saw *Witness* on a plane, the same with *Baby Boom*. Two entirely different films, yet you could understand them without hearing any dialogue.

It's a good exercise. Try it the next time you're flying. It illustrates what the studio executives are up against when they buy a script to produce. All we do as an audience is focus on what we don't like about the film. And that's the way it should be, because we're the ones paying the price of admission.

"What *is* the market?" the studio executive repeats questioningly. "I don't think you can tell. I think the most important thing is to avoid what's familiar. Avoid the trends that exist. If you follow the trend, you will usually fail.

"If you avoid what's familiar, and search for what is quickly engaging, then I think you'll find what the new market is.

"I'm on the receiving end of the creative end. And to be attuned to what to buy is the same as what it is to be attuned to what to write. There is very little recognition of what a starved community this is. What a starved business this is. We're always searching for more movies to make. We never have enough. We say we're going to make fifteen movies a year and I don't know whether we ever will. We never did at Paramount, and we said it the entire four years I was there. We never made fifteen movies a year because we didn't have the material.

"Everyone's scrambling for the next movie. And they don't care where it comes from."

When you talk about the market, or about selling your screenplay, you have to know what the bottom line is. And after talking to all these people about *the market,* it seems to me that the bottom line is simply choosing a subject to write about—wanting to write a screenplay because you're passionate about it, because it's something that interests you, because it intrigues you.

Then research the market to see what films are currently in production. Choosing a subject to write about is no longer jumping into a character, situation, or experience. It's more than that.

Know what the market is before you begin writing. And as you're writing, don't focus on selling the screenplay, and how much you're going to get for it. Don't focus on the results of your actions. In the famous Eastern text, the *Bhagavad-Gita,* one of the major themes is learning not to be attached to the fruits of your actions. In other words, don't write your script because you want to sell it for a lot of money.

Write your script because you want to write it.

That's your job as a writer.

When you really think about it, the bottom line is simple: what you write is really the market. You can talk about it, discuss it, argue with it, condemn it, or fight it, but:

You are the market.

2

Agents and Agenting

"Fresh and original, with a twist."

Every year, as I crisscross the country giving lectures and seminars on screenwriting, I'm asked the same question over and over again: "How do I get an agent?"

And I sarcastically reply, "Write a screenplay."

It's true. An agent's got to have something to sell before he or she can do anything. A treatment doesn't count, an idea doesn't count, even a book that you have the rights to doesn't count, *unless you have a screenplay* you can show as a sample of your work. I mean, why would anyone give you forty-odd thousand dollars or more to write a script if you've never written a screenplay? You wouldn't do that, why would you expect someone else to? You have to have a completed screenplay for an agent to answer a simple question: "Can I *sell* this material?"

But I've written a treatment, people say. Can't I get an agent with a treatment?

No.

You can't sell anything with a treatment. You need a screenplay to show as a sample of your screenwriting ability. Whoever says otherwise doesn't know what he or she is talking about.

Assuming you have a completed script, how do you go about getting an agent? There is no simple answer. It's a process, just like finding a house, an apartment, or a new job; as simple as it is frustrating. Somehow, either by chance, referral, persistence, hard work, dedication, a good writing sample, or just plain luck, people find agents to represent them.

How hard or how easy it is depends on what you've written, and how well you've written it.

Some things are easier to sell than others. Selling a screenplay in Hollywood is almost as difficult as getting a movie made; it's a roll of the dice. There are some who say you have to be in the right place at the right time. Chance, coincidence, timing, and some grace from above is the key to getting an agent.

Agents. Most people have the illusion that an agent can work miracles for them; they can sell your screenplay or get you an assignment. Nothing is farther from the truth. A good agent can do a lot, open a lot of doors, position you in strategic situations, can help you in any number of ways. but in the last analysis can't write the script for you.

Being an literary agent in Hollywood is tough. They work hard for their 10 percent commission. Plus, they deal with an unspoken attitude that a literary agent in Hollywood is like a real-estate agent or a used-car salesman: when they know they can sell something, they're your best friend; but if they have a difficult time, forget it, they won't even return your phone calls.

To be a literary agent in Hollywood means you have obtained a license from the state to represent writers and be their legal representatives, and that means they collect a commission on whatever they sell.

An agent's job is to represent his or her client; either to sell a screenplay, get a writing assignment, or find a buyer willing to "develop" his or her idea into a screenplay, then negotiate the deal. Sometimes agents "package" material: from a client's screenplay the agent puts together a "package" of talent—a producer, director, and star from the same agency—then walks into the studio and says we have all the elements, let's make this movie. The agency, of course, gets a commission on everything. *Legal Eagles* was a packaged movie, set up by CAA, Creative Artists Agency.

My experience with agents—I've had six of them—has not been the best. I've always expected them to do something for me, either selling a script or getting me an assignment, and of course my desire for success led to expectations which always led to anger, disappointment, and frustration. But that was *my* problem. An expectation is simply an expectation. It has nothing to do with reality.

An agent has a tough enough job as it is. He doesn't need to deal with his client's unreal expectations. And it's tough. It's a job that requires knowing how to generate "heat" on a script. And if the agent doesn't believe in the material, you've got another problem. The agent puts in a lot of time with a client, makes his daily rounds, either on foot or by phone, and tries to determine what the studios, producers, or production companies are looking for, and then supplies them, ideally, with one of his agency's clients.

It's strictly a business of dollars and cents.

When I started my screenwriting career, I thought if I had the "right" agent all my problems would be solved. He or she would sell my material, get me assignments, counsel me, and be my friend and confidant.

That was then.

In the last few years my attitude toward agents has changed; I've become cynical, deprecating, and judgmental. When I'm asked about agents, whether in Maine, Atlanta, Seattle, L.A., Brussels or Rio de Janeiro, my standard sarcastic reply is "Agents are great, but I don't know what they do!"

That was the way I was going to approach this chapter. What does an agent do?

But when it actually came time to research this chapter and conduct my interviews, I knew this approach would never do. It wasn't fair, honest, or truthful. If I wanted to get any information at all I would have to modify my concepts, and go in simply as the objective observer, and try to find a common ground that would answer my questions about agents and agenting.

With that in mind, I interviewed five literary agents. When I came away from these interviews there was one thing I was absolutely sure of: I was impressed. These professionals are dedicated, hardworking, and intelligent people who work the script market with skill and expertise, and all are highly successful.

Brenda Beckett attended Carnegie-Mellon University and Stanford, worked as a dialogue coach and secretary, and finally became an associate producer on a number of TV movies. After working in a small literary agency, she formed a partnership with Jeffrey Sanford, and opened the Sanford-Beckett Agency in 1981.

Jim Berkus, of Leading Artists, began his career as an attorney, then became an agent-trainee at IFA (International Famous Agency), and when that company merged with CMA (Creative Management Agency), he went to work for Eisenbach-Greene-Duchow, where he stayed for several years. He left there to work for the prestigious Zeigler, Diskant and Ross Agency, and then formed Leading Artists with his partner, Robert Stein.

Jim Crabbe, of the William Morris Agency, was a banker in San Francisco, then moved to Los Angeles, where he attended graduate school at USC, getting a master's degree in business. After working in the film distribution department at Disney, he joined the William Morris Agency as a trainee and soon became an assistant to Stan Kamen, then head of the motion picture department, which represented such clients as Robert Redford, Al Pacino, Goldie Hawn, Sylvester Stallone, Alan Pakula, Michael Cimino, and Chevy Chase. Crabbe remained with the Morris office for several years, negotiating with studios, attorneys, and talent.

Linne Radmin of ICM (International Creative Management) was a theater and English major at George Washington University, then went to Columbia where she got her master's degree in business. She worked in publishing and advertising in New York, then moved to Los Angeles in 1980 with a vague notion, she says, of becoming a producer. She got a job at the Chasin, Parks, Citron Agency, at that time one of the finest agencies in Hollywood, stayed there for a little more than a year, then left to join the Henderson-Hogan Agency in January of 1983. From there she went to APA (Agency of Performing Artists), and soon after joined ICM.

Nancy Roberts became an agent strictly by accident. She got a B.A. from Scripps College, Claremont, majoring in history and humanities. Upon leaving, she went to UCLA, enrolled in the master's program in art history, and worked part-time as a secretary for one of the top interior design firms in L.A., specializing in luxury homes, hotels, and major complexes. After ten months, the head designer started his own business, and hired her to run it. She was twenty-two. Three years later she became interested in biorhythms, and soon she and her partner were the leading authorities on biorhythms in the United States. Knopf commissioned them to do a book, they appeared on *The Tonight Show, Today,* and other talk shows, and soon began working with such notable institutions as Cal Tech, the Jet Propulsion Laboratory, and the UCLA Neuro-Psychiatric Institute. After her partner suddenly died, she began running her husband's independent production company. Almost a year later, she decided to open her own agency, The Nancy Roberts Company.

Cindy Turtle went to Queens College, then joined station KOR, New York, working in production, then left for RKO, where she did sports, *Firing Line,* and network specials. In 1976 she came to L.A. and joined Eisenbach-Greene-Duchow. After several years she joined the advertising agency of Needham, Harper and Sears, developing shows for Xerox, McDonald's, and Arco. Later she became director of development at Showtime, a movie channel, where she stayed for three years. Upon leaving, she decided to go back into agenting and with her partner, Michael Rosen, formed the Rosen/Turtle Group.

Of course, the first thing I wanted to know was "What does an agent do?" Jim Crabbe replied that "the agent's job is to facilitate our clients achieving their own goals. I won't tell any client what they should or shouldn't do. What I do is simply lay out the possible results of their actions, whatever it is they choose to do. Once they know what the options are, they have to decide for themselves."

What do agents look for?

Basically, they said the same thing. Good writing; that is, strong action, good characters, and solid structure, with a strong beginning, middle, and end. "Good writing," Nancy Roberts says, "makes you want to turn the page. You can't put it down, you're absolutely hooked into the subject, it elicits a visceral reaction from you. I mean, what is entertainment? You go to James Bond movies for escapism and hardware. You go to *Robocop* for escapism, vengeance, and excitement. It's a visceral response, and you're entertained.

"Occasionally," Roberts continues, "you'll get a script and you'll say, God, this is a great story. That doesn't mean it's a movie. You could be at the dead wrong time; you could make all the right moves and get all the wrong responses. And then it joins the list of great scripts not made. Sometimes, if it's good enough, it might get made. Something will open up and people will listen. Look at *Platoon*."

When I was a free-lance screenwriter, I wanted to write what I wanted to write. Being somewhat headstrong, stubborn, and independent I found I couldn't get into writing something that was somebody else's idea. Most of the time I wrote "on spec," which means I wrote without being paid for it. I had good luck in my screenwriting career: in seven years, I wrote nine scripts; two were produced, four optioned, and three nothing ever happened to—they weren't bought or optioned. My goal was to write two original screenplays a year.

When I worked on assignment, it was only to get money to write an original. As far as I'm concerned, a writer writes. He or she sits down and works three or four hours a day, or more, whether they're getting paid for it or not. We're spoiled in Hollywood; it's the only place in the world where a writer expects to get paid *before* they put one word down on paper.

Times have changed of course. "If somebody wants a career today," Nancy Roberts says, "they should write their brains out. If they get a deal, they should write the assignment, then take time off to write something on spec, then write an assignment, then write on spec. You have a lot more control over a spec script that becomes a hot script. It can put you on the A list faster than waiting four years to get something developed."

Because I wrote what I wanted to write, my decision on what to write was based on personal preference, not market conditions; I made only a cursory examination of the marketplace. At that time, studios bought scripts they thought would make good movies.

When I was head of the story department at Cinemobile and Cine Artists, I learned what I hadn't learned as a writer. The material I was looking for was something fresh, different from the current box-office hits. I always felt you had to "hit 'em where they ain't." If the trend was for war movies, like *Platoon* or *Rambo*, I would look for a small, personal story, or a wacky romantic comedy. In fact, when the trend was for action detective stories like *Bullitt* or *The French Connection*, I was trying to get the rights to a zany, wacky comedy by Olsen and Johnson called *Hellzapoppin*.

"I think the worst thing a writer can do is try and second-guess the marketplace," says Jim Berkus. "The worst thing. The minute a writer tells me he's written a commercial script I know he's in big trouble. The worst thing you can do is to try to second-guess what question the teacher's going to ask on the exam instead of just studying the material and knowing the course. You can't do it. Any script that comes from your gut, that you write with passion, has a much better chance than a script you're writing because you think that's what people want to buy. I mean, what Steven Spielberg is excited about and the movies he personally wants to make seem to be more universally accepted than perhaps the movies that David Lynch [*Blue Velvet, Dune, Eraserhead*] personally likes to see and make."

In the past I, too, would fall into the trap and think "commercial," and it never worked out.

It's a common mistake.

"I was sitting with a potential client," says Brenda Beckett, "and I could see he was the classic case of trying to figure out what 'they' want; he had written several screenplays and hadn't sold any. He kept asking me, 'What do they want?' I said the two most important things you need are having an idea that can be told in a *TV Guide* version. People call it high-concept but it's really having an idea which you can tell in a couple of sentences, so the head of the studio can call the marketing guy and pitch it, and the marketing guy can say, Yeah, I can sell that.

"The second thing is a strong three-act structure. I think you've got to have an active first act, a solid second act, and an effective resolution. Right now, both of those are very important in getting a movie made."

Getting the movie made. Over and over again, I heard that refrain. It was only a few years ago that most agents wanted to sell the script for as much as the market would bear. That could be anywhere for $350,000 to $500,000. The attitude around town was let's take the money and run and it doesn't matter whether the movie gets made or not. Today it seems more important for the movie to get made in order to expand the client's career.

"I spend very little time today trying to auction scripts," Jim Berkus says, "because my experience has been that it doesn't necessarily guarantee the movie's going to be made, nor does it guarantee the movie's going to get made by the right people. A lot of money doesn't equate into a quality film. My philosophy is this: selling the script for a lot of money is great, but getting a script made into a good film where the writer has sole credit is even better."

"One of our clients, Carol Black, and her partner, Neil Marlens, wrote a script on spec called *Soul Man*. We went from studio to studio trying to get a deal. Finally we got Steve Tisch involved as executive producer and ultimately we sold it to New World for not a huge amount of money. But what we had in the deal was that Carol and Neil were to be involved as coproducers, and they had access to the set at any time. More importantly, nobody else could rewrite the script. The only rewriting that could be done had to be with their approval. If they weren't available, then only minor line changes could be done without them. And to me, that's a more beneficial route to go than just writing a script and having it sold for a lot of money."

Writing the script and selling it are two different things. So many times in my screenwriting workshops I see people making creative choices based on what "they" want, of what "they" think is commercial, (whoever "they" are), and each time it doesn't work.

What does work?

Good writing. "On Monday morning," Berkus continues, "all the agents in the office get together for an hour, and we talk about what we've read over the weekend. And inevitably someone might say, this is a well-written script, but there's no story. And my comment is that an essential part of being a well-written script is a story. By nature, it can't be well written if there's no story. You're not writing prose, you're writing a screenplay. You're writing a story for a movie. And if there's no story, then you haven't done your job. So don't tell me it's well written but there's no story.

"Every executive and producer in town takes home anywhere from five to ten scripts over the weekend," Berkus says, "and the ones they like are the ones where they can say, yes, that's a movie. They can see it. Even if parts of it need work; maybe some of the jokes don't work, maybe some of the characters are a little cliché, maybe some of the stuff is a little repetitive. But if you can see the movie, there's a chance it might get made, even if they have to rewrite it or do more work on it."

Whenever the agent has a script they "see" as a movie, they put the word out around town, they "hype" it, weaving an aura of excitement and enthusiasm around the script. The *buzz*. Hollywood, more than any other industry, turns on information. And since the basic operating system in Hollywood is set up to say no, "you have to give the buyer a reason to buy the product," says Nancy Roberts. "You have to create a presence, some sort of heat, something that makes people want to read it and return your phone calls."

If an agent finds a script that he or she wants to send into the marketplace, they don't send it out with a form letter and expect to get results. They've got to generate *heat*. And that means they've got to have a plan, a strategy.

This is what Linne Radmin does: "When I have a script to sell, I let it leak out that I read something really great, but I can't talk about it. I talk about not being able to talk about it. You slip it to from three to six very powerful producers. When you know you have at least one producer interested, then you start slipping it around to the studios. And what you do is slip it to the senior vice president at each studio whom you most trust, and the drill goes like this: I will slip you this screenplay. There must be no coverage. If you don't love this screenplay, you've never seen it before. And if you do love this screenplay, we'll figure out what to do next.

"Some executives will say, it's not my cup of tea, but per our agreement I won't block you at the studio. Feel free to give it to another v.p. Or if you want to, send it directly to the president of production.

"Sometimes, the people at the other end will take the attitude that if we don't buy this script somebody else will, and maybe it'll be a great movie and be a hit. And we missed out. It's very much a feast-or-famine mentality in this town, either you can't get arrested or you can't have five minutes alone."

The strategy for a screenplay going out into the market has to be carefully planned and orchestrated. You can't send anything out in a haphazard shotgun manner. You have to assess the situation. You should know, for example, what's in development around town, who's doing what films for which studios, who's likely to buy it, who's likely not to buy it. The agent's job is to have as much information as possible. Therefore, each move has to be carefully calculated to achieve the maximum result. The life of a studio executive is short, maybe four or five years. So the studio executive always has to cover himself or herself in any decisions they make. And a lot of studio executives operate on a "cover your ass" basis.

"And that goes with the territory," Jim Crabbe says. "An executive may only be there for a little while and he better prove himself or he's out. If the film he's responsible for ends up being a flop, he has to be able to justify why he made it in the first place. I mean, that's one of the main reasons that film packaging has become so predominant, even at the expense of the film. Unlike television, where you have spaces that have to be filled, there's really no reason for having to say yes to a motion picture. If the movie bombs, the average studio executive's going to want to turn to whoever it is that he or she answers to and say, wouldn't you have made this film with such and such a director attached, or this actor?"

That's what happened with *Ishtar*. Who wouldn't want to make a movie with Dustin Hoffman and Warren Beatty, written by Elaine May? The whole thing simply got out of hand, but it would have been crazy for a studio executive to turn down *that* film with those elements attached.

Put together a plan.

"When I'm ready to put a script into the marketplace I establish a game plan," says Nancy Roberts. "Often it's dictated by the material. What I look for is an advocate, someone who believes in the writer and the material. In most cases I look for a producer, because producers don't change when the head of a studio is fired. Is the producer committed to the writer? That's my first question. Do they have a good rapport? Will the producer go to the wall with the writer and keep the writer on the project, even fight the studio, if need be? If you know there's a producer who can execute that idea and has a track record for getting a movie made, that certainly is a way to go."

Evaluate the situation. It's just good, common sense. In corporate lexicon it's called market research. The agent wants two things when he or she sends the script into the marketplace: to sell it and get the movie made. That, perhaps, is the more important of the two. If it's a good script, even if it doesn't sell, the material can be used to get the writer an assignment. The writer will be paid to write something for a producer or a studio, or possibly rewrite a script in development. In either case the writer is a gun for hire.

A good solid screenplay is the easiest way to break down the barriers of Hollywood. "Agents cannot work miracles, contrary to popular belief," says Nancy Roberts. "If you give the agent a $1.98 script, the agent'll probably get you $1.98. If you give the agent a $400,000 script, the agent'll probably get you $400,000, if the agent's any good," she emphasizes.

"*Kindness of Strangers* is a good example," says Linne Radmin. "This was a first script, written by an acting client of APA's [Agency of Performing Artists], Karen Leigh Hopkins. Her acting agent called me one day and asked me to do him a favor and take a look at the script. So I read it, and the script was breezy, funny, and pretty quirky. This woman has a definite voice and a definite point of view. It's been described as an *After Hours* for girls, a compressed time romp about one young woman's struggle to get to a job interview.

"I knew the market might be a little soft for this kind of a project. I mean, we've had *After Hours*, *Who's That Girl?*, *Blind Date*, and *Adventures in Babysitting*.

"The first three or four producers I sent it to liked it but did not want to buy it. So I started thinking of it as a writing sample. I knew an executive who had just started working at Interscope [a company that specializes in the development of screenplays], and very often the management is looking to make a new executive feel good about joining the organization. So if a new executive is very excited about a project, there's a good chance it might go through. Well, I sent it over and she got really jazzed on it; she in turn 'sold' it to her boss, in terms of Interscope's getting behind the project. He felt the script needed a lot of work, which I didn't disagree with, but I could already feel the heat starting.

"So we split up the town: he slipped it to some executives and I took it to some executives. The next thing I knew it was the food-fight of the week. We got tremendous response. We saw where we were getting our executive, vice president level of support, and we went after all the presidents of production on a given weekend, and everybody was crazed when they got the script, because we wanted our responses on Monday.

"It became a feeding frenzy. Ned Tannen [then head of production at Paramount] got hold of the script Thursday night and pounced preemptively on Friday. Ned had been given the script earlier by David Madden [a v.p. of production] and it wasn't clear in his mind that he couldn't bid on it until Monday. I did my damnedest to keep the flood gates open, but it was very difficult to do. We ended up selling it to Paramount for $300,000.

"Ironically, at the present time, the studio feels the script is too quirky and off center, so maybe we ought to make it a little bit more normal. So it's like you buy a light comedy about a guy who gets elected president, and now what they want is a drama about a woman who links up with a goat."

"It's foolish to shotgun material without a strategy," emphasizes Nancy Roberts. "I think a superior piece finds its way to the top very quickly because everybody wants superior material. That's what reputations are made on. Lesser material has to be guarded carefully, because it's not going to stand on its own.

"*Short Circuit* is a case in point. I received a call one Thursday morning from Sally Merlin-Jones, a screenwriting teacher at UCLA Extension, and she told me I was one of several agents who had been recommended to her by the Amblin people and others, and would I read a screenplay. Well, I did. And I loved it. *Short Circuit*, written by Steve Wilson and Brent Maddock, was a movie. You could tell immediately. The characters were wonderful, the situation unique, and it had a lot of humor. It was fun. You laughed when you read it. You can always tell you've got something going when you read a script and it elicits a visceral, nonintellectual response. I mean, that's what the moviegoing audience is going to do. It was the story of a baby that had to learn all over again in an alien world. A fish out of water. And it was the way it was done, the references they brought to bear and the style and humor with which they wrote it. You couldn't put the pages down.

"Occasionally you'll get a script like that and you'll finish it and you'll say, God, this is a great story. Which doesn't mean it's a movie. *Short Circuit* was always a movie. If you, as a writer, don't write up to the material, the agent can't sell it."

"An unsold writer is only really exciting if they've got a screenplay that comes within an inch of being bought," says Linne Radmin. "It doesn't have to sell but it has to come close so people clamor to want to get into business and make other deals." Everybody in town is always looking for new, hot writers, to change, polish, develop, and rewrite screenplays.

"Many new writers feel they should be able to get assignments easily," says Nancy Roberts. "Writing assignments go to people who deliver movies. And people who deliver movies are people who have a track record. I'm constantly amazed when I hear new writers talking about how they want an agent to get them an assignment. Getting a new writer an assignment is one of the hardest things to do.

"Number one," she continues, "you have to create in the buyer a reason to hire the writer. If the writer has no profile, it's not easy. When an agent puts somebody up for an assignment, the company is looking for someone to invest money in, somebody who will hopefully help them get a movie made. And if that person has no track record, it can be a hit or miss, and quite possibly a costly proposition. If, for example, there is a rewrite assignment open, and it is a page-one rewrite, the company already has several thousand dollars invested in that project. If they want to go forward with the rewrite it's going to cost them several thousand dollars more, so hopefully they're looking for somebody to make those dollars pay off, otherwise they're further in the hole. The company's not there to hand out assignments for people who may or may not be able to hit the ball. So it's hard. That's why it's easier to launch a writer's career from a spec script that gets a lot of attention."

On an assignment the writer usually writes a first draft along with a set of revisions, and at that point the company has an option to cut off the writer. If they keep the writer on the project, then there's an optional set of revisions and polishes. There are cut-offs all along.

"The writer isn't on for the whole ride," Roberts explains. "The writer can turn around and do a good, bad, indifferent, or mediocre job, and he will be vulnerable. And if he does a good job, he may or may not go on with the project, depending whether the studio executive who put him on the assignment stays or leaves. Because writers on assignment aren't in turnaround positions, they don't get their projects back, they're guns for hire."

"Turnaround" simply means this: if the studio buys your material, and they decide not to do anything with it, they will sell it back to you within a certain period of time. And during that time the writer or producer or whoever owns the property has the right to try and set up that project with another studio. Whoever the producer sets it up with simply pays back the studio who originally bought the material for their total costs plus some interest and overhead.

Most writers don't realize what it takes for a screenplay to be made into a movie. "In order for it to be made," says Brenda Beckett, "somebody's got to read it and say, this would make a great movie and millions and millions of people would want to see it. And if the agent can't see that in the material, then it's not going to get sold and it's not going to get made."

At least not at this time.

Many writers I talk to seem to believe that when they finish their screenplay it should sell immediately. Nothing could be farther from the truth. Just look at *Platoon, An Officer and a Gentleman, Witness, Terms of Endearment,* and scores of other films. These scripts made the rounds for many years before they finally got made into movies; ten years for *Platoon,* seven for *An Officer and a Gentleman.*

What's important is to use your screenwriting experience as a learning experience, sharpening your skills, perfecting your craft.

"I heard an interview on National Public Radio a couple of years ago," Brenda Beckett reflects, "and they were interviewing a woman novelist and she was being hailed as an 'overnight sensation.' They asked her, do you have any advice for writers? And she said she had a note taped to her typewriter saying, 'Write what only you can write.' I thought that was wonderful. Don't try to write what you think they want you to write.''

"As a writer, I don't think you can research the market and get a definitive answer as to what to write," says Cindy Turtle. "There might be 'market trends' like action-adventure, or romantic comedies, that are currently selling, but if you're like Stephen King and your true talent lies more in the horror genre, then you'd be better off writing horror films than writing something according to the current market trends. Don't be a 'slave' to market research; write what you have to write, because if it doesn't sell now, it may sell later.''

It's true.

When you complete your screenplay, and before you put it out into the world, you better put on your armor just like Don Quixote did when he challenged the windmill. You have to be prepared in case nobody wants what you've written. And in case that happens and nobody is interested in what you've got, either agent or buyer, you've got to rethink your position. Objectively.

Do a self-inventory. Take out a piece of paper and ask yourself some hard questions. Number one, what kind of screenplay have you given the agent to sell? What kind of script is it? In terms of the present market is it salable? Try not to lie to yourself, be as truthful as possible.

Who do you see playing the major characters? Who do you think would be interested in it? What studios, what production companies, what producers? Write these down on your list. How many agents have you submitted the script to? What's the response been? Favorable or unfavorable? Have you made up a list of people you know in the industry? Are you going to contact them about the script?

These are questions you must ask yourself. How good or how bad it is is irrelevant; the only question is whether or not you can sell it. The two are not synonymous.

What are you going to do?

You've got some choices. Number one, you can continue sending the material around to the agents listed on the Writers Guild list of authorized agents. This goes for anyone else you can think of—stars, directors, producers, companies, friends, anyone who has access to somebody in power.

You can give up, too, that's another choice. Or you can choose to pull the script off the market and wait for another time and another set of circumstances before you send it out again.

And you can sit down and start another screenplay.

"I can think, I can wait, I can do without," Siddhartha says in the Herman Hesse novel of the same name.

Are you up for that? Can you take the heat of rejection? If you can't take the heat then you better get out of the kitchen.

3

The Attorneys

"The first thing I do is draw a can of worms on a piece of paper."

When I first began my screenwriting career, I had a lot of unrealistic expectations about the way Hollywood worked.

I believed that when I became a member of the Writers Guild of America, they would somehow be able to get me work, like writing assignments for films and TV.

Wrong. It's the old catch-22. To be eligible to join the Writers Guild of America you must be "employed" by a motion picture or television production company who has signed the Minimum Basic Agreement of the WGA. You must have a written contract to write a film or television show; it is that written contract that makes you eligible to join the guild and pay the initiation fee of $1,500. As a member of the Writers Guild you are entitled to the benefits and protection the Guild offers in terms of pension and health plan, establishment of a minimum basic fee (called *scale*) for television and motion pictures, collection of residuals by a qualified staff monitoring foreign and domestic sales, a script registration service that allows you to register your material (which is proof of authorship) for the minimum fee of five dollars as a member (ten dollars for nonmembers), and a lot more.

The Writers Guild of America, west, is run by a board of directors consisting of nineteen members—including president, vice president, and secretary-treasurer—who have been nominated and elected by the nine thousand members of the Guild. The administration of the WGA, w, is carried out under the supervision of the executive director, who at this writing is Brian Walton.

The Writers Guild of America exists for the protection of the writer. It is not an employment agency. If you want to get work in Hollywood, you need an agent. But do you need an attorney? An agent, as stated in the previous chapter, must be licensed by the state of California to sell his or her client's work. But an entertainment attorney in California is not licensed to sell material or seek employment for his or her clients. "An attorney cannot solicit work for their clients," says Susan Grode, a noted entertainment attorney in Century City. But "if I know someone is looking for a particular kind of script, and I can put that person together with a writer I represent, I will try to make the introduction.

"But I will not solicit. I will not call a studio. I will not call a producer. It's different in New York. In New York, a lawyer can go out and hawk somebody's talent to get them employment. Until the federal government addresses that issue," she continues, "it is a state by state situation."

Then, what do you need an attorney for, if the agent gets you jobs, negotiates the deal, and the Writers Guild protects your rights as a writer?

That's what I wanted to find out. What is the relationship between the writer, the agent, and the attorney? So I went to interview Eric Weissmann, head of Weissmann, Bergman, Coleman and Silverman, a prestigious entertainment law firm.

Eric Weissmann was born in Zurich, Switzerland, grew up in Europe and Mexico, came to the United States when he was sixteen, attended UCLA, and graduated from the UCLA Law School. After a short stint in the army, he started working in the legal department of MCA (now the parent company of Universal Studios), then moved to the large and prestigious law firm of Kaplan, Davis and Livingston. He became vice president for the world in business affairs at Warner Brothers, then moved back to Kaplan, Livingston, Goodwin, Berkowitz and Selvin to head up their entertainment division. In that capacity he trained many lawyers who have gone on to become top entertainment attorneys in Hollywood, "much to my detriment," he says, "because they take clients away from me."

Now, heading his own firm, he represents some of the top writers, directors, and producers in the industry: Paul Mazursky, Terry Gilliam, Gene Wilder, Bob Rafelson, Kenneth Ross, Mark Rydell, to name a few.

What's the difference between an agent and an attorney? I ask.

"An agent does three things," he begins. "An agent sells, gives career advice, sometimes makes suggestions to the writer about the screenplay, like tighten up the first act and make the main character stronger, and then negotiates the deal when he either sells the script or gets an assignment for his client."

An agent, depending on his or her ranking in the community, will also do a variety of things for their clients, like helping them shop for clothes, picking up their cleaning, getting their names in the trades, and so on. After all, they do get 10 percent of what their clients make.

The attorney, on the other hand, says Weissmann, "reads the contract and checks to see whether the agreement conforms with the deal made by the agent, and tries to improve it whenever necessary. The attorney makes sure that the writer is protected against any potential lawsuits that might be based on infringements of rights of privacy."

The second thing a lawyer does is negotiate the deal, or helps the agent negotiate the deal. Deals are money, as well as credits, and the writer's credit is determined by the Writers Guild of America.

"But there are some things that are beyond the money aspect of the deal," Weissmann continues. "All kinds of technicalities. Do you get less payment if there's a split credit? If so, how much less payment? Can you exclude from the split credit somebody who wrote the original screenplay or a prior draft that you can't do anything about?

"The third thing the attorney can do is give career advice. Yes, do this script for less money because it's going to be Paul Mazursky's next movie, and that's better than doing another script for more money and not knowing whether the movie will get made or not.

"Along with that, you do all the services that lawyers render, which is to help with the divorce, or the premarital agreement; to give advice if the maid is drunk and hits somebody's car, or the maid needs to get into the country legally. Or your client buys a house, or sells a house, or there's a fire and your client's out of town and you've got to go to the house and water down the roof, which I've done. Or a client is dying of cancer and you have to figure out whether the will is appropriate; or your client sets out to break the land speed record and you want to know if he has a will.

"I've even gone to China with a client," he says, "to visit the location and help negotiate the deal.

"Now, there are some lawyers who don't do all these things; they simply say I'm a lawyer, I don't make the deals, I don't give career advice, I just look at the contracts.

"That's not my way. I love my clients and foster a very special relationship with them."

Susan Grode says "counselor" is an appropriate term for the attorney. Grode, a native of New York, started as a painter, then became a vice president of the Harry N. Abrams publishing company. When she moved to California she entered USC Law School, knowing that "all the past experience I'd had working with writers in publishing was really the best preparation in the world for becoming a lawyer who represents writers."

Many of Grode's clients write screenplays as well as books, both fiction and nonfiction, and many end up writing books and then doing the screenplays based on their books.

"As a result,"she says, "I try to communicate to people who I negotiate with that my clients are not just a commodity; their talent and ability is unique, something generally not flowing in commerce. It is a very important part in putting a film together. Without the original words, you don't really have very much to build a film upon.

"One of the things I offer my clients," she says, "is the ability to sit down and outline a three- or five-year plan. I'm interested in knowing where my clients want to be in the next three to five years. Where they want to go. It helps me understand what they need in terms of the contracts they enter into. An agreement really is not worth the paper it's written on if there isn't a basis of understanding between the two parties. It is essential that I understand what it is my client ultimately wants from his or her career."

The issue of the client's career goals has been coming up over and over again during my interviews for this book. When I was pursuing my career, we—my agent and I—were always after the short-term goals, that is optioning and selling the screenplay, or getting an assignment for one.

Today it's more important to get the movie made.

"I have several clients," says Grode, "who want substantial control over what they write. There are a number of ways to do that. The classic process is to turn that writer into a producer. Or director.

"That takes planning. If there is an agent, I work with him or her and share what the plan is going to be. So if three or four assignments come up, we can use them as building blocks that will lead to the next step. On the first screenplay, for example, maybe the writer will get an associate producer credit, and when the next screenplay is sold there may be a coproducer credit. Now we might get stuck for two or three screenplays in that coproducing capacity until the writer gets enough experience to become a producer."

The attorney, as mentioned, usually works hand in hand with the agent. The legal aspects of the contract are not the agent's responsibility— unless, of course, the writer's agency has a legal department to guarantee the contract. But if that's not the case, the writer usually needs an attorney to look over the contract.

If you want to get an attorney, "I think you should go shopping," Grode says. "Especially if you take your professional life seriously. And that initial meeting with the lawyer should not cost any money.

"I am not a decision maker," she emphasizes. "I tell my clients I will not live their lives for them, and I'm not going to make decisions for them; I'm an information giver, a counselor. I think it's my job to give them the best information I possibly can, both legally and experientially. If I see, for example, that the nature of a screenwriting deal has changed over the last six months, it's important that my client get the benefit of that knowledge. If percentages are changing, if certain clauses are creeping in or out of context, my clients should benefit from that experience and information."

How much does an attorney charge for his or her services?

It depends. "Lawyers, with some clients," says Eric Weissmann, "have an arrangement where they simply get paid for their time. Or, they can charge a premium, a reasonable value for their services. In terms of lawyers who work on percentages, it ranges from 5 to 10 percent."

On the other hand, an attorney may say to a client, you don't have an agent so I may charge you 12 percent, because I'm not only working as an agent (by putting people and material together) but also by doing the legal services involved.

As a matter of fact, there are rumors circulating around Hollywood that certain agencies are cutting their commission from 10 to 6 percent for some of their star clients. Real estate agents do this all the time, but it makes sense in some situations in the Hollywood community as well; 6 percent of Robert Redford's salary and percentage, or Sylvester Stallone's salary and percentage, is better than 10 percent of a well known actor who does not happen to be a superstar. It's a question of negotiation.

What about negotiation? How does an attorney structure a deal that benefits his or her clients? Is there some kind of procedure to follow, some rules or guidelines that would help you prepare to negotiate? What can an attorney do that would benefit the writer?

The structure of negotiation is "to protect the writer," says Eric Weissmann. "The first goal is for the writer to make a living; to make a sale and to make a name for himself or herself. The second goal is to preserve the integrity of the screenplay. So, you do whatever you can to do this.

"If it's a first-time script you try to sell it with an element component [like a producer or director] attached that is responsive to the writer and sees the same things in the screenplay the writer sees. It doesn't mean the screenplay can't be changed, but if it's going to be changed, it should be changed by the writer.

"Therefore, you try to give the writer the opportunity of making the first set of changes or revisions."

The first step may be that a producer, production company, or studio may option the screenplay. Or they may buy it outright, then commission the writer to do additional revisions; this is called a "step deal," where the writer receives a down payment, a payment upon completion of the first draft, another payment for any additional revisions he or she might do, and a final payment, depending on whether the writer gets sole credit or a shared credit when the picture is done. And then there are those "production bonuses" which can also be negotiated into the contract.

"When I negotiate," Weissmann continues, "I try to find out who the other negotiator is. If I know the person, it's better. We can enjoy the process, and still protect the interests of our clients. Some negotiators you have to defer to, you can't hit them head on. It doesn't mean you have to sell your client down the river, but you have to be attuned to the other person's problems. Maybe you can find a solution to his problems without endangering yours. And then, there are some negotiators you have to hit head on, punch them out, set up a situation where you beat them, just like a game of tennis.

"You have to know your strength. A good negotiator is like a good jockey; he has a very good idea of what kind of horse he's riding. A good jockey knows not to burden his horse. He doesn't come out of the gate too fast, he doesn't come out too slow. By the same token, you have to know the strength your client has in the negotiating posture; if he's written a Western, you have to know whether there's seven cowboy pictures either in development or out right now and nobody wants them in the first place; or whether it's a high-concept script that is exactly what Steven Spielberg is looking for.

"You have to know whether the studio has a new head of production. It may be very important for that person to establish his position in the company by getting that particular script, because with that screenplay he can get Alan Pakula as director, or Steve Martin as actor.

"The other thing you have to know is the psyche of your client. Can your client take a siege? Can he endure a long negotiation? Is he a fighter, or somebody who's going to collapse and it's not worth your while holding out and endangering the entire negotiation for an extra $30, or $30,000.

"You've got to make sure your client does not have unrealistic expectations," Weissmann says. The price someone pays for anything is always subjective, and Hollywood is notorious for being enslaved in a system that bases the price of a brand-new screenplay by what the writer got for his last one. If the writer got $300,000 for his last script, that means you can ask $350,000, maybe $400,000 for this one. The new script, however, may be worth $700,000. So the question that is always being raised is why the cost of the last script should influence the price of the new one.

"So you have to plan your strategy," continues Weissmann. "Certain questions have to be asked: How much does the picture cost? Are there any other interested bidders? How badly do they want this screenplay? Who do we have that we can attach to the project? We have an important director. What about financing? Can we contribute something to the cost of this picture? It's possible, for example, that we might have a studio in Germany that's willing to invest in this deal. Have there been any other deals in town like that recently? That's where the agent has a big advantage because there are some agencies that know every deal in town."

If you find yourself in a situation where a producer, or production company, is interested in something you've written, and you don't have an agent, you should not negotiate for yourself. Hire an attorney to do it for you. An entertainment attorney; someone in the business who knows what they are doing. It's worth the investment, whatever it may be. Hourly rates for entertainment attorneys vary, anywhere from $150 to $300 an hour.

What about writing a screenplay about a person who is the subject of a newspaper or magazine article? How do you go about getting the rights to that material, and what does it entail? It is a question I get asked over and over again.

What do you do if you see a story in a newspaper, or magazine, or hear of an interesting event or experience that happened to someone you know, and you think it would make a fantastic film, or movie for television? What do you do?

If this happens, and it does for most writers, "the first thing I do is draw a can of worms on a piece of paper," says Susan Grode. "I graphically explain how urgent it is that they pay attention to what I'm going to say. They must own that material before they write anything, and that doesn't happen until I say they own it. Until I tell them we have all the necessary signatures on the dotted line; that all considerations have been paid, and I'm satisfied that there are no legal ramifications that would prevent them from owning it and going forward to develop those rights."

How do you go about getting the rights to a person's story you see in a magazine or newspaper?

There are several ways to do this. First check the city the person lives in. Then call information in that city and ask if there is a listing for the person the story is written about. If there is, prepare what you're going to say, and then call and explain what it is you want to do.

If you can't find the person this way, then the best way is through the reporter who wrote the story. Sometimes the reporter has the rights to the person's story, but that's not very often. In most cases the newspaper or magazine reporter will turn you on to the person because "number one, reporters usually aren't wealthy enough to option the lives of the people they're writing stories about," says Grode. "And two, there is an ethical question about reporters saying to their subjects that 'I want the rights.' It taints the interview. After the story is written, reporters may join forces with their subjects and work with them on selling their stories to the movies."

One of my students does just that. A reporter for *The Washington Post,* he's written stories about some of the major evangelical scandals recently, and has sold some of them to television production companies. He's just been retained as a consultant for a CBS movie of the week.

"The thing I recommend to my clients," Grode continues, "is to bring the article writer along with you by taking an option on his or her article so someone else won't option it and compete with you."

After you locate the person, see whether they are represented by an agent or attorney. Sometimes they are, sometimes not. In my experience, it's been more difficult dealing with someone who's not represented; their knowledge of negotiation and the way things are done in Hollywood are based on rumor, hearsay, fantasy, old movies, and gossip columns.

One time I was researching the Fatty Arbuckle scandal that occurred in 1921. Fatty Arbuckle was one of the most famous silent comedians. A 1920 popularity poll found Charlie Chaplin, Fatty Arbuckle, and Harold Lloyd to be the three most popular silent comedians. At 5'6" and 255 pounds, Arbuckle was the original Keystone Kop in the films that became so famous under Mack Sennett, and was the man who invented the pie-in-the-face routine.

In 1921, he had just signed a three-million-dollar contract with Paramount. To celebrate, he and his friends drove to San Francisco over Labor Day. They had a party at the St. Francis Hotel. It was the time of

Prohibition and bathtub gin, and the era would soon become known as the Roaring Twenties. At Arbuckle's party was a Hollywood starlet, Virginia Rappe. During the party, it was claimed, Fatty Arbuckle raped her. A few days later she died.

The city of San Francisco brought manslaughter charges against Arbuckle, and after three sensational trials, he was finally acquitted. But when he tried to resume his career, it was too late. Citizen groups, vigilante groups, religious groups picketed his films, and Paramount, under public pressure, had to withdraw some twenty-six Fatty Arbuckle films from distribution. His career was over. "Nobody loves a fat man," he once remarked.

He died several years later, a broken man.

I wanted to do something with this story. According to the San Francisco court records, the files, evidence, and transcripts of the trials had either been lost, stolen, or destroyed. So I began digging, doing research, trying to find leads that would help me locate material on the scandal.

After many weeks of fruitless research, I located the only existing copy (as far as I knew) of the transcript of the first trial. And then I had a further stroke of luck: I managed to locate the grandson of the defense attorney. He told me that he had three full filing cabinets of his grandfather's material (the entire defense file) stuck away in his garage. I, of course, wanted to see what was there; once I knew what he had, I could make him an offer for whatever I found and wanted to use. Or, if I couldn't do that, the producer I was doing this for would purchase the entire file from the man.

But first I had to see what he had. I couldn't negotiate blind. The first thing he said was that I couldn't see anything. What I would have to do was write questions about the material I was looking for, and then he would go through the files to see if the document was there. And for this service he would only charge me $200 an hour for his time.

A real bargain. Even at an auction, you get to check out the merchandise before you make a bid. Not knowing what, if anything, was there, I passed. The man did not understand the process of negotiation as it relates to the film industry.

* * *

If you want the rights to the person's story, you negotiate with that person. "The classic situation is that an option is taken for the life story rights, and a release is signed," says Grode. "The thing the writer usually forgets if he gets the rights himself is to ask the person to get releases from the other important people in the story. This is a potential source of legal liability."

"There are times when a person is involved in a civil lawsuit or is being prosecuted for a crime and is still waiting for the outcome of the trial. Frequently," she says, "the attorney in charge will require a proviso saying that the story may not appear on TV, or in a film, or anywhere in the media until the outcome of the trial has been declared.

"The reason is obvious. Did any members of the jury watch this on TV, or read about it in the newspapers and therefore form an opinion about the case? Will certain facts damage the outcome of a civil case if they are disclosed? Even a TV show that doesn't do well reaches 20 million people.

"Of course, the classic horror story is when the project goes forward and at the last moment someone pops out of the woodwork and says, 'I know you think that's a fictional character, but that's really me.'

"It's one of those exquisite tensions. You have a choice at that point; you can offer what you would have offered had you known about that person, which is compensation, a contract, and a release.

"You cannot be too careful going in to make sure that all the rights relevant to a story have been obtained. Are you getting the rights from a minor? If you are, you must make sure the parents or guardian has acceded for the best interests of the minor, and one now has to have that confirmed by the court. Because minors are really not considered competent to enter into a contract," concludes Grode.

Sometimes there are exceptions. The singer Tiffany, for example, at sixteen, recently went through the courts and managed to get control of her career.

What if you read a book you like, and want to write a screenplay based on that book? To find out if the rights to that book are available, call the publisher of the hard-bound edition. Ask for the motion picture and theatrical rights division. They will tell you if the rights are available; if they are, they will refer you to the author's agent.

The next step is to contact the author and see if he or she would be willing to give you the rights to adapt the material into a screenplay. If they refer you to their agent, the chances are you'll have to option the material; it could be anywhere from $500 or $5,000 for a year, with an option for a second year. Make an offer and see what happens. If the book has been newly published, the price for the rights will probably be out of your reach. But if the book has been out for ten or twenty years, you have a chance.

One of my students found a novel she liked, tracked down the author in New Mexico, and talked with her about the possibility of doing the book as a film. The author gave her the rights to the novel for one year for one dollar. There would be no option for the second year unless the author approved that option. My student jumped at the opportunity. She wrote the script but did not get it optioned or sold. But she had the opportunity for a year. You can't ask for more than that.

"If you are going after the rights for a book," Grode emphasizes, "there must be, in addition to a detailed contract with the author, a publisher's release to insure that in the publishing agreement between the author and publisher, the publisher does not retain the rights you just negotiated for, and has the right to negotiate for them, or the right to actually receive some payment for them."

It's those little things, the things you think don't make a difference, that, if left alone, can blow a deal. In law school it's called "the parade of horribles." The lawyer's job is not only to protect the writer but to protect the project.

In the event that things go forward, and the author or agent is willing to negotiate with you for the rights, you might offer a small payment up front and possibly defer the major part of the option until after you get a deal. That is, if you manage to negotiate a deal with that point included in the agreement.

A lot of writers I know are avoiding the expensive news stories and looking for smaller, more personal stories. In any event, if you find a story you would like to use as the basis for a movie, you must be careful.

In a recent legal decision, the court ruled that you can write a work of fiction and yet somebody might claim that your work of fiction has damaged their reputation by portraying them. In this particular case the name of the person was changed, the way the person looked was changed, the location was changed; the only thing that was the same was that one of the fictional characters in the book happened to be a therapist who arranged nude, therapeutic sexual encounters. The author had attended one of these sessions and had in fact signed something saying she would not write about it. And she did.

What you might have to do is generalize the facts. As Grode says, "Authors draw upon their own life experience as well as research for elements of their work." Therefore, if you have any doubts about whether there may be any legal repercussions, it is important to give some careful consideration as to whether a story of character is too close to a real-life situation, and could possibly raise problems dealing with right of privacy, defamation, and so on.

In this particular case the court found against the author and against her publisher. This ruling established a precedent that can greatly limit a writer's use of investigative research in works of fiction and nonfiction. It can make things very complicated and very, very messy.

When you come right down to it, you, as writer, must use your discretion accordingly, act responsibly in the particulars of the situation, and legally try to cover yourself as much as possible.

Suppose you have an idea, write it up in script or treatment form, send it to the person you think would like the idea, and they send it back, either unopened, or with some kind of rejection letter, and then a year or two later you see what you think are your ideas on the screen? It does happen occasionally, but it doesn't mean that the studio, production company, writer, star or director has deliberately ripped you off and stolen your idea. For a number of reasons.

"The copyright law states that you cannot copyright an idea, only the expression of that idea," Susan Grode explains. The classic example, of course, is boy meets girl, they fall in love, and trouble ensues because of their different backgrounds. That's the story of *Romeo and Juliet, Abie's Irish Rose,* and *West Side Story.* The original idea of that story can't be copyrighted, but a new expression of the story can. Use that as your guideline.

Several times I have been called upon to be an expert witness on copyright infringement cases. A movie was made, someone claimed the movie used elements found in their unproduced treatment, script, or novel, and they sued. In every case except one, I thought the claims were unfounded. Yet the studios or production companies settled out of court, and I think it was a terrible mistake. Financially it made sense, because it is cheaper to settle out of court than to bring a case to trial, lawyers fees being what they are. But I would like to see a case like this go to trial—and lose—in order to set an important precedent.

As of this writing, I am involved as a witness in a case dealing with *Rocky IV*, written and directed by Sylvester Stallone.

A man in the Rocky Mountain region wrote a thirty-one-page outline that has Rocky fighting an East German fighter. The man wrote to Stallone, then sent this unsolicited outline to the studio, where an executive read it and tried to set up a meeting with Stallone. Once the star knew the treatment was about *Rocky IV*, he refused to read it and only reluctantly took a meeting.

Rocky IV was made and released; the man in the West claimed that certain elements in his treatment were used and that his copyright had been infringed. In his treatment, Rocky fights a giant East German fighter behind the Berlin Wall near the Brandenburg Gate. In the movie Rocky fights Drago, a Russian. Other claimed infringements: Adrian comes to be with Rocky before the fight; Rocky and his son have an emotional good-bye scene before he leaves for Russia; the East Germans at first boo Rocky, then end up cheering him for his courage.

All of these incidents are similar to the treatments. But the law says you cannot copyright an idea, *only the expression of that idea*.

Sylvester Stallone had already created the structure, form, and characters of the Rocky films. He had created Rocky's relationships with Adrian (Talia Shire), Apollo Creed (Carl Weathers), Mickey (Burgess Meredith), and Paulie (Burt Young), as well as all the other relationships and dramatic ingredients that go into the Rocky series.

The man in the West did not study the Rocky structure sufficiently to see that in his treatment, at least in my opinion, Rocky does things that Rocky would never do, like jeopardize his family in any way, shape, or form. The other characters likewise depart from the foundations formulated in the previous three Rocky movies. His structure is wrong, he's really telling two different stories, the relationships are unreal and contrived, and the general Rocky "form" is violated all over the place. It goes on and on.

Yes there are some similarities, but they are based on the characters and relationships that Stallone had already established in *Rocky I–III*. I hope this case goes to trial and is not settled out of court. A precedent has to be set, after what I think to be many unfair rulings, that the creator of the original material, the action and the characters, must be protected. Writers draw from their own experience; their point of view is subjective and individual, and they should not be limited by any fears of legal action.

4

Top Guns

*"I stand on top of the heap and control
everything."*

With these words, Jerry Wald defined the role of the producer in the moviemaking process. Wald, a writer as well as a dynamic Hollywood producer in the '40s and '50s, produced such films as the classic *Key Largo* (Richard Brooks), *Mildred Pierce* (Ranald MacDougall), *Peyton Place* (John Michael Hayes), and *Sons and Lovers* (Gavin Lambert and T.E.B. Clark), to name a few. He was considered to be the model for the crudely ambitious Sammy Glick in Budd Schulberg's classic Hollywood novel *What Makes Sammy Run?*

Traditionally, the producer in Hollywood was responsible for making a movie from inception through completion. The producer found the material, bought it, developed it into a screenplay, raised the financing—either independently or through the studio—hired the director, cast the roles, supervised the shooting, approved the dailies; in other words, made all the decisions necessary for bringing the film in—on time and on budget. Many of the Hollywood producers during the '30s, '40s, and '50s were moviemakers.

The role of the producer changed in the '60s and '70s, became more specialized, more fragmented. Today the producer plays a different role, wears many different hats. A studio producer, for example, is under contract to a specific studio and "contracted" to produce films. He gets offices and overhead paid, and when there's a script that needs a producer, the studio assigns him the project. He becomes the producer of credit. That's one kind of producer.

Another kind of producer, generally known as the executive producer, is involved with the financial aspects of the movie. He or she raises the money and puts together the necessary elements—writer, director, and stars—to get the movie made. Such producers are packagers. They buy or option the material, hire the writer to write the screenplay, and at a certain point make a decision about what is going to be done to get this script made into a movie. They have lunch with a lot of people and persuade them to do the project, then scurry around and procure checks from other people or write checks themselves. It's not moviemaking, it's deal making.

There are deals and there are deals. I once heard Peter Guber, the producer of such movies as *The Deep, Midnight Express, The Color Purple,* and *Missing,* say that nobody drives down Hollywood Boulevard on a Saturday night to see the best deal; they want to see the best movie.

In the '70s and '80s Hollywood movies, generally speaking, were better deals than they were movies. Producing a movie from inception through completion is a *process*. It can take many years.

Today, very few producers actually make movies. Most of them are associated with *some aspect* of making movies. They don't get into the nuts and bolts of filmmaking, the everyday decisions that must be made on the spot; cost of production is high, something like $15,000 a minute on a major studio production.

But there are two producers in Hollywood who make movies the "old-fashioned" way. They develop their own ideas, work hand in hand with the writers getting a shooting script ready for production, hire the director, cast, crew and everybody else, and attend to the everyday details required on the set day in and day out. They control every phase of the movie, including release, distribution, and advertising. In terms of the 120 to 144 Hollywood films produced and released each year, these two producers lead the pack in terms of selection of material—and the resulting box-office receipts.

You can always tell a Don Simpson/Jerry Bruckheimer film: interesting subject matter played against a strong visual background, characters who combat their own inner demons and overcome many obstacles to achieve their dreams or desires.

The movies Simpson and Bruckheimer have made—*Flashdance* (Joe Eszterhas), *Beverly Hills Cop* (Dan Petrie, Jr.), *Beverly Hills Cop II* (Warren Skaaren), *Top Gun* (Jim Cash and Jack Epps, Jr.)—are successful on two levels: dollar grosses (over a billion dollars in rentals so far) and quality. These movies all have a unique and contemporary visual style. Their point of view is consistent, their subject matter is interesting and different, and the way the plots are worked out is simply good drama. Finally, their expert packaging of music and other elements into a cohesive orchestration of marketing savvy is skilled and knowledgeable.

Yes, these films have been criticized as being too "sensational," or too "slick and superficial"; many say the films are thin, their characters glib and one-dimensional. Indeed, one critic called *Flashdance* a "toxic waste dump of a movie."

But you've got to give credit where credit is due. Don Simpson and Jerry Bruckheimer are trendsetters. Innovators. Pathfinders of the contemporary marketplace. And it shows at the box office.

What makes these two moviemakers so successful? What do they have that other producers don't? Who are these guys?

With that in mind, I went to interview them. I couldn't go to their offices on the Paramount lot—the Writers Guild forbids any member of the Guild to cross a picket line unless you're a hyphenate (a writer-producer or writer-director), and at the time the Guild was on strike—so we met at a local restaurant.

I had met Don Simpson before, when I was head of the story department at Cinemobile and CineArtists. At that time he was working in the publicity department at Warner Bros. We were doing a picture with Floyd Mutrux (*Aloha, Bobby and Rose,* with Paul Le Mat and Diane Hull), and he used to drop by and hang out with Floyd.

The one thing I remembered was that he was direct and outspoken, whereas Jerry Bruckheimer, I heard, was quiet, more reserved. I didn't exactly know what to expect from the interview or even what to ask, but I knew there were certain things I had to take into consideration. The first thing I had to acknowledge was that Don Simpson and Jerry Bruckheimer are moviemakers. Not filmmakers, because, while they develop their own material, and orchestrate the writing of the script, formulating concepts, characters, ideas, sometimes scenes and dialogue, they don't direct their material, at least not yet; that, too, they told me, is coming.

Don Simpson grew up in Anchorage, Alaska, where "the first skill I had in life other than walking was reading." After attending the University of Oregon, he moved to San Francisco, where he studied acting at ACT, then migrated to L.A., where he had dreams of becoming a writer-actor.

To make ends meet he went to work at Warner Bros. in the early '70s in the publicity department, as "the first in-house hippie in Hollywood, officially designated as the youth expert. I had long hair, a beard, spoke the jargon, but was never really a hippie." He worked on such films as *Mean Streets* (Mardik Martin), *Woodstock, Performance* (Donald Cammel), and *A Clockwork Orange* (Stanley Kubrick), and started hanging out with members of the writer-director program currently in progress at Warner Bros.

At this time in Hollywood, after the enormous success of Peter Fonda and Dennis Hopper's *Easy Rider,* Warner Bros. (now the Burbank Studios), wanting to cash in on the potential youth market, began a writer-director program for talented newcomers. That meant, if you were under thirty, and had long hair and a beard, you could probably get a development deal somewhere, John Milius, Paul Schrader, Marty Scorsese, Terry Malick, and Michael and Julia Phillips were all part of this program.

Simpson, after an argument with a major director, quit his job in publicity, and went on unemployment. While hanging out at Schwab's Drugstore one day with Paul Bartel, a director working for Roger Corman, he happened to see a magazine article about an automobile race called the Cannonball 500. He skimmed it and pitched a story to Bartel. Within hours he had a screenwriting deal. He ended up cowriting the script, acting in the movie, and being associate producer. "There's no tool like reading and information," says Simpson.

Simpson heard about a job at Paramount, so he borrowed a sport jacket from his friend Jerry Bruckheimer and went on the interview. He got the job and started working as a production assistant to Richard Sylbert, then head of production. During the next few years, Simpson moved up through the ranks of the studio hierarchy, and soon was senior vice president of production. In 1981, at the age of thirty-five, he was named president of worldwide production.

As head of production, Simpson was responsible for films like *Urban Cowboy* (Arron Latham), *48 Hours* (Roger Spottiswoode, Larry Gross and Walter Hill), *An Officer and a Gentleman* (Douglas Day Stewart), and *American Gigolo* (Paul Schrader), produced by his friend Jerry Bruckheimer. It was a movie originally budgeted at $11.5 million with John Travolta, but Bruckheimer brought it in, with Richard Gere, for under $5 million.

Bruckheimer appears shy and quiet in contrast to Simpson. He was a photographer before he started producing commercials, then moved into film; he produced *Thief* (written and directed by Michael Mann, of *Miami Vice* fame), one of my favorite films, and *Cat People* (Paul Schrader), among others.

Simpson and Bruckheimer first met in 1970 and have been friends ever since. They formed their own company in 1983 when they produced *Flashdance*. It's a film that bears the unmistakable story and visual imprint of Simpson and Bruckheimer. They complement each other like ''two sides of the same brain,'' as they're fond of saying. How do they do it? What's their secret?

First of all, Simpson and Bruckheimer make their own movies, movies that are conceived, developed, and produced from their own ideas. What's interesting is the way they find and develop material. *Top Gun* was a magazine article Jerry Bruckheimer read. He immediately saw ''a strong visual arena'' and gave it to Simpson, who was immediately attracted to the characters and situation.

That's their start point. They search for their stories everywhere, from situations and life experiences, and by reading magazines, all magazines, anywhere ''from fifteen to twenty magazines a day'' Simpson states emphatically. ''We have somebody on staff whose job it is to stay in touch with the new magazines coming on the market and subscribe to them for us. They subscribe to everything. I'll just read the headlines and see what the articles are dealing with. I'll go through a certain chronology about the material and in that way you can find subject matter that inspires story ideas.''

"Let's face it," Simpson adds. "Most of the key information in the world is available in magazines.

"Our job is to tell stories. Not be producers, not directors, not actors. Our primary function on all our pictures is always a function of the stories we've created.

"What's fascinating for me," Simpson goes on, "is plumbing the depths of other areas and then finding those common ingredients that pull it back into the middle. It's not reading mainstream magazines like *Time* or *Newsweek,* which frankly is old news. By the time it hits *Time* or *Newsweek,* I'm not interested. I'm interested in character, story, and arena."

"We make movies for ourselves," Bruckheimer adds. "We don't make movies for the audience. We make movies we want to see. Not parking-lot movies." When I asked him to explain what that was, he told me, "When you go see some movies, by the time you walk to your car in the parking lot and put the key in the ignition, you've already forgotten what the movie's about." So true. I call them "cotton candy" movies.

So how *do* they do it? First of all, "we look for an arena we find interesting," Simpson continues, "something that's visually exciting, and then we try to invest that background, or venue, with characters we like. At that point the arena lends itself to the story. The arena doesn't always have to be great, but it's got to be strong, because it's the arena that dictates character. There's got to be a match between arena and story."

I was intrigued by his use of the word *arena.* And using that arena as a start point for character and action. Thinking about that, I went back and took another look at their films.

When I examined *Flashdance,* I began to see what Simpson meant about defining the arena. You have a woman who's a welder during the day and an exotic dancer at night. Look what happens visually: you've got the visual dynamics of the steel plant juxtaposed against the clean filmic line of the dance. It's erotic and stimulating. One visual venue contrasts with the other. Put them together with a character trying to overcome her own fear of failure, and you have an arena of struggle and conflict.

In *Beverly Hills Cop* you've got a black cop from Detroit in Beverly Hills; that's almost a contradiction of image, and it creates an arena that heightens the character's development. *Top Gun* takes place in a high-tech jet training school, a visual arena that literally hasn't been seen since the 1940s.

It's the same with *Witness* (Bill Kelley and Earl Wallace), another of my favorite teaching films. It opens with a contradiction of image; Amish people, in horse and buggy, going to a funeral in what could be the early nineteenth century—only we learn it's 1984. When Rachel (Kelly McGillis) leaves the rolling hills of Lancaster County, Pennsylvania, to visit her sister in Baltimore after the funeral of her husband, the train is delayed in Philadelphia. We enter the world of the twentieth century as she does. The contradiction in image is emphasized when a huge truck rig followed by several cars trail the horse and buggy down the highway leading to the train station. When John Book (Harrison Ford) learns his superior officer is responsible for the murder of an undercover policeman, he has to flee and is cared for by the Amish. The tough Philadelphia cop has to adjust to the ways of the Amish, and learns something about himself he had buried years ago. The contradiction of image sets up the familiar "fish out of water" situation. It's no accident the original title of *Witness* was *Called Home* (see Chapter 19).

It's this arena, the area of struggle and conflict, that generates the strong visual dynamic that heightens the tension between characters and background and drives the story from beginning to end. "What happens when you combine arena and story and character and theme," Simpson goes on, "is that you have those four elements manifesting characters into a strong, single, and unified point of view. You can keep the film on an even keel. Because from the day you start development to the day you finish the edit, that point of view has framed the entire process. It's what keeps the producers, the director, the actors, the screenwriter, on the same course.

"It's been my experience as a production executive," Simpson says, "that what derails many, many movies at many different stages is a specific lack of a cohesive, coherent point of view. And point of view is a function of all those elements."

Remember, point of view is defined as the way a person views the world. The *Yoga Vasistha*, an ancient Sanskrit text, says, "The world is as you see it." That means what's inside of your head—your thoughts, feelings, memories, and emotions—are reflected outside, in your every-day life. It is our mind, not the world, that is the source of our experience, joy or sorrow, success or failure, abundance or scarcity. The subject and object are the same. How do you separate green from a leaf, heat from fire, or mind from body? We attract those things we subconsciously project into the world. The movie inside your head is the same movie that plays outside, in your day-to-day reality. Which is, of course, life, the big L.

It's the way we view the world. It *is* our point of view: victim or hero, humanitarian or thief, charlatan or specialist. A world bursting with the mysteries of God and creation, or a world troubled with violence, pain, and suffering. You choose. "The world is as we see it."

Take *Beverly Hills Cop*. "We knew we were doing a cross-genre picture," says Simpson. "Not a drama, not a comedy, but a dramedy. The original idea came out of two things. When I first came to Hollywood I had long hair and a beard, and I'd drive through Beverly Hills in my '56 Chevy, and the cops would stop and pull me over. They used to roust me, because they thought I was an outsider. And, indeed, I was an outsider." (That was his point of view.)

This was about the time that I met him, and he was hanging out with Floyd Mutrux, who was preparing his script on *Freebie and the Bean*. One day Floyd took him into the barrio to show him around and meet some of the gangs that were in East L.A.

Later Mutrux took some Latino cops he knew, along with a few gang members, out to dinner to a swank restaurant on the west side of town. Simpson was with them. "This was a big deal for them," Simpson recalls, "because they never got out of the barrio and Floyd had them jacked up on tequila shooters and they had guns in their waistbands and in their ankles. These cops were going to the bathroom with the guys who were the Mexican Mafia; the cops and robbers were at the same table and Floyd was getting them all drunk.

"While we were sitting there, I had this sudden idea. What happens, I said to myself, if I take one of these cops from East L.A. and transfer him to Beverly Hills? Wouldn't that be an interesting arena? That was my original idea."

That was the start point, the foundation, of *Beverly Hills Cop*. For over ten years, while Simpson was an executive at Paramount, he carried this idea in his head. He even had Danilo Bach write a first draft with the cop being from Detroit. That didn't work. Neither did a second draft. Simpson dropped the idea, but when he formed his partnership with Bruckheimer, "Jerry said it was the best project I had in my New Ideas Book, a book I jot down ideas in. Jerry convinced me to revise it and start working on it. At that point we pitched it to Mickey Rourke, and he accepted, so we started rewriting it for him."

When they started working on a screenplay they went through some "twenty-two drafts of the script, and maybe six screenwriters," Bruckheimer says. "Until Dan Petrie, Jr., got on the script, nobody could get the balance right; all those other scripts were all right, about a funny, tough cop in Beverly Hills. But there was no balance of comedy and action." (Remember *Dog Day Afternoon,* written by Frank Pierson? It was really two movies; the first two acts were wonderful comedy, but Act III, where Al Pacino is killed, is all drama. It was unbalanced.)

Then Sylvester Stallone got involved, and he wrote a draft that altered the concept too much, so they didn't go forward with the project. When Eddie Murphy became interested, Simpson and Bruckheimer saw they could make the contrast even greater, so Axel Foley became a black cop from Detroit, Bruckheimer's hometown.

"We built in certain scenes to set up certain structural pillars in the first act so the relationship between the black cop and his white thief friend could reverberate throughout the rest of the piece.

"For example," Simpson adds, "remember the bar scene in the pool hall where Axel says to his friend, I want to ask you a question. When we were sixteen and stole that car, he says, and the cops were after us, we ran down that alley. When you fell down, you stayed behind. Why'd you do that? You got arrested, I didn't. And, his friend replies, don't you know why, man? Axel says no. He says, because I love you.

"That scene drove the entire movie. It was purposefully constructed and placed in Act I for that specific reason. Now, you take that basic situation and move it to the next level," Simpson goes on, "by having a black man going into an alien environment. Then you crank that up by having his best friend not only a young white guy but a guy who's a crook. Axel's a cop and his friend's a crook to this very day.

"And he still comes back to his hometown and goes to the cop's apartment. They drink beer, they're gonna get laid, they're buddies, and then the crook gets killed.

"Well, guess what," Simpson says. "This is a movie about brotherhood. It's about loyalty and professionalism. Those are the issues at stake. It's about Axel Foley, a guy who's going to be a best friend, a best brother, and the best cop he can be regardless of any other circumstances. And that's a theme we're personally drawn to in life."

If Simpson and Bruckheimer are so involved in building the story line, how do they work with writers?

"What we try to do, in a sense," says Simpson, "is make the writer a partner of ours. A writer understands when he or she gets an assignment with us that the movie is coming from our point of view. So we sit down together and bat it around and nail it down. It's a collaborative effort. And when everybody's comfortable with all the strokes, first act, second act, and third act, and this is what happens, here's why it happens, and here's where it happens, then the writer will go and write the screenplay. There're no surprises that way.

"It would be foolhardy of us to hire somebody who doesn't agree with our point of view," Simpson continues. "If a writer comes in and says, I understand what you're trying to say but I don't agree with you and I want to do it another way, we simply say, thank you for your time, and what you should do is go make that movie. We're interested in the team approach in making movies. So if the director (like Marty Brest, in *Beverly Hills Cop*), Jerry, and I can establish the course of action in the story and all the elements that are involved, then when the writer turns in the pages, there're never any arguments about why did you do this and why did you do that. We've already told him, this is what we need, this is what we don't need, and this is how we'd like it."

"It's not writing by the numbers," Bruckheimer says, "in any way, shape or form. What it is is adhering to a preconceived course of action.

"Everything in that story line becomes a function of that original line of action. I learned that from a wonderful film editor, Elmo Williams. He taught me a lot about storytelling and editing."

"There are some cases," Simpson says, "like *Top Gun,* where we let the writers [Jim Cash and Jack Epps] do the first draft by themselves, after we all had agreed on the story. In that case, it didn't work. They wrote an excellent first draft but the girl didn't work at all, so we had to reconceive the girl and restructure the entire first act."

"We knew we wanted to get an inside look into the world of Maverick [Tom Cruise]," Bruckheimer adds. "His camaraderie, his ability to triumph in the end over his dark side."

"*Top Gun* is about nobility, courage, and honor," Simpson continues. "It's about warriors of the heart. It was an internal battle, the struggle of a man overcoming his own obstacles, the same thing that Jennifer Beals had to do in *Flashdance*."

"We worked endlessly in defining Maverick," says Simpson. "Story grows out of character. So naturally we approach our stories from a thematic point of view. What's this thing about? Who are the characters? We don't come at them from the outside in, which is the way high-concept movies work: 'Let's do a movie about a guy in Top Gun school.' "

Actors work in much the same way. Some actors approach their characters from the outside in. They focus on physical elements, or certain traits, or clothes the character would wear, and then start building a history of that character. Other actors approach it from the inside out, where they start from the emotion in the scene and build the character by the surges of emotion that connect the character to the story line.

When Simpson and Bruckheimer start working on their stories, "We decide first who the main character's going to be," Simpson says. "What are his obstacles? What does he have to overcome and how does he go about it? What's the price he pays and what does he achieve?"

With *Flashdance* it was difficult because the situation was different. "We were shooting in three weeks," says Bruckheimer, "and the script we bought didn't work at all, so we just kept the title." Basically, they kept the idea of the girl dancer and reinvented what she did. Simpson did a precise and detailed outline of the story, redefining the dancer's goals and the dramatic needs of the script.

"Then we sat in a room with Joe Eszterhas, an excellent journalist," continues Simpson, "because we needed somebody who would sit at a typewriter and turn out pages. And Joe delivered pages on a nightly basis. It was my first movie, and Jerry's fifteenth, and he was teaching me how to produce. We were in preproduction during the day and then pages would come in at night. We'd read the pages, meet with Joe, and then he'd go back to work that night. He'd work all night and give us new pages during the day.

"Joe had to start from scratch with an idea we had using the girl. Yet the process remained the same because the principal players—the director, Jerry, and I—wouldn't be working together unless we shared the same perspective."

When *Flashdance* was finally released, it was a smashing success (grossing some $185 million at the box office), sold more than 17 million soundtrack albums, and created a fashion craze for leg warmers and ripped sweatshirts that is still evident today.

When you get right down to it, the key to Simpson's and Bruckheimer's success is that they believe in the basic essentials of storytelling. "In the first ten minutes of the movie the audience wants to know what they're sitting there for, and what it's going to be about," Simpson explains.

In the same way, "if I read a screenplay and I see stage direction that's overwritten, I immediately start to get negative, because I'm not interested in stage directions; that's not what the script's about. A screenplay should be clean, it should be economical, it should be precise.

"Sometimes you read a screenplay," Simpson continues, "where the prose in the stage direction is very clean and economical and strong, and the dialogue is excellent, but the story's flat. The narrative's flat. You're reading and reading and get to page 52 and nothing's happening.

"When I start reading, I look at the dialogue," Simpson says. "I get a feel for it. If I start reading language that is cliché, obvious, or flat, I get turned off very quickly. No matter what the story is, I'm not very interested. If the screenwriter hooks me with stage direction and dialogue pointing toward a story that's interesting in the first ten or fifteen pages, I'll continue reading to see if they've got a narrative that works.

"And sometimes," Simpson adds, "you'll find a writer who has a strong ability with narrative and they'll pop you in the first three or four pages. Quality television writers have the facility for this. They really pump it in the first ten pages. Than all of a sudden you see the characters are predictable. You don't care about the people. It's a television-oriented thing.

"What happens when you get a good screenplay is that the quality of writing reflects the quality of thinking. Writing a screenplay is not like writing a novel; in a novel the prose functions in a cumulative way. It's a word medium. Screenwriting is a story told with pictures; it is the writers fusion of word and image. When someone reads a screenplay and sees the movie in their head, it's manifested immediately, by page 2 or 3. And if it's unique and original, you want to turn that page. Like a good novel is a page turner. You don't want to put it down."

They read so many screenplays looking for new writers that they know immediately whether the screenplay is working or not. "The one thing that's a major tip-off of an inexperienced screenwriter," says Simpson, "is the element of convenience they use in the story. Using something conveniently works to solve a problem, but that's not drama, that's device."

I asked why he thought that was, and he replied that during the last decade "a lot of writers have been *film schoolized*; their ability and point of view is really an extension of old movies, not of life. And movies are not about old movies. Movies are about life. They're supposed to be drama.

"That's it. No more, and no less."

He's right. Movies are larger than life.

That's what makes these two Top Guns so successful. The qualities that drive them in their films are the same they employ in life; both are persistent, dedicated, and determined professionals who make films they want to see. And they infuse these films with their drive, their persistence, their ambition, and above all, their point of view.

"The world is as you see it."

5

The Producers

*"Getting a film made is a combination of
inspiration and perspiration."*

Getting a film made is the keynote of success in Hollywood. How
good it is, or how bad it is, is irrelevant. Hollywood, as one journalist
commented, is a "town where you fail upward." If you get a deal to
make a movie budgeted at $10 million, and it's a colossal failure, the next
film you produce will probably cost $15 million. If you get $100,000
salary for the film that bombs, you'll get $150,000 for the next one. And
it keeps on going.

There are lessons to be learned from the people who get movies made.
For a producer, buying a screenplay is one thing; getting the script made
into a movie is another. And that's the bottom line.

As producers, Don Simpson and Jerry Bruckheimer represent the
hands-on approach to moviemaking; they conceive, create, and design
their projects from inception through completion.

But there are some producers who represent a more entrepreneurial
approach, working on many projects simultaneously at different stages of
the process, assembling the material—either script, book, novel, or
article—then bringing together the writer, director, and star or stars, then
presenting this package to the studio for financing. They make their deals
based on the quality of the "package." These producers are called
"packagers."

Producers who package their movies can be selective about which properties they put their energies into. Some projects may take a year or two to put together; others, up to seven or eight.

Peter Guber is the quintessential producer, the man who stands at the hub of the creative process and puts all the elements together to make a movie. He calls himself a "creative entrepreneur."

Guber, with his partner Jon Peters, has individually or collectively produced, or executive-produced, such highly acclaimed films as *Midnight Express, Missing, The Deep, The Color Purple, Flashdance, An American Werewolf in London, Gorillas in the Mist,* and *Rain Man.* In short, Peter Guber is a mover and a shaker. He gets things done.

We met for our interview in the conference room of his new offices across the street from the William Morris Agency in Beverly Hills. Guber and Peters recently merged their company, the Guber-Peters Company, with Barris Industries, creating a diversified entertainment complex specializing in films, TV, music, and the print media.

Personable, lean, and trim, with a substantial ponytail, Guber looks younger than his forty-odd years. I was impressed with his manner and presentation. He's a man who radiates confidence, success, money, and power.

While pursuing an M.B.A. degree at New York University's Graduate School of Business, Guber was recruited by Columbia Pictures. After two years in Casting and Creative Affairs, he became worldwide head of the studio, overseeing the development and production of such films as *Tommy, Shampoo, Taxi Driver, The Way We Were,* and *The Last Detail.*

In 1976 he left Columbia Pictures, formed and became co-owner of Casablanca Records and Filmworks with the late record entrepreneur Neil Bogart. At that time Casablanca, under Bogart's leadership, had a tremendous roster: Donna Summer, Kiss, The Village People, Cher, Mac Davis, Robin Williams, Woody Allen, The Captain and Tennille, Giorgio Morodor, and more.

After Bogart's death Guber formed the Guber-Peters company with Jon Peters and has undertaken production of such films as *Innerspace, The Witches of Eastwick, Batman,* Tom Wolfe's *The Bonfire of the Vanities,* and Carl Sagan's *Contact.* As of this writing, Guber-Peters have many projects in different stages of production. *Batman* is to be shot in the fall in England; *Contact,* directed by Roland Joffe, will be shooting soon;

Capa has a script by Menno Mejyes (*The Color Purple*), and Oliver Stone will direct; *Rain Man,* written and directed by Barry Levinson, stars Dustin Hoffman and Tom Cruise (the winner of several Academy Awards).

Guber-Peters has purchased the rights to *The Bonfire of the Vanities,* the number-one best seller by Tom Wolfe.

Among his other accomplishments, Guber is a member of the teaching faculty at UCLA, and is a member of the California, New York, and Washington, D.C., bar associations.

It was a rainy and overcast day in L.A. when I went to see him. Billowy clouds swept across the western sky as we sat in the plush conference room and talked about his role in making movies.

Guber underscored his close collaboration with partner Jon Peters on all business and creative affairs. "I see myself," he began, "as a producing filmmaker, a creative entrepreneur. Our business is not called show show, it's called show business. It's that blend of understanding you have to have in order to get your movie made, so you have to be entrepreneurially sound. You have to be willing to take a risk economically as well as creatively.

"The geography of every project is different. On some, you take only a creative risk, like acquiring the rights to a book; others, you develop yourself. Some projects you have to be willing to share the proprietorship of the project, and how that is shared determines what role my partner and I play and what credit we end up taking.

"Sometimes," he continues, "I'm simply an executive in my company; we may, for example, acquire a piece of material that already has a producer attached, and we assist him or her in the execution of the project. We help lay out the strategy, raise the financing, package it, generally assist and support them in their needs, and after that's all done, they go off and make their film.

"Other times, we become intimately involved in the development and acquisition of material, participating in the creative process. I'll find the material, and commission the screenwriter, either by myself, or with my partner and another producer, or possibly with a studio executive.

"There are many times when we become directly involved in an actual production capacity. On some films we may not stay on location but are involved in the post-production phase, conceptualizing and managing the marketing of the film," something which Guber is particularly adept at, and for which Guber-Peters will take an executive producer credit.

"And then," he goes on, "there are those special projects where my partner and I actually produce the film. We become intricately involved with every element of producing and marketing the film. We may find a book before it's published and decide to acquire it with our own funds. Then we'll begin the delicate process of finding the writer and developing it into a screenplay. Sometimes we'll bring in the filmmaker at this stage, and we'll be with the project on a day-to-day basis, and then we'll take the producer credit. So I define the credit we take by what job we do on the picture.

"After all," he emphasizes, "if you don't get the film made, you don't have anything. You don't hear someone saying I hear there's a great script playing in Westwood. The only criterion you can use about a producer is, did he or she get the film made; then you can ask, is it good or not?"

Though Guber-Peters purchased the rights to the novel *The Color Purple* "in order to get it made," he says, "and to get Steven Spielberg to do the picture, we had to step aside because he wanted his people to produce the movie. So we became the executive producer. I would have preferred to stay on as producer, because I had a lot invested in the project. While it wasn't in our best emotional interests to do that, it was certainly in our best economic interest, and in the interest of the project. So we did what we had to do to get the film made with the best creative talent."

The first job of the producer, Guber reminds us, is to get the film made. "It's a function of melding circumstances and opportunity together and knowing what to do with it," he continues. "It's a process of selection, as well as creation. A good creative producer, or executive producer, or creative entrepreneur, has the vision and the determination to see it through. He must have the romance to convince the director, the studio, and the talent to go along with that vision. He must have the tenacity and wherewithal to bring these elements together and coalesce them into a unified whole. He must have the drive and enthusiasm to keep it all together through whatever bumps and grinds occur during the process of getting the movie made."

This certainly sounds good—passionate and dedicated—but words are cheap in Hollywood. How do you go about applying it and making it work? What is it that attracts a producer like Peter Guber to a script, book, idea, or article?

"I'm moved by something emotionally," he says. "I don't figure it out, it doesn't start in my head, it starts in my heart, my gut, my groin."

What happens then?

"At that point, I begin to develop a strategy to translate what I feel. Whether it's a play, a book, or an article in a newspaper, like *Midnight Express*, or an original idea somebody pitched, like *Flashdance*, where you had an unknown director [Adrian Lyne], a first-time writer [Joe Eszterhas], and an unknown star [Jennifer Beals]. Or a song or rock opera like *Tommy* that provides the basis of a story line or situation for a movie. Whatever it is that makes me laugh, or cry, or become emotional in some way becomes the motor for the whole thing.

"What spurs me on is very simple; I want to see this as a film."

I found this simple statement expressed in interview after interview after interview. What intrigues anybody in Hollywood, what propels someone into an active mode, whether an agent, development executive, producer, or reader, is something that strikes them emotionally.

A short time ago one of my students called me from New York. She wanted my advice, she said, and then went on to explain that she had written a screenplay that a number of people in L.A., agents and producers, had read and liked, "but they all said it didn't 'live' for them; it didn't leap off the page."

They said it was different, interesting, and unusual, but they were going to pass on it, but they would be happy to read anything else she cared to submit. As soon as I heard that, I knew it was a setup. I already had an idea of what was coming.

We talked awhile about the script, about her writing, and the comments of the agents and producers. I was testing the waters up to then, and just before we hung up (in screenwriting, you enter the scene at the last possible moment), I asked her what her story was about. So she told me. It was a story about a professor at a Midwestern university doing nuclear research who accidentally stumbled onto a very important find which became a political issue for a nuke-antinuke confrontation, and of course the CIA and KGB become involved. The professor goes through some past-life regressions and learns the source of his discovery, and so on.

I stopped her right there. No wonder, I said. The subject matter, the use of the political situation, nuke-antinuke, CIA, KGB, is old hat. That subject matter has saturated this town like a wet sponge and no one's interested anymore.

But what about his past life regressions? she asked. What about them? I asked. That part of the script is certainly new and novel, I said, but the readers of the script were getting turned off by the political issues just the way I did. They made their decision before they finished reading the screenplay.

No matter how it's done, no matter how interesting it is, or how well written it is, it's old stuff. You need a fresh look, a fresh environment, a fresh approach. "Fresh and original, with a twist."

I'm beginning to understand that the choice and selection of the subject matter is the most important thing in selling the screenplay. Once you have found your "arena," action, and characters, and weld them into an interesting story line, and you have a good, solid first-draft script, then you can plan a strategy that helps you get it to the people who can say yes to a project.

What does Peter Guber do when he finds a script he likes? After all, he is both buyer and seller. How does he plan a strategy?

The first question Peter Guber asks himself when he responds to a script is "What would the film look like? Is it lighthearted, drama, slapstick, or science fiction? Is it going to require special effects? Is it going to be a big-budget enterprise? So the first thing I do is define what it is. Recognize what it is. You always ride the horse in the direction it's going.

"If this picture is a $20 million film shot with animals on the top of a mountain in Africa, it's unlikely a new young director from UCLA will be a good selection. That would be wasted energy. It's just too hard to swim upstream. So what are we going to do to pull this off?

"Number one, we'll need a top director—like Jim Cameron, who did *Aliens,* or Oliver Stone, who did *Platoon*. The real key is to make sure the project has a shape and direction to it, so the financier, or the studio/distributor, can see the project as a film as opposed to development."

The key factor is to determine what will be the hub of the project in terms of getting the film made. Such is the case with *Gorillas in the Mist* (Anna Hamilton Phelan), the story of Dian Fossey, the famous anthropologist who was studying gorillas in Rwanda when she was mysteriously murdered. No one knows who did it, or why.

"This story," explains Guber, "takes place in Central Africa, on an extinct volcano some eleven thousand feet high, in the dense jungle, with eight-hundred-pound silverback gorillas; it is a monster project, both figuratively and literally. At an early date, it was determined that the key to this movie would be the director; someone established, who could deal with animals, the logistics of handling a large crew in foreign terrain and under difficult conditions."

At this same time Warner Bros., Universal, and an independent producer, Skip Steloff of Heritage Entertainment, were all developing projects about Dian Fossey. Once she was murdered, there was a feeding frenzy. The studios threatened each other, Skip Steloff had news conferences, and ultimately everybody realized they either had to work together on this project or not at all. So Universal and Warner Bros. joined forces and Steloff, the independent, was forced out.

Arnold Glimcher, who developed the Fossey project at Universal with Anna Hamilton Phelan's screenplay, and Peter Guber got together. After an initial clearing of feelings, "we hit it off pretty good," Guber remarks. "He was from Boston, I was from Boston. He was a sailor, I was a sailor.

"So we joined forces and ended up agreeing to use his director, Michael Apted, and his script. Arnold went off to Rwanda and produced the film. We are the executive producers, and Arnold Glimcher the producer.

"Ironically, the element that provided the momentum for this project was something quite different. I describe momentum as being the critical element in getting the picture made. In *Gorillas* the momentum was achieved by securing the natural-history rights in Rwanda so we could photograph the actual gorillas, then getting support from such groups as the African Wildlife Foundation. They were instrumental in this regard.

"While this was a true story, we felt it was critical that we have legal releases from the people we were going to portray. Since Dian Fossey had been murdered [still unsolved at this writing], we could avoid the normal requirement of certain clearances. Since we had these clearances as well as permission from the country and the National Park System of Rwanda, we created the hub that held everything together.

"Formulating a strategy and executing it requires a combination of inspiration and perspiration. In this case the key was to create a critical mass, to secure enough elements to get the project breathing.

"It's not only inspiration. You need the perspiration and the experience and the tenacity to see it through. I get my point of reference from where I want to be at the end, what I want it to look like. [Just like writing a screenplay—you've got to know how it ends before you begin.]

"So we set up the strategy of how to get there, plug in the success element that will generate the critical mass, and unleash the momentum of how we're going to achieve it, which hopefully will lead us to the gold at the end of the rainbow. What we do, really, is buy other people's dreams and make them our own. One has to be a dreamer to be a really top producer; to be successful you have to have a goal, and a goal is simply a dream with a time limit."

Organizing and planning a strategy. Notice how Guber first defines what he wants to do, then searches for the pieces he needs to put together, determines the "success element," then visualizes the path, the process, by which he can get it made.

"The key," he says, "is not to get in your own way and let yourself be overcome by your own ego. The producer must deal with thousands and thousands of details that have to be looked at and handled in concert with an overall plan. God, as they say, is in the details.

"No one really knows how a project will turn out, whether the ingredients will work. After all, the same ingredients that go into a chocolate mousse may go into making a soufflé.

"Some projects take a long time to put together and the sheer weight of it tests your commitment. That's what happened with *Batman*."

After Guber and Peters acquired the rights to *Batman* from D.C. Comics, they spent years going from one deal to the next, putting their own money into a number of screenplays. Nothing happened until Tim Burton (*Pee Wee's Big Adventure*) expressed some interest in the project.

A new writer, Sam Hamm, was commissioned to do yet another draft, and during the writing Burton decided to do *Beetlejuice*.

The budget for *Batman* was estimated at $20 million; it would be a "big" film, and would require stars to get it off the ground. Through the efforts of Jon Peters, Jack Nicholson was signed to play the Joker; at the same time Michael Keaton agreed to star as Batman. *Beetlejuice* opened, did well, and all ingredients blended together to keep the project alive.

"The trick," Guber says, "is to stay out of the way and let other people help you make it happen."

"What is it that's marketable about this project?" he asks rhetorically. "How do you give it momentum, breathe some life into it? And how do you present it so everybody sees the same vision you do?

"The farther out you go, the more exposure you'll have and therefore more opportunity. If we really go far out, and put money into it, we'll have a director, script, and star, and we'll be sitting there with maximum clout to make an unbelievable deal.

"We know, for example, that if we went to the studio and said here's the book *The Bonfire of the Vanities,* the number-one best seller in the country, winner of the Pulitzer prize, we could get a deal. If we wanted to add Michael Cristofer, the Pulitzer prize screenwriter who wrote *The Witches of Eastwick,* we could get a better deal. And if we wanted to wait until the script was completed, financing it ourselves, we could probably fold in a filmmaker like Larry Kasdan, Mike Nichols, or Adrian Lyne, all people we've talked with about the project. Then we could say we're going to make this picture at a modest price by today's standards, $15 million, and we'll have it for you by November 10, before the Christmas season, and pre-Academy Awards.

"At that point, you can be sure every studio in town will be knocking at our door, asking what do we have to do to get this picture? And we'll say, you don't have to do anything. We'll finance the whole picture ourselves. And they'll say what do we have to do to get this picture?

"Now you're sitting there making a killer deal on the picture. A killer deal.

"So, you ask, why wait?

"Simple. To develop the project to that point you have to establish what the risk-reward ratio is; each one of these steps requires a large investment. A screenplay by an established screenwriter can cost anywhere from $300,000 to $400,000; attaching a director on the project is probably another $150,000 to $200,000—just on development alone.

"If the script doesn't work, and the director takes on another project, you're sitting there with a lot of unrecouped costs which the studio doesn't want because they would have to start out with a financial burden. Then it's not momentum you're dealing with, it's resistance—drag—and that might bring the project down. But if it works, it's magic.

"If we had started all the way back and just made a deal for the book, we could have made a nice deal. But you've not taken any of the risk, therefore you won't get the reward."

It is not uncommon in Hollywood for certain projects to take several years before the script is bought and the movie made. Twenty years ago, Dennis Shryack (see Chapter 1), wrote a spec screenplay called *Count a Lonely Cadence,* based on the novel by Gordon Weaver. Shryack had optioned the book with his own money ($500). At that time, he was a literary agent by day, a screenwriter by night. The response to his first draft was enthusiastic, but nobody felt it was the right time for this type of picture.

The story, about a rebellious young man in an army stockade and his relationship with five black prisoners and the commander of the stockade, is a solid character piece that addresses the concerns of young people everywhere. Every year some studio, producer, director, or star would express interest in doing the material and would pay the option money. And every year the result was the same. Kenny Hyman, formerly head of Warner Bros., was the first, followed by Phil Feldman, producer of Sam Peckinpah's *The Wild Bunch* (Walon Green), then Marty Erlichman. Even Kirk Douglas encouraged Shryack not to give up hope for this project; after all, Douglas told him, he had spent fifteen years trying to bring Ken Kesey's *One Flew Over the Cuckoo's Nest* to the screen, and it was his son, Michael Douglas, who finally accomplished it. One of the first actors interested in it was Martin Sheen, but at that time, 1968 or 1969, he did not have a big enough name to get the project off the ground.

Shryack put it on the shelf and continued writing screenplays; *Gauntlet* and *Pale Rider* are just two of the thirty screenplays he's written during the last twenty years. With his new partner, Michael Blodgett, author of *Captain Blood*, four of his original screenplays are scheduled for production or release in 1989, including his favorite, *Turner and Hootch*, a story about a cop and his dog.

Shryack kept getting phone calls about *Cadence;* he would send it out and there would be interest for a while, but the person or company would pass. Then one evening when Dennis Shryack and his wife were in a restaurant having dinner, Martin Sheen and his wife and a few friends came in and sat down in the next booth. After debating with himself, Shryack finally got up and introduced himself to Sheen as the screenwriter of *Count a Lonely Cadence*. Sheen became excited and spent the next twenty minutes talking about the script.

A few days later, Sheen called. He wanted to activate the project but was no longer interested in playing the lead; he wanted his son, Charlie Sheen, to play the lead, and he would direct. As this book goes to press—twenty years after Martin Sheen first expressed interest in *Count a Lonely Cadence*, Sheen is raising the financing in Canada and hopes to begin shooting within a year.

Twenty years. A labor of love sometimes pays off when we least expect it.

Peter Guber told me that several of his favorite projects, now in various stages of preproduction, took many years to get off the ground. *Batman* took more than ten years to get made. *Capa*, the story of the famous war photographer, has occupied Guber for more than eleven years; I asked him why he would spend so much time on one project. He replied that Capa was "an amazing man who made a career of looking death in the face.

"Why did he do that?" Guber asks. "What was it about him that made him do that? Was he a hero or was he just confronting his own mortality? What makes somebody be like that? He went through three of the great wars, the Spanish Civil War, World War II, and Vietnam. We see in him the face of death, and we experience in him the face of life, through the women he loved. It's *The Way We Were*, it's *Out of Africa* in Europe. It has all the same elements, almost epic in stature. There's real strength in *Capa*. It's not topical, or trendy; it'll be in this year, it'll be in next year, it'll be in the year after that, like *Gandhi* or *The Last Emperor*. Whenever you make it, it'll be in. It's not like *Dance Fever* or *Salsa,* you know. That's only in this week.''

Though the Guber-Peters Company has more than fifty projects in development, *Dangerously,* from a screenplay by Jim Cash and Jack Epps, Jr. (*Top Gun*)—a story about a cop who's been kicked off the force and has to solve a twenty-year-old murder—has been in the works for seven or eight years. *Innerspace* took more than six years of active pitching and presentation before it got the green light to be made into a movie.

You'll usually find that anything of value, anything of substance or quality, usually takes a long time before it's sold, or made. There is no such thing as an overnight success in Hollywood. A script that is written, sold, and made into a movie within a few years is the exception, not the rule. Patience, persistence, and determination is what works in this town, the same way it does in life. Maybe that's the lesson we all need to learn. A freshly planted fruit tree doesn't bear fruit immediately. It has to grow, mature, and blossom, and after a certain period of time, when it's ready to bear fruit, it does. It's the same with selling a script, and getting it made.

As we were finishing up our interview, I nonchalantly asked Guber why some films get made and others don't. He laughed and said, ''Why does this woman love this man and not another? Why are you wearing this jacket and not another? Why do you like this car and not another?

''There has to be a leap of faith for every movie that gets made. There is a pusher, someone who goes around and pushes the project forward, from place to place. Usually that's the producer. Then there's a leaper, someone who reaches out, whether it be a studio or financier, and says I'm going to make that. The leaper says, I believe in this, and I believe in you. The louder the push, the bigger the corona surrounding it, and the more likely the pusher will find a receptor for it.

''So the question of why one film gets made instead of another has any number of answers. It's usually because the critical mass of one film seems to be hotter. It's got a hotter director, a hotter writer, it's got somebody who has just come off a successful picture, so somebody at the studio feels that this particular film has a greater chance for success than another.''

By the same token, some films get made because of luck, circumstance, and timing. Not to mention the fact that a director is broke and can't make his alimony payments or his house payments and needs a project, any project, to pay off his debts. Or, as is so often the case, a star needs work, and whatever script is around that suits his image, gets made. It doesn't have to be the best around, and it usually isn't; it just has to available.

Timing is everything in Hollywood. Not luck, though that sometimes helps, but persistence and knowledge of how the industry works. That information can be power. One day when I was at Cinemobile—it was right after the success of *M*A*S*H*—my boss walked in the office, threw a script on my desk, and said read it immediately. I said I'll do it after lunch, and he said no, do it before lunch. So I read it.

It was not very good. As a matter of fact, if I recall correctly, reading it on an empty stomach, and finding it necessary to cancel my lunch appointment, I gave it a 4 out of 10. When I finished reading it, I called my boss and gave him my opinion. He said okay, and hung up. Then he started making a lot of phone calls.

Later I found out the circumstances. Elliott Gould and Donald Sutherland, the stars of *M*A*S*H* (Ring Lardner, Jr.), wanted to work together and there was a six-week break in their schedules. So they were looking for a script. This was the only script around at the time that fit their needs. It ended up being called *Spies*. It was a dreadful movie and a dismal flop at the box office.

That's why some movies get made and others don't.

"The quality of the screenplay," says Guber, "is critical to the success of the film. When all is said and done, and you see the fancy dailies with great production values, the wonderful locations, and beautiful costumes, what is up on the screen is the story. But getting it made requires four skills on the part of the motivator of the project. *Commitment;* the person has to be totally committed to getting this movie made. *Enthusiasm;* there's so much drag on a project, so many reasons for people to say no, so many obstacles to overcome, you've got to be your own cheerleader to see it through successfully.

"Then there's *inspiration;* you've got be inspired. It can't just be hard work, it's got to have some magic about it. There's something more than just the words that keep you going. If you just wanted to shoot the script you could stand it up and take pictures of it! The script is the start point, the blueprint, the foundation, but the magic comes with the filmmakers and the actors and the director and the production designer and the location and all those elements that go into making a movie.

"So what pushes it across the line? *Momentum.* Momentum means that the project looks like it's going to get made. It may be a studio hearing about something, tracking it down and then intercepting it from going somewhere else. They have to chase it, court it; it has to be valued. Now, everybody wants something that somebody else wants, especially in Hollywood. So it's got enough elements in it to keep it moving forward.

"There's a balance between inspiration and perspiration. Now, if you get a brilliant script that's a 10, it doesn't need anything; what's on the page is on the stage. I could give it to my dog and I can go to a studio and say this dog is the producer and the studio would say okay.

"But that's the exception, not the rule. The writer has to understand that the elements he or she needs to add to this project are more important than just selling it to someone for a price. He's betting on those people's capabilities to get the movie made, because once a film gets made, the more chance he has of being successful."

Today it's not enough to sell the screenplay. What's more important is getting the movie made. And you have to do whatever it takes to get the job done. Selling the screenplay, as Guber emphasizes, is a combination of inspiration and perspiration. That's what we can learn from someone like Peter Guber. How to overcome all those obstacles that drag a project down and keep it from happening. How to be persistently relentless.

There's a great line from Larry Kasdan's *Body Heat,* where William Hurt accidently meets Kathleen Turner and her husband, Richard Crenna, the man they're planning to murder, at a restaurant. During their conversation, Richard Crenna tells William Hurt that what stops most people from being successful in their lives is "that they don't know the bottom line."

"What's the bottom line?" Hurt asks.

"Doing whatever it takes to get the job done," Crenna replies.

It's something we all need to remember.

6

The Independent
Producers

*"It's never a risk when you believe in
your own taste."*

In 1986 some 511 major motion pictures were produced in the United States, and of those, 144 were made by major Hollywood studios and production companies; the other 367 were made by independent producers. Many of those films were both critical and commercial successes. In fact, films like *Platoon, A Room With a View,* and *Kiss of the Spider Woman* seem to be ushering in a new era of Hollywood production.

The rise of the independent film is a relatively recent phenomenon. The last few years have seen the videocassette creating a major new market for home viewing. Recent research shows that children and young people are not going out to movies the way they used to. Instead, they're staying home and watching cassettes, and an older audience is emerging. The money from this market caters to an older, more sophisticated audience, and therefore taps a new source of financial funding dedicated to producing films. Companies like Vestron and HBO are both exhibitors and producers of product. Add to this the new Cineplex multitheaters that have as many as sixteen screens, and you have a need to create product that will feed both theaters and television screens.

Because the studios are such large corporate entities, they cannot afford to produce the small, serious films that often win awards and critical acclaim. The cost of running a studio is so enormous that a "major motion picture" must gross about $100 million at the box office to show any kind of a profit at all. Do you know how many films gross $100 million a year? You can count them on one hand.

The average studio film costs about $16 to $18 million to make, and another $7 to $9 million to market. That means prints and advertising. And the figures keep going up and up and up. The Hollywood studio today is looking only "for home runs, not doubles," says one studio executive.

The low-budget film, on the other hand, has an ability to present daring and innovative material, and seems to attract a producer who can function either within or without the normal Hollywood channels of production.

To be independent means to stand alone, or to be self-sufficient. Most independent producers do not have overall studio deals or access to huge sums of financing, or the power of a large agency like CAA to help package their material. They are independent because they are on their own. And to survive in the wilds of Hollywood, they must exhibit the patience of a fox, the cunning of a coyote, and the courage of a wolf. Most of them prefer it that way.

Tony Bill is an exemplary example of the independent producer. Bill searches for talent and material in a unique way, "and most of the movies I've produced or directed," he says, "have been first scripts, such as *Steelyard Blues* by David Ward [Bill also produced *The Sting,* David Ward's second script, which Bill commissioned him to write]. *Deadhead Miles* was a first script by Terry Malick, who later went on to write and direct *Days of Heaven,* a contemporary classic; *Taxi Driver* (Paul Schrader) was a first script, as were *Harry and Walter Go to New York* (John Byrum), *Hearts of the West* (Rob Thompson), *Boulevard Nights* (Desmond Nakano), and *Five Corners,* written by John Patrick Shanley, who went on to write *Moonstruck,* nominated for an Academy Award for best original screenplay."

The way Tony Bill found John Patrick Shanley is typical of the way he finds material. "I was auditioning some student actors," he says, "and I saw a two-minute scene from a play I'd never heard of [*Danny and the Deep Blue Sea*], by a writer I'd never heard of. Even though it was a two-minute scene, I started listening to the quality of writing. Though I was auditioning the actors, I thought the dialogue was interesting. So I tracked him down and said I think you ought to write a screenplay. *Five Corners* was the result.''

It's not an easy process finding new writers. "It's like 3M searching for gold," says Bill. "They move mountains of earth to find one little ounce of gold. And that's how I do it.''

Bill receives between twenty and thirty screenplay submissions a week. They come from all over, from agents, through the mail, by special delivery, occasionally by limousine. One writer even sent a script by armored car (see p. 7).

Tony Bill is the exception in Hollywood. He or someone on his staff will cover the material submitted. What he suggests is sending a letter describing what the script is about, "so I don't have to handle spaceship movies that don't interest me, or monster movies I don't want to bother with. If I get a letter that introduces the script in a novel, witty, and unpretentious way, and it gets my attention, I may read the script. But if somebody sends me a script and says, 'This is very commercial and it's going to make a lot of money for you,' I won't even bother to read it.''

In Hollywood, presentation is everything. From the words on the title page, to hard leatherette covers, to a script submitted wrapped in a rubber band instead of three-hole punched paper bound with brads, there is a right way, and a wrong way, to submit your material. You have to approach the presentation of your screenplay the same way an independent producer must present your script to get it made.

How do you do that? It's different with each script. And each producer approaches it differently.

"Should I go for the actors first, or should I look for financing?" asks Tony Bill. "Or do I try to get a director? I don't think anybody can tell you what the next step should be.

"I just optioned another first-time script, and I think my next step will be to go to the actors before I go to a studio. On another project, for example, it may be just the opposite. Each script is different, and you have to handle it in an original way.

"But I won't go anywhere with a script that needs apologies. What you don't want to do is let the studios do your casting for you, either for director or actors. That's your job as producer or director.

"Then you ask them if they want to make that movie. Rather than go ask what kind of movie they want to make out of your script. *My Bodyguard,* for example, was turned down by every studio in the business. It was finally made by the Mel Simon Company. If you let the studio do your thinking for you, you sometimes get in trouble."

Howard Kazanjian is the producer of *Raiders of the Lost Ark, Return of the Jedi,* and more, and has been associated with George Lucas ever since they attended the USC Film School in the '60s.

After leaving the USC Film School, he entered the assistant director's program at the Directors Guild of America, and worked with such noted directors as Joshua Logan on *Camelot,* Sam Peckinpah on *The Wild Bunch,* Billy Wilder on *The Front Page,* Robert Wise on *The Hindenburg,* and Alfred Hitchcock on *Family Plot.* Is it any wonder George Lucas wanted him to produce all his pictures?

Kazanjian is a man who knows how to make movies. When George Lucas took his much-needed hiatus from moviemaking, Howard Kazanjian became an independent producer. "He had been working nonstop for ten years," says Kazanjian. "*Return of the Jedi* was probably the most difficult picture ever made. It had 963 special-effects shots. *Empire* had more than 500. Every day while in postproduction, and sometimes on Sunday, we were there seeing dailies; we were there at 6 A.M. designing what effects we were going to shoot that day, seeing dailies at 8 A.M., then seeing dailies again at 6 P.M. The lab had to stay open on weekends around the clock and I never slept the last couple of weeks before we put *Jedi* into the theaters."

When *Raiders of the Lost Ark* was being realized, story conferences were being held with Lucas, Spielberg, and Kasdan. They had all grown up on the old serial, and they knew that every ten minutes or so you need to have something happening on screen.

The first ten minutes of *Raiders,* for example, is one of the most exciting openings in modern film, and it's followed by perhaps the dullest ten-minute expository scene, which is essential because it sets up the rest of the story.

It works because of the opening. Indiana Jones (Harrison Ford), makes his way through a series of booby traps seeking an ancient statue. With the sheer bravado of a larger-than-life character, he manages to escape the giant boulder thundering down a ramp that could crush him like a bug. As he's lying there, lucky to be alive, his old nemesis appears and forcefully takes the statue from him. It's great filmmaking.

The next scene, the long exposition scene, shows Indiana Jones back in his classroom, when he is summoned to the auditorium by two federal agents who ask him questions about the lost Ark. He explains, they ask more questions, he explains, and by the end of this scene we know everything we need to know about the temple of Ra and the lost Ark.

Even though it's dull and talky, it works because the opening was so powerful. We need to catch our breath and understand what the story is about, just the way a bottle of fine red wine needs to breathe before pouring.

When I first started working at Cinemobile and Cine Artists, I worked for a man who never read anything. Fouad Said, my boss, was the location cameraman for the old TV series *I Spy,* starring Bill Cosby and Robert Culp. When I first started working for him, he always told me he wanted a lot of "whammos" in the scripts I submitted to him.

What's a whammo? I asked.

He hemmed and hawed and couldn't explain it. But over the next few months, I kept hearing him talk about the essential needs of whammos in a screenplay. This from a man who never read anything except budgets! He would always say "ten pages and a whammo, ten pages and a whammo."

At first I though he was crazy. But after a while I figured out that a whammo must be some kind of action scene, something that grabs the audience and keeps them pinned to their seats.

Sometimes after work we would sit around and talk, and he kept saying when he was filming *I Spy,* you always need a whammo after a few pages of dialogue. You need something to keep the audience interested and involved in the action of the story line.

Then, one day, out of the blue, he asked me to "make a whammo chart."

I looked at him, dumbfounded. "A whammo chart," I gasped.

He nodded, and walked away.

I didn't know what in the world he was talking about. "When in doubt, do nothing,'' is my motto, so I did nothing, hoping he'd forget about it. But every week or so he'd ask me how the whammo chart was coming, and I would smile weakly, and say nothing. But I knew he was serious, and the only way I could do what he wanted was to figure out what a whammo was and define it.

I seriously thought about it, and finally came up with a definition I felt okay about: a whammo, I reasoned, was a piece of action, or anything that impeded the action. It could be a car chase, it could be a love scene, it could be the silence of waiting for someone to open the door.

Suppose you're dramatizing a bank robbery. It's tense, terse, taut. That's a whammo. Now, suppose the robbers race out of the bank, and the car is gone. That's a whammo. Or they race out of the bank, and the car won't start. That's a whammo. Or as they race away, the street is suddenly blocked by a huge streetweeper. That's a whammo.

Either a car chase or a kiss.

What makes the opening of *Raiders of the Lost Ark* so great is that it's one whammo after another. If you go back and count the individual whammos, there are at least six of them that keep you pinned to the edge of your seat. It's that opening that makes the following exposition scene work.

Once I defined a whammo, I set about creating the whammo chart. I drew a graph, and on the left side of the page I drew a vertical line with numbers ranging from 10 to 1, 10 being the highest. On the bottom of the page I drew a horizontal line and put page numbers, 1 through 120. That way I could locate the whammo by page number and rate it on a scale of 1 to 10.

The opening of *Raiders,* for example, would be a 10. The next whammo is when Indiana Jones gets on the old seaplane and flies to see his old girlfriend, Karen Allen, and the Nazis show up and in the ensuing fight you have another 10-rated whammo.

Ten pages and a whammo. Ten pages and a whammo. With this chart you could go through any film and find any holes that slow down and impede the action of the script. I used the whammo chart for all kinds of films, knowing, of course, they worked best on action-adventures. Whenever I pitched a script to my boss for possible financing, or production, or completion funding, I always presented it with a whammo chart.

As I'm writing this, I'm remembering the absolute absurdity I felt about what I was doing. You can't measure a screenplay in terms of how many, or how few, whammos there are. I was just doing my job. Yet, there was a certain, insane logic to what I was doing.

My boss would look at the whammo chart and start evaluating the script based on the graph I had drawn. And he would say: Look at Act II. For twenty pages, from page 35 to 55, there's not one whammo. It's all talk. We need a whammo here. And he would go and mark on the chart where some kind of whammo should go. Of course, I had to convince the writer of this, and help guide him or her to the whammo that would work in that particular screenplay.

He didn't care about the story. He didn't care about the structure. All he cared about was making good film. And he knew, intuitively, that you can't have a movie with talking heads. You've got to have "ten pages and a whammo, ten pages and a whammo."

That's what George Lucas, Steven Spielberg, and Larry Kasdan knew intuitively from watching those old Saturday morning serials on television. If you examine any good action film, like *Raiders, Jaws, Beverly Hills Cop,* or *Top Gun,* they are all built on this principle of "ten pages and a whammo."

But you have to be careful. More is not better. *Indiana Jones and the Temple of Doom* has too many whammos; it starts with a strong whammo and then it continues on the same level through the entire film. You've got to give the reader or audience time to catch their breath.

When the script of *Raiders* was finished, the first studio they took it to was Paramount. Howard Kazanjian set up a meeting with the then head of production, and stipulated they were giving the studio first shot at it, "but I've got to have it back to tomorrow, Thursday," recalls Kazanjian. The head of production took the script but called later to say, "I'm not going to be able to read it tonight because I've got to go to a preview, but I'll read it over the weekend, and give it back to you on Monday morning."

"He already knew it was going to be a tough deal," says Kazanjian. "Spielberg had just completed *1941,* and the town was filled with rumors of how much *1941* was overbudget, from $18 million to $28 million to $48 million. That weekend the studio head saw a sneak preview of the Spielberg comedy and didn't like what he saw.

"We met on Monday morning, and he said to me: 'We're going to pass, but I want you to know that this is a terrific screenplay.' He paused dramatically, then said, 'But I have one suggestion.' I said, 'Yes, what is it?' And he said, 'Take the Germans out of it!' "

Take the Germans out of it!

"I looked down at the script in my hands and thought maybe I had given him the wrong script."

How can you do that! Taking the Germans out of *Raiders* is like taking the heat out of the sun, or the wetness out of water. If you start changing your material to suit everybody's needs, you end up with nothing.

It happens to screenwriters all the time. You spend a year or so working on a screenplay and submit it to an agent. The agent says this or this should be changed. So you go back and dutifully change it the way the agent suggested, only to learn he's not going to represent it anyway. So you go to a producer, who says the same thing, and you go back and make the changes he or she suggests, only to discover that they're really not interested in optioning the property anyway. You keep on doing that and you end up with a screenplay that is not the script you originally envisioned, and you are definitely confused about what to do to fix it.

Sometimes an agent or producer will read the script and say it's similar to something being done at one of the studios. When you investigate, you learn that a similar film is in development, production, or soon to be released. One of my students was writing a story about a man and woman who work together, compete with each other, and hate each other. One day, while playing in the company softball game, they collide at home plate and are knocked unconscious. When they wake up, he wakes up as her, and she wakes up as him. It's a delightful story as both try to get back to themselves.

It turned out that a few similar films had just been completed— *Nothing in Common, Big, Father and Son*—so no one would touch the script, no matter how good it was. She had to use it as a sample of her writing, and managed to get a very good agent to represent her on future projects. But her goal in writing *that* script had been to have it made into a movie, and that she was unable to do.

In the same way, the goal of every producer is to get his or her film made. Since the independent usually has no studio deal, they follow no rules, no set line of action, to bring their project to fruition.

Midge Sanford and Sarah Pillsbury are independent producers who select individual projects and then work to get them made, sometimes spending years to do so. *Desperately Seeking Susan* (Leora Barish), *The River's Edge* (Neal Jimenez), and *Eight Men Out* (John Sayles) are small, personal films that are both critically and commercially successful. More than that, they are films that are original, thought-provoking, and different from a studio film in theme, execution, and style.

I interviewed Midge Sanford (Sarah Pillsbury was unable to be there as she was about to deliver her baby) in their small offices in Westwood.

Midge Sanford is a graduate of Sarah Lawrence, and "grew up at a time when women really didn't think about careers, unless they had a particular talent like writing or painting. So I got married and had children. When I became restless, I went to graduate school, got a teaching credential, and taught elementary school for five years." Feeling it was time for a change, she took the summer off and thought about a career. Married to Jeff Sanford, a well-known and respected literary agent (the Sanford-Beckett Agency), she had read and commented on scripts for years. So that summer she did some free-lance reading for three independent producers. Then she met Bob Estrin, a former film editor who had just started an independent production company, and worked for him for several years, learning about the development process.

At that time she happened to meet Sarah Pillsbury, a graduate of Yale who had come to Hollywood by way of documentaries; she worked on *With Babies and Banners* and *Rosie the Riveter* and spent time at AFI and the UCLA Film School. She coproduced a short film called *Board and Care,* which won an Academy Award.

The two of them met casually, liked each other, and started talking about forming their own independent production company. After a year and a half, they managed to raise enough capital to do so.

At first, of course, "nothing happened," laughs Sanford. "There were days when we just picked up the phone to see if it was still working.

"We knew it was going to be tough in the beginning. We were calling ourselves producers, but most of the agents wouldn't send us scripts or writers because we weren't established, didn't have a lot of money to spend, and didn't have a studio deal.

"The first script we optioned was *Desperately Seeking Susan*. We knew Leora Barish, and she showed us a draft of the script, which we responded to immediately. Even though her agent was sending it around to other places, and there were two option offers on the table, Leora chose us because she felt she'd be given a chance to stay involved in the filmmaking process. And she was. We had meetings, we went over directors' lists, we talked about casting; we were working on this together.

"Sarah and I sent the script everywhere: to directors, studios, executive producers, anyone who would look at it. Finally, Susan Seidelman agreed to do it and we set it up at Warner Bros. A completely different version was written for them, with a kidnapping and bad guys, and a McGuffin" involving a forged stamp; it got too quirky for them. They passed, and put it into turnaround [see page 32]. Orion, who had been interested in it before, asked to see it. We went right back to the first draft and started over again.

"By the time we went into production, Leora had written nine drafts of the script." The result, of course, starring Madonna and Rosanna Arquette, was a thoroughly delightful, captivating, and original film.

Eight Men Out was a different story. But it is a good example of the various routes an independent producer must follow to obtain material. Originally, Sarah Pillsbury's brother told her about someone he knew in Texas who owned the rights to a script based on a book called *Eight Men Out,* written by Eliot Asinof in 1963. Sarah contacted her brother's friend and he sent her the script. The story is about the notorious Black Sox scandal of 1919. In that year, eight members of the Chicago White Sox conspired to fix the World Series. They were called the Black Sox because the owner of the team was too cheap to clean their uniforms.

Midge and Sarah liked the story but didn't want to use the existing script, so they optioned the book and started thinking about who could write a new script. "About a month later," Sanford recalls, "John Sayles [the writer-director of *The Return of the Secaucus Seven, The Brother from Another Planet,* and *Matewan*] called up and said, 'I hear you have the rights to this project. It's something I'd like to do.' We loved *Secaucus Seven* and thought if we could get John Sayles attached to *Eight Men Out,* either as a writer or director, we could get an immediate development deal.

"We couldn't get arrested. After about two years, the option period on the book was expiring and we either had to drop the project or buy the book outright. We had so much faith in the project that we bought the book with John and became equal partners.

"We tried for seven years and couldn't make a deal anywhere," Sanford continues, "because it was a baseball movie and it was an ensemble piece and a period piece, and everybody thought it would be too expensive. Add to that [the fact that] it had a downbeat ending, and you can see why nobody wanted to make it." At that time, baseball movies had a reputation of being notoriously bad box-office.

Sanford and Pillsbury persisted, and started sending the script to actors to see if they were interested in doing the piece. "We had a budget of about $5 million," says Sanford, "and at one point we had Emilio Estevez, Kevin Bacon, and Tom Cruise interested. We still couldn't sell it.

"Finally, Barbara Boyle, an executive at RKO [she had been instrumental in pushing *Desperately Seeking Susan* through when she was at Orion], got her company to option the script. She took it to Orion and was able to make a deal with them to finance and distribute the movie if we could get four name actors. We got D. B. Sweeney interested [Orion had just made a film called *No Man's Land* with D.B. and Charlie Sheen], so now we had D.B., Emilio, and Kevin Bacon interested.

"We always knew this would be an ensemble piece, and if Orion was really going to make this film, we had to tell all the agents that everybody would have to work for scale. Nobody gets a trailer, nobody gets a driver, nobody gets any extra perks.

"Ultimately, Emilio Estevez didn't want to do it. But when Charlie Sheen found out D.B. was going to do a baseball movie, he became interested, because Charlie Sheen is an incredibly good baseball player.

"We offered him the part of one of the eight guys involved in the fix. He said 'probably' yes. So now we had D.B. and maybe Charlie, but we didn't have Emilio or Kevin anymore; we only had one definite out of four names.

"When Emilio dropped out, we went to John Cusack and offered him the part. But because it was an ensemble piece, he wanted to know who else was going to be in the picture. Fortunately, there was a screening of *Matewan,* and we got Charlie and John Cusack to see it, and though they were in different screenings, they were both so impressed with the acting that they called immediately and made a definite commitment to the project. Even though they didn't know what other actors would be in the movie, they knew they would be in good hands because John Sayles is so wonderful with actors.

"So now we had three of the four names Orion had insisted upon. It was time to make a move. I called the executive at Orion and said we're running out of names of people who are approved. We've got three of the four. Are you *not* going to make this movie if we've got three names and not four?

"And he paused and said, 'No, we'll make the movie.' And then Chris Lloyd finally committed to the part, and we ended up with four names after all.

"It took seven years to get that final go-ahead, and by the time the movie was released, it was eight years. And the truth is that *Eight Men Out,* while ostensibly a baseball movie, is really a story about corruption, about gamblers, and about lost dreams. [F. Scott Fitzgerald, in *The Great Gatsby,* has Nick, the narrator, have lunch with Waldheim, one of the gamblers who was in on the scandal.] These characters are so interesting; one man has an idea and seduces, in some cases easily, in some cases with difficulty, other people into the scheme. Some people were in a couple of meetings and didn't do anything wrong. John Cusack plays Buck Weaver, who happened to be in a couple of meetings but never took any money and played his hardest. And he was banned from baseball for the rest of his life."

When an independent finds material, he or she may not be able to get studio financing to get the picture made. Where does the independent producer go to secure the monies needed to get his movie made?

"We go to film companies for financing, we don't go to film investors," says Midge Sanford. "We tried to do it on *Desperately Seeking Susan, River's Edge,* and *Eight Men Out;* we had some Broadway producers who were committed for a year or so, but when it came time to making the deal, they dropped out. And going to a consortium of dentists and real estate developers hasn't worked at all for us. In the beginning we get encouraged that something's going to happen, the money's going to come through, but it never works out. So we go to studios and independent financing companies."

Tony Bill agrees. "I've never gone out and tried to finance a picture with financing that isn't already committed to making movies. I think it's crazy to find a rich industrialist, or doctor, who wants to make movies. If you're looking for financing outside the professionally committed areas, then you're looking for a crazy rich person. They've got to be rich, and they've got to be crazy to give you their money. And they probably didn't get rich by being crazy.

"It's a different story with development money. I'm always looking for people who would like to invest in developing projects and think they can make a lot of money."

Isn't that the way it always is? Everybody's looking for the quick score. You write a screenplay you think would make a terrific movie. If you're lucky to get it optioned, the producer may have to spend years working to get it made. And they don't get paid until they make a deal somewhere.

The process is the same. Both involve selling the screenplay. There are plenty of people who believe that success in Hollywood is a combination of luck, connections, and power. But that's only the first step. The remainder of the journey takes patience, persistence, and determination. With the rise of the independent producer becoming more of a force within the Hollywood scene, the values that bring a project to fruition remain the same.

Tony Bill sums it up this way: "To second-guess what other people want to see is a real waste of time. I wouldn't want to build a house I wouldn't want to live in, and I wouldn't want to own a restaurant I wouldn't want to eat in, and I certainly wouldn't want to make a movie I wouldn't want to see."

The Executives

"In the dark, what people really come together
for is the community of emotion."

The business of show business is an open marketplace where buyers and sellers get together and exchange goods or services. Only in this case, instead of being clothes, jewelry, or fruit and vegetables, it's the production of movies. The major studios and production companies in Hollywood are in the business of making movies; that means they must produce a product that makes a profit so they can stay in business.

It's the biggest crap shoot in the world. Nobody really knows for sure what an audience will buy or not buy. "The market," as Sidney Ganis says (see Chapter 1), "is anything an audience wants to see." The stakes are high and the decision on which movies to make and how much to spend making them is the job of the executive.

A good executive must have special skills. He or she must be passionate about film, have a good story sense, and be able to read and evaluate screenplays for their quality and execution. The producer must be able to anticipate audience trends at least two years in advance, because that's how long it takes to make a film, from the initial go-ahead to final release; through preproduction, production, and postproduction.

On a day-to-day basis, a good executive must know how to structure deals, attract the best talent, maintain relationships with the creative community, and know what's going on in all the other studios and production companies around town. The jobs are tense and high-pressured;

the pay is good, the hours long, and the cost high; the average job span of an executive in one place is only about five years. They either leave, get fired, or go to another studio or production company.

The major studios and production companies receive about 5,000 submissions a year—that's about 65 or 70 submissions a week. It includes scripts, treatments, novels, and resubmissions but does *not* include pitches. The average executive listens to about five pitches a week; depending on the studio and executive, sometimes it's a lot more. The sheer volume of material an executive in Hollywood must wade through each week is staggering.

Each studio establishes a slate of ten to twelve films they want to produce each year. It is a far cry from the days of MGM, when Mayer and Thalberg were turning out fifty-two movies a year. One executive, now at Disney, told me that when he was at Paramount they tried to make fifteen pictures a year but they could never find enough material.

Because the cost of production is so high (and getting higher), the job of the executive, says Mike Medavoy of Orion Pictures, is to be a "selector" of material, "to make the right film for the right price."

Of course, that's almost a contradiction. Many executives "select" movies to make for the wrong reasons; sometimes there's a situation where the deal is so good it's hard not to take the gamble and make the film. Sometimes a star is available only for a brief period of time, so whatever script is convenient, regardless of quality, might be greenlighted for production. Because of the high interest rates, there are certain times, like the end of the studio's fiscal year, when it becomes financially imperative to make a film, any film. So just because a film gets made doesn't mean it's the best script; it just means it's the script that got made.

When a script is greenlighted for production, it is the executive's job to keep the costs down, make sure the film is on schedule and budget, and generally oversee the film's production without necessarily being involved in the day-to-day shooting. A line producer does that. And he or she usually reports to the executive in charge of the production.

David Kirkpatrick is president of production at Touchstone Films at the Walt Disney Studio, and was formerly president of the Motion Picture Division for the Weintraub Entertainment Group. He started his career as a screenwriter for Roger Corman, worked in television writing episodes for series like *Nancy Drew* and *The Hardy Boys,* then worked for Paramount, starting out in the story department reading scripts. It soon became apparent that Kirkpatrick had a good, solid story sense, and it wasn't long before he moved into development, sitting in on story sessions, taking notes and making story suggestions. During the next eight years he moved up through the executive ranks at Paramount to become a vice president of production. He was the executive in charge of such projects as *An Officer and a Gentleman,* established the multitalent deals that brought stars like Eddie Murphy to Paramount, and was the executive for Simpson and Bruckheimer on *Beverly Hills Cop,* as well as the *Star Trek* series.

I asked Kirkpatrick to define what an executive does. "First of all," he explained, "we would clock between 4 to 5,000 submissions a year at Paramount. At Weintraub Entertainment, we got maybe 50 or 60 submissions a week, approximately 2,500 scripts a year. At Touchtone we get 5 to 6,000 a year."

"As an executive, we do five things. The first thing we do is try and identify a good idea. We have tons of pitches a week, so we try to isolate the unique ideas. What does unique mean? It means that which is different in the marketplace, and is easy to grasp from the standpoint of the audience. Some people call it high-concept. [*The Car,* for example, was sold as *Jaws* on wheels.]

"The second task in our job is to take that project and develop it into a screenplay. We need to get those ideas on paper to the point where we can shoot them.

"The third thing is to creatively package a movie. We try to put together the most interesting elements from the standpoint of director and cast.

"The fourth thing we do is supervise that script and those elements in such a way that it is fiscally responsible for our studio. So we can bring it in at a price and, if necessary, oversee any schedule delays or production overloads. We want to be able to make that picture and deliver it into the marketplace at the price we agreed upon.

"The fifth thing we do is make sure the concept we started with is identified in the marketing campaign. So the movie we deliver, and the concept we agreed upon, is sold in the marketplace with a similar viewpoint. There's no point in developing a romantic thriller like *Fatal Attraction* and having it sold as a 'bang, bang, shoot 'em up' picture.

"Half the process of an executive is making a good picture, the other half is being able to sell it in an interesting way in the marketplace. Which goes right back to identifying a good idea, because a good idea means it's easily sold in the marketplace.

"*Foul Play* [Colin Higgins] was a good idea in its time," Kirkpatrick continues, "but after *Hanky Panky* and fifteen other generic rip-offs of *Foul Play*, it was no longer an interesting idea. It therefore became difficult to sell unless it was distinguished by really top star talent.

"Those basically are the five cornerstones of an executive's life."

Like most executives, Mary Anne Page, vice president of production at United Artists Pictures, doesn't have time to read scripts during her long working day. She's too busy soliciting material, having production meetings, talking on the phone, and listening to pitches, to read scripts. The story department sifts through the sixty or seventy submissions a week that UA receives, and anything worth pursuing is given to the executives to read.

"I've read up to twenty-five scripts over a weekend," says Page. "The average now is about fifteen." Page graduated from film and business school at Yale, came to Hollywood, and got the first job she interviewed for, working in development for Tom Hanks at Columbia. "It was just one of those one-of-a-kind luck stories," she says. From there she went to work for Ray Stark at Rastar, working on *Nothing in Common, The Secret of My Success,* the late John Huston project *Revenge, Peggy Sue Got Married, Biloxi Blues,* and others. From there she went to UA Pictures.

Because she reads so much material in such a short time, I asked her if she feels obligated to read the entire script.

"No," she replied. "If it's not working, I'll stop on page 30 and read the coverage.

"The main thing is to see the story," she continues. "Very often you'll see what seems to be a heavy-handed, flashy kind of writing, extravagant when it doesn't have to be, calling attention to itself by making jokes and trying to be clever. You get turned off right away."

"Sometimes," adds Dan Rogosin, UA's story editor, "you get to the point where there's a discrepancy between the story and the writing, and I'm enjoying it more for the sake of the writing than the story. That's when I say this guy's a good writer, but he needs a better story.''

And story, of course, is the foundation of the entire screenplay.

Executives buy scripts and make films for different reasons. If you have a script, for example, that costs $6 million to make, says David Puttnam, former head of Columbia Pictures, you have to ask yourself if the script works and the subject matter is really interesting. If a script costs $10 or $12 million to make, you look for a level of professional skill and competence on the part of the filmmakers. But if you have a script that is in the $20 to $25 million range, Puttnam goes on, you need a big star, and "that represents a safer, more risk-free situation than a $2 or $3 million film made with unknowns."

At Cinemobile and Cine Artists, I would sometimes recommend a low-budget script with an interesting idea, characters, and locale. My thinking was simple: this is a pretty good script, and if it's done for the right price, you can presell the video rights and European distribution rights, and you've paid for the cost of production before you begin shooting. Put this into a few select markets and you could be in profit within a few weeks.

Aloha, Bobby and Rose was just that kind of film. It cost $750,000 to make in 1973 (today it would cost between $1.5 and 2 million) and grossed domestically (without merchandising the Elton John sound-track album) some $20 million.

If an executive at United Artists Pictures finds a script that he or she thinks is good, copies are given to the other executives to read. They read the material over the weekend and discuss the material at the Monday morning meeting. At UA "it's more a team approach," says Page. If everyone likes the material, a deal is considered. "Usually four people like it, and two don't," says Page, "and in that case, we discuss it and find out how soon we need to have an answer. I brought a script back twice on weekend reading, a comedy, and four or five of us thought it was very funny. But our boss didn't think it was funny at all. So he asked me what the high points of the script were. I listed them, and the others who also liked the script agreed, but he still didn't find it very funny.''

UA finally passed on the script and "I accept that," says Page. "Humor is so subjective, you can't argue whether this is a funny scene, or a funny line, or a funny piece of business. You do what you can do, and that's it.''

That's why an executive will tell a producer, or director, or writer, or star, that while they love their script and will do everything in their power to push it through, they're not going to lose their job over it.

There are some scripts that are really well written and make the rounds from studio to studio yet everybody still passes. There's just no interest in buying the material. ''There seem to be two reasons for this,'' says Mary Anne Page. ''First, we'll read a script where people have gone to see a crime movie, and then say, I can write a better script than that, so they go off and write a better version of that. But it's old hat; it doesn't make any difference because it's already been done. Whatever the reason the other script got bought and the picture made, it's not an indication for you to go out and try and write a better version of that.

''Secondly, there are a million different reasons why things get made. All kinds of scripts get bought for different reasons, and there are no specific rules you can measure things by. Sometimes you get the feeling that everything you read is based entirely on old movies and TV shows, and that it's a retread. By its very nature it's derivative.''

Then what does an executive look for when he or she is looking for material? ''What tends to excite me,'' says Frances Doel, vice president of production at Price Entertainment, ''is something different, something that goes against the grain of whatever is currently popular at the present moment. As a reader and moviegoer, what thrills me is the sensation of a fresh experience; what disappoints me is to say yes, it's decently written, or well made, but so what—I've seen it before.''

Doel came to Hollywood with a degree in English literature from Oxford University when she started working for Roger Corman in the mid-sixties. ''Roger did not believe in buying scripts,'' she says, ''because he didn't feel anybody would sit down and write the kind of movies he wanted to make. Low-budget, contemporary genre films that delivered what television could not: sex, action, and violence, fueled by a story idea that implied some comment on contemporary society, and spiked with humor, intentional or otherwise. Corman's New World Pictures made and released about twelve pictures a year, and we developed all the scripts.''

After working initially as a secretary, production assistant, and script girl (continuity) during shooting, Doel was promoted to story editor. Her job was to work out stories based on Corman's ideas, sometimes to write first-draft screenplays (an experience she feels should be mandatory for any executive supervising the work of writers), and finding writers to write those Roger Corman films that started so many careers in Hollywood: Jack Nicholson, Robert Towne, Francis Ford Coppola, Peter Fonda, John Sayles, Martin Scorsese, Jonathan Demme, Joe Dante, and many, many others.

As a development executive for Corman, Doel's job was to look for talent rather than material. "Roger believed there were two kinds of writers: *real* writers, writing short stories, novels, or plays; and Hollywood writers, people who wrote scripts only because they wanted to direct, or make money from writing. For me, the excitement was reading talented young writers and persuading them to bring their gifts for character development and dialogue to our story ideas. In this way I was lucky enough to find work with people like John Sayles [*Eight Men Out*], Rita Mae Brown [various TV movies] and William Hjortsberg [*Legend*].

Doel then moved to Orion Pictures as a production executive. Orion was a company that "didn't believe in developing material initiated by executives," she says; "they believed in looking for screenplays developed by producers. They frequently encouraged revisions, but essentially they set out to help package the best material they could find.'' While there she worked on *Desperately Seeking Susan, The Falcon and the Snowman, At Close Range, Terminator,* and *Robocop.*

Later she moved to Disney as a creative executive, and began working more in development because the emphasis at Disney has always been developing original screenplays. Especially comedy. "And we were always looking for situations that had an interesting hook," she says, "because Disney responded to a strong premise, figuring the story and conflict could be worked out and resolved in development.'' While there she was involved in *Outrageous Fortune, Three Men and a Baby, Ernest Goes to Camp,* and others.

At present, Doel is vice president of production at Price Entertainment.

(Frank Price is the former head of Columbia and Universal Pictures, and made films like *Tootsie, Out of Africa, Gandhi, Tess, The Verdict,* and *A Soldier's Story.*)

"The goal at Price Entertainment," she says, "is to produce six films a year, eighteen over three years, each with a budget of $6 to $18 million."

What kind of material is she looking for? Is she given any kind of directive, or any specific genre requirements? "The directive is very simple," says Doel. "We want to make hits. So we look for characters with interesting conflicts, rather than any kind of particular genre. For example, there may be new situations and stories to be mined in the triangle story, which can provide taut drama with a surprise ending." Like *Fatal Attraction.*

Doel told me she loves to develop original material, and notes there is a lot of waste in the development process in Hollywood. "Most first-draft screenplays need rewriting; every good writer knows how much better it can be. The development process for the writer is brutal because they have to go through several sets of revisions, and *then* find themselves replaced by another writer. In the past, I've noticed that when a screenplay passes through several writers, or teams of writers, and still remains 'in development' [as opposed to undergoing revisions for production], it's generally a sign that the problem with the project is conceptual. For example, it may have a 'hook' or premise that sounded great in a verbal pitch but has nowhere to go.

"A lot of time and money is lost when executives or writers don't keep the concept firmly in mind that excited them in the first place. A good story, with a strong conflict and unique characters, should not be tinkered with to accommodate the wishes and prejudices of everyone who happens to read it; it should not be homogenized so it doesn't offend or displease anybody.

"Sometimes a project will come in," Doel says, "and everybody agrees we'll do a rewrite to solve a glitch in the plot, or strengthen the relationship between the two leads, or make the ending better; but the truth is, it may not make it better. So another writer is brought in, or team of writers, and yes, the lines are better, little plot points are straightened out, but in the end, everybody forgets why they wanted to make the movie in the first place. That initial excitement, that initial response to the idea of the script, can sometimes disappear in a lengthy revision process.

"It doesn't happen on purpose. I don't think anybody sets out to sabotage the script," she continues, "but it does happen. The script you read that gives you that special feeling for a movie you want to make is essentially the script you're going to end up making. You may be able to improve part of it, but it's going to remain the same animal, and I think trying to turn it into an animal that hopefully will please everybody results in a script nobody really wants to make or a movie that ultimately doesn't please anybody."

Unfortunately, this is common occurrence in Hollywood. Many times a studio or company will buy a book, a script, or an idea, work on it, change it, restructure it, and then find out it doesn't work. So they decide to put it into turnaround, and "one of the first things we do," says Mary Anne Page, "is to put it back the way it was in the first draft."

The strength in your screenplay is its originality. Something that is new in the marketplace, or something "that goes against the grain," says Doel. "I'm always excited after I read, or hear, or see something which is the opposite of what any current cycle seems to be. I'm less interested when I read something that simply dramatizes what the pop psychology of the media tells us is on our minds this month. I'm very drawn to material where a writer puts to dramatic use his or her concrete experience of the world; this material might or might not be based on a true story, it might be based on personal experience, or on research, but I'm more ready to suspend my disbelief when I recognize a story is being unfolded by a writer who really knows the world he's talking about.

"I also find a character who has a strong attitude, or someone who bears a strong grudge, interesting. I also like a character with an eccentric point of view that gets him into trouble, or lands him in a strange and unusual situation. Somebody who comes in with an ax to grind, like Jack Nicholson in *Chinatown* [Robert Towne] or Paul Newman in *Absence of Malice* [Kurt Luedtke]."

Because the cost of moviemaking is so high, and getting higher, it puts a lot of pressure on executives to find hits. By the very nature of their job they are put in a pressure-cooker situation to find material that will be financially successful at the box office. So they look for what they think are interesting characters, situations, or story lines that will attract an audience.

When an executive presents a script to his or her boss, he or she must pitch and articulate the reasons why they think this movie should be made. It's no easy matter to greenlight a movie.

"Production heads around town cannot greenlight movies," David Kirkpatrick explains. "What they try to do is put together scripts from good ideas and assemble them in a way that makes sense. The right film for the right price. That means from the standpoint of budget, cast, and director. The person who greenlights the movie is generally the chairman of the board. If a film costs $20 to $25 million to make, the chairman of the board will usually have to go to the parent company to get approval. So even he, at times, has to sell.

"The higher you get within the executive ranks," Kirkpatrick continues, "the harder you have to sell; you're not talking about a $50,000 development deal, but a $20-million movie."

When an executive receives a submission, "you have to says yes or no fast," says Frances Doel, "because the market for good original screenplays is very competitive. Essentially, you say yes or no to the premise.

"There are times when the script a number of executives read and love for the writing doesn't get bought because the premise doesn't appeal," she says, "but it can get the writer a job."

Sometimes that works to your advantage. Sometimes it doesn't. The writer always takes the fall in Hollywood for a bad movie. If it's a great script, and changes are made in it by the director and/or star, and the picture bombs, it's the writer's fault; it was a lousy script, everybody says. If it's a great script, and the movie turns out to be successful, the chairman of the board, the executive, and the director all take the credit.

One of the executives I interviewed showed me a bookcase filled with leather-bound scripts, movies that had been made while he was an executive with the company. It was very impressive. Then he pointed to a special shelf and pulled out five beautifully bound scripts. The titles, all Academy Award winners, were printed in gold leaf. He paused dramatically, then told me they were "his" films. That's show biz.

It's important to remember that Hollywood runs in cycles. Therefore, the arena you choose to write about can be a major factor in selling your screenplay. "If there's a great thriller, for example," says Mary Anne Page, "and it's set in Vietnam, forget it. We have very good scripts about Vietnam, but there's a ton of them, so forget it. I read a lot of police stories, and as a rule, they generally keep working, but personally, I've had it with them too. Change it, do something different, make it a T-man or something, anything, just don't write another police story.

"I've also read so many scripts recently taking place in Japan that I'm sick of them too," she continues. "There's a good rule to remember: If it's been on *60 Minutes*, don't bother writing about it."

Recently, after the success of *Wall Street*, a lot of scripts deal with real estate scams, and executives tell me that the most popular character this year is a cartoonist. "They're everywhere," says Page. "Writers have to search for new and different arenas to write about."

That includes historical films. "There's a wariness about period movies," says Frances Doel, "partly because of cost, but primarily because it's very common for an executive to believe that the American public is not interested in the past anymore. I know Orion was very disappointed in *The Bounty* but subsequently did very well with *Amadeus*. Even though the executives there were personally attracted by historical movies, they were reluctant to make them because they didn't believe there was an audience for them.

"At Price Entertainment, we're open to period movies, if we think the story and characters have a strong emotional appeal to a contemporary audience. It wouldn't be enough, I think, that the story and characters make the past come alive; the experience of the past needs to illuminate the present and speak to our concerns now.

"The most frequent reason executives say no," continues Doel, "is not that the scripts aren't well written, or the writer isn't good enough, or it isn't structured correctly; most executives know that if there's an interesting premise and conflict in the story, with appealing characters, they will be able to help solve the structural problems. It's possible to improve a script by doing a rewrite, but you can't get a better idea than it had in the first place.

"It grieves me that there are so many screenplays written on familiar ideas and premises in which neither the characters nor the setting make it different, or stand apart; there is no fresh ingredient from the contemporary world to bring it to life. It's almost not worth writing them as far as the hope of getting them made is concerned."

What can we learn from all this? How can we make our screenplay presentation more acceptable, more salable, more marketable?

David Kirkpatrick sums it up best. "We will always buy a great concept in a screenplay. It doesn't necessarily have to be beautifully executed; but it does need to have a strong story behind it. We would never buy a beautifully written script that has no unique idea to hang its hat on. We might hire the writer to come in and do a rewrite on something, but we would never buy a script that doesn't have a strong concept behind it.

"A screenplay should be entrenched in an emotional genre because an audience needs to know when they pay their six-dollar admission price, they're going to go on an emotional roller-coaster ride. And they need to know what level it's going to be on.

"So we look for a good story with strong story beats, with great characters cast in an interesting way.

"No matter what kind of movie it is," Kirkpatrick continues, "whether it's a suspense story, a comedy, or tearjerker, you've got to be able to deliver about five big moments that have the audience either laughing, crying, or getting scared half to death."

I asked him to elaborate on this.

He paused for a moment, then said, "You can't just give an audience a great ending. You've got to deliver it again and again and again through the course of the movie. That requires five or six memorable scenes within the emotional sphere of the tearjerker, the suspenser, or the comedy.

"And if you don't have those five or six set pieces, then I don't think you have the potential of making a real commercial movie."

Interesting. That's why screenplay structure plays such an important role in screenwriting. Because you can design and incorporate those five or six elements into the screenplay before you start writing. That's why you start with structure when you're preparing your screenplay. Then you follow up with your characters. And that means castability.

"It's true there are A, B, and C lists with actors," Kirkpatrick continues. "Sometimes, if you have an action-adventure, a bang, bang, shoot 'em up, there are only about five or six names you can use on the A list to get the film made; you may decide not to buy the script because Clint Eastwood, Sylvester Stallone, Arnold Schwarzenegger, and Mel Gibson are not available, and are committed for the next two years. And if you can't get them, you don't make the picture. It's as simple as that.

"Sometimes, when somebody's really hot, you need something strong for them, but if you have to pay an arm and a leg for the script, you pass because you look down the line and see that you probably can't put it together.

"When we were trying to put *48 Hrs.* together at Paramount," he continues, "it was originally conceived for Burt Reynolds and Richard Pryor. They elected not to do the movie. Nick Nolte at that time was a bit cold, and Eddie Murphy was hot after *Saturday Night Live* but he had never done a picture before. We figured that together they might add up to one star, therefore we tried to make it for a certain price and maybe, just maybe, we'll connect in the marketplace." Which it did, of course. It made Nick Nolte "hot" and Eddie Murphy a "star."

"So from the standpoint of selling the script," Kirkpatrick says, "it's sometimes nice not to have a one-star-part vehicle, but a script where two or three people can possibly add up to one star; that way you can avoid the A list syndrome of being able to sell it only to five or six people."

So many producers in Hollywood option or buy a screenplay, then spend up to a year learning that those "A" actors, the "bankable" stars, are not available.

"A good executive has to look down the line to see that," states Kirkpatrick. "But it's also important to remember that there are also people who believe a B list character (like Dennis Quaid, for example) put together with somebody who is slightly original (Ellen Barkin, for example) with a slightly original notion, may add up to 'A' casting. Like *The Big Easy*. Or *Down and Out in Beverly Hills,* or *48 Hrs.,* or *Three Men and a Baby*. Collectively, the cast adds up to a star.

"What's so important for a writer to know," says Kirkpatrick, "is that he or she must think like an executive. They have to know what's out there now, and what will be out there in the future. From there, they have to search and find those areas which have not been tapped. The writer needs to see if there's an absence of buddy action movies, romantic thrillers, or just a great love story. Right now there's been a complete absence of major tearjerkers in the marketplace. That's today. 1988. And there's nothing coming down the pike in the near future.

"I think a major tearjerker, put together with interesting elements, would score even if executed on a secondary level; nothing like that has been out in the landscape for a while and the audience has been deprived of that."

The absence of a great love story is a common lament in Hollywood right now; Twentieth Century Fox has been trying to remake *An Affair to Remember* (Delmer Davies and Leo McCarey), originally with Cary Grant and Deborah Kerr, for more than a decade now. The same with MGM and the great love story *Forever*.

"It's really that Jungian notion of what people want to dream about in the dark," says Kirkpatrick. "And then you've got to find that original idea and execute it so you can fulfill the dream they've been having all along.

"The classic example of that," Kirkpatrick continues, "is George Lucas and *Star Wars*. Intuitively he knew there was not the kind of big, blustering boys' adventure movie he had grown up with. So he embarked on *Star Wars*.

"When you get right down to it, people respond to the transcendent value of the story. It doesn't have to be hell on wheels or a space opera. It can be about a little boy who's got a friend down the street who happens to be an alien. It can be a mother whose daughter is dying of cancer, like *Terms of Endearment*. It can be anything.

"Because in the dark, what people really come together for is the community of emotion."

8

The Readers

*"Listen to your heart and be true
to your vision."*

When I was a reader at Cinemobile, I was reading three scripts a day, plus a novel or two on the weekend. For each script I had to write a "brief" (a three-sentence *TV Guide* log line), along with a synopsis of the story, and a few paragraphs of personal comments. As mentioned in *Screenplay,* I only found one in a hundred I liked well enough to pass on to my superiors. The brief, synopsis, and comments are called the *coverage.* Before any executive *reads* the screenplay, he or she will read the coverage. And based on his or her reaction to the reader's coverage, he or she will either read or not read the screenplay.

You can't sell a script if no one reads it. Somebody's got to read those scripts and sort out which are good and which are not. That's the reader's job.

The reader is a pivotal person in selling the screenplay. Heard but rarely seen, the reader is responsible for making a preliminary evaluation of the material. It is the reader's coverage that lets the executive know what to say in those encouraging rejection letters. If the executive likes the script, the agent or attorney is called, the interest stated, and a meeting set up.

Some companies have designed a form for the reader's report, providing the reader with a checklist for rating structure, action, character, story line, marketability, and audience appeal. If "elements" are added to the script—for example, if a certain star or director is attached—the reader must give his or her opinion of the "package."

The reader's coverage is perhaps the most important document the executive considers when a screenplay is being evaluated. Most readers read ten to fifteen screenplays a week, and if they find one they like it's a major "win."

When you submit your screenplay to be read, you are triggering the Hollywood system into the active mode. The script, as they say, is "in the hopper." The main function of the reader is to say no, to provide the necessary information for the executive to write "an encouraging rejection letter." That's just the way it is.

How do you get the reader on your side? What does he or she look for in a screenplay? Is there anything the writer should or shouldn't do to avoid the reader's wrath? Any traps or pitfalls you need to know about?

With that in mind, I interviewed three Hollywood readers. As a former reader, I had my own expectations about what I would find hidden behind the wall of studio heads and production executives.

Dayle Michele is a graduate of the USC Film School, worked as a secretary for PBS (the Los Angeles station KCET), then worked for Martin Scorsese as a production assistant on *Taxi Driver; New York, New York; The Last Waltz;* and a documentary called *All-American Boy*. As director of development for Lily Tomlin's company, she worked on *The Incredible Shrinking Woman* and *9 to 5*. From there she became vice president of creative affairs for the Mel Simon Company (*Love at First Bite, Stuntman, My Bodyguard*). Needing a change after a few years, she starting writing original screenplays, sold a few, and helps support herself as a free-lance reader for Columbia, the David Geffen Company, Dino De Laurentiis, and a few other production companies.

Janaki Symon started in theater and advertising in New York, moved to L.A., and got a job working for a TV executive at CBS. When the executive became a v.p. of production at United Artists, she stayed with him at the studio for several years, working on *Heaven's Gate* (Michael Cimino) and *Arthur*. From there she went to work for the Ladd Company (*Night Shift, The Right Stuff* [Philip Kauffman], *Once Upon a Time in America*). After a few years she left the Ladd Company and started reading for Tri-Star. At present she is a free-lance reader; her clients include Lorimar Studios, Embassy Home Entertainment, and Odyssey Pictures.

Kim Ohanneson went to UC Santa Barbara, studied film theory, then worked for Ralph Edwards on *People's Court*. She joined Embassy Pictures and stayed there through the formation and disintegration of six different regimes ending with the time Dino De Laurentiis had control of the company. She began as a secretary, became literary manager, was then placed in charge of acquiring books to be made as movies. At present she is an independent writer-producer, and reads for CarolCo (*Rambo*), the Geffen Company (*Risky Business, Little Shop of Horrors*), Odyssey Pictures, and Embassy Home Entertainment.

How is it that the reader has become such a pivotal cog in the Hollywood system?

"Originally," Janaki says, "the function of the story department and the story editor was really to develop the stories. Their input was critical to the writers, directors, and producers. The production executives brought in the talent and put the picture together. That's changed now. Studio heads are basically agents who put the proper elements together to make the movie."

The volume of material the reader reads is enormous. The average reader reads between ten and fifteen scripts a week, or about five hundred scripts a year. "The reader," Janaki says, "is hired to give an honest analysis of the material. If they don't give it, they're not earning their money.

"If I have a job with a company I've never worked with before, I sit down and talk to them in terms of what they specifically want, what the philosophy of the company is, how they want me to do it. Some companies," she continues, "want high-concept projects, something that's salable in one line, that doesn't cost a lot of money. So I'll recommend anything from a low-budget imaginative horror story to a period love story, as long as it can be done inexpensively. By period, I mean something set in the '50s or '60s."

The first ten pages are the most crucial for a reader. In all my seminars and workshops I stress the importance of setting up your story within the first ten pages. By the time I have read these ten pages I have to know the main character, the dramatic premise—that is, what it's about—and the dramatic situation, the circumstances surrounding the action.

Your screenplay begins on page one, word one, paragraph one. You must grab the reader's attention immediately, because "I look for imagination, ambition, and creativity," says Kim Ohanneson. "If I don't get a feel for the story in the first ten pages, if I'm not riveted by it, I'll just skim and read for story."

"If I'm not caught in the first five pages, then it's time to go buy popcorn," Janaki emphasizes.

"When you look at a script, you know where everything is supposed to fall; if the first act is under twenty pages you know there's going to be a problem," Dayle states. "That's why you keep going back to structure. Because nothing else really works; no matter how avant garde your script is, it still has to be in that structure. And when you're reading a large number of scripts, that's one of the first things you look for.

"If I can't read a script in an hour and fifteen minutes, then there's something wrong," she continues. "When I read a script, and find I'm reading it instead of watching it in my head, I begin looking for what's wrong, why it's not working. I know a movie will be forty-five minutes longer than my reading time. When I'm reading, I have to see those pictures."

A screenplay is a reading experience before it becomes a visual experience. When I was reading at Cinemobile and Cine Artists, my boss always told me he "had to see the script" in his head. First and foremost, a screenplay is a story told with pictures, in dialogue and description, and placed within the context of dramatic structure. Most people in Hollywood want to see the movie they're reading.

"I read a script all the way through," Dayle says, "because I'm a writer and my scripts are getting submitted, and if I thought someone was just reading page 1, page 30, page 50, page 90, and the last page, I don't think that's right. Some scripts are so bad, I can hardly read them, and those are the ones that are the toughest to read because somebody sat down and wrote it."

Most staff readers, working for production companies, are not so generous. They'll make a decision based on the way the story is set up, introduction of characters, premise, and situation. And they'll make their decision by the end of the Act I.

Most readers focus on what they like or don't like about the screenplay. "During the read," Janaki says, "I look for classic things: structure, point of view, justifiable characters, and credibility.

"The most important thing for me is the psychology of the characters: are they believable characters who are sympathetic or do they become sympathetic during the course of the story? Do you understand them? Or do you hate them for the right reasons? Is the psychology of the character sound? Does the character grow or change as a result of his or her experience? That's what gives something a sparkle."

Kim agrees. "I respond to characters. I love unique characters. Characters we haven't seen before. If there's one character who's brilliant, and the rest of the script is awful, I'll make a note of that."

"There are some screenplays I read," says Janaki, "where the action is not credible. If the writer doesn't respect the reader to the point where they don't make the action follow in a credible manner, then I totally dismiss it. I can tolerate some of the incidents being contrived, I can even tolerate the action being derivative, to a point, but not those things that are just basic sloppiness and don't follow the line of action."

Action and character. If structure holds the story together, the characters bring it to life. Real people in real situations.

"I like dialogue that sounds like it's coming out of people's mouths," says Dayle. "Many times I get the impression that when the writer's thinking about the scene in his head he's got some great dialogue going on. But something happens between the brain and the fingers, and the dialogue seems to be self-conscious when it gets on paper. I see this all the time." The first thing that comes out of your mind should be what you put down on paper. Later, during the rewrite, you can change it, accent it, freshen it up.

"What drives me crazy is when characters are not true to themselves," Dayle emphasizes. "If a character does something that's out of character, or if a character talks in a way that is not justified, it turns me off.

"It's the same with plot. If you're going to create a story and characters, then stick with it; don't try to come up with a special twist ending, because it doesn't work."

The screenwriter's job is to keep the reader turning pages. "I respond to scripts that develop themes, that have subtext, says Kim. "I went absolutely bananas over *Blue Velvet* (David Lynch) because it was about things underneath the surface. It was one of those scripts I had to put down and walk away from because it just got too intense.

"Our job, I think," she continues, "is finding people who are unique. Certain writers make their living being good technicians. Being able to come in and fix a script. Being able to write something quickly. Being able to punch up a bad idea that somebody's uncle came up with and at least make it somewhat interesting. But the people who touch you, the people who engage you emotionally, those are the people you're looking for.

"You know when the writer has sweated over his script; it's going to show, no matter how seamless it appears to be. Sometimes you read a script and the structure's fine, there's a nice little first act, a not-too-long second act, a punch in the third act. It has characters you like, and the dialogue's not bad; it's all fine, but so what!

"The writer has to be passionate about his material. I think it's easy to find people who can write a script by the numbers. There are enough books out there that tell you how to do that. But the one thing a book can't teach you is to listen to your heart and be true to your vision."

It's true. It's the writer's passion for his or her material that grabs the reader's attention, even though the script may be less than perfect. Everybody I interviewed agreed. It's that element, that passion, that makes the reader enthusiastic. You're not going to sell a script in this town without the help of a reader.

"I read scripts all the time," Kim reflects, "where the writer tries to second-guess the executive. I always get the impression that there's this overwhelming group of writers out there who have the illusion that a good script can't be sold. Or they think they have a better chance of selling it if it's somehow mediocre.

"I see script after script after script where people are trying to write what they think the studios want to buy. And that's death."

This happens all the time when writers try to write to current trends. After *Top Gun* did so well, there were *Top Gun* type stories all over town, on land, on water, on the racing circuit, you name it. The new TV series *Supercarrier* is based on that *Top Gun* trend.

"A lot of readers don't recommend any material because it gives the executive a problem," says Janaki. "They have to read it. They have to consider it. One executive, who I like very much, knows a lot about exploitation movies. One day she said to me, 'Janaki, I'm getting very upset.' I said, 'What's wrong?' 'I know a lot of these scripts aren't very good, but a lot of them get made. When you're evaluating stuff, could you not be so critical?'

"I was floored. She pays me to do a job, so I'll do what she wants. So now, when I'm reading for her, and I read something that has a certain amount of horrible scenes, an appropriate amount of blood, and some good sex scenes, I simply note it in my comments and say, 'This script has the appropriate number of necessary scenes.' "

"Sometimes," Janaki continues, "I recommend things I don't like. I've recommended things that I personally find appalling and offensive, and I've recommended them because they've fulfilled the requirements of the genre and that's my job."

The reader's job is to find material. In one of my screenwriting workshops I was working with Anna Hamilton Phelan when she was writing *Mask,* and after she had completed the first draft, I called another of my students, then head of Silver Screen Productions for HBO, and told him about the script. I sent it to him, he gave it to one of his readers, and a short time later he called me and said he was sending me a copy of the reader's report.

When I received the report, I was amazed. This particular reader had stated that the writing, characterizations, structure, visual dynamics, and story were excellent, but he felt the company should pass on the material because it wasn't "commercial."

I immediately told my student at Silver Screen that he better keep an eye on this particular reader. Any reader in Hollywood who finds an excellent screenplay must recommend it to the next person in line. The reader's judgment, though personally right for him, was wrong from the company's point of view. He didn't do his job.

We all know what happened with *Mask*: it was a big hit starring Cher and Eric Stoltz, directed by Peter Bogdanovich.

Sometimes readers—or producers, or studio executives—will pass on a screenplay for no other reason than they're caught in a personal crisis of some kind, with a friend, a lover, wife, or ex-wife, or they're caught in some kind of a money crunch, and that's reflected when they're reading the script. It has nothing to do with the quality of the script at all.

"One time," Janaki remembers, "the company I was working for wanted to do a deal with a well-known producer who had several major hits, including one that won an Academy Award for best picture. They gave me seven projects the producer had developed. When I read them, I got sick; each one was worse than the other. Only one was interesting, a book written by a sportswriter. I didn't know what to do. Needless to say, I was very nervous. After a couple of sleepless nights, I called the executive who had given me the assignment. When I told her my evaluation of the material, she became very nervous. So I wrote up the coverage and dropped the scripts off at her office.

"I knew my job was on the line. But in all honesty I could not recommend any of those projects. When the executive finished reading the material, she called and said, 'I will never doubt your word again.' Because they were terrible. I mean, if I didn't give an honest opinion I would have lost my job. If you don't put yourself on the line, you don't stand for anything."

This is tested all the time. One day, at Cinemobile, my boss came in and gave me a rush script to read. I read it and, to my dismay, found it to be so complex and confusing it was almost unintelligible. I simply could not recommend it.

When I walked into my boss's office, I found two of the other executives there with him. I knew something was up.

"So what do you think?" my boss asked.

"Is it good? A ten?"

I told him the truth: it was well written but was so stylized and complex, with so many characters, I couldn't recommend it. I saw the executives look at each other, and I knew, somehow, that this script was very important. I began to get nervous. There was no title page on it, so I had no idea who had written it. But from their looks I knew it must have been written by a "hot" screenwriter.

After a moment, my boss told me the script had just been purchased by

Warner Bros. for $450,000. I didn't know what to say; that fact didn't change my opinion at all. It was a great lesson. Most good executives will throw in a script like this once in a while, just to keep the readers on their toes. (By the way, the movie *was* made, and bombed within two weeks.)

A reader always has to be objective. The reader can only give his or her opinion, and then take responsibility for it.

Remember the person who took the script of *Casablanca* (Julius and Philip Epstein), retitled it *Rick's Place*, and then sent it all over town to see if it would sell? He sent it to over 180 different agencies, production companies, studios, and executives. Only a few people recognized the script; the rest passed for various reasons: too wordy, too dated, not enough action, unbelievable love story. "There would be no audience for this kind of film," one executive was quoted as saying.

At Cinemobile, as mentioned, I found only one script out of a hundred that I could recommend. Janaki says, "I'll give some kind of a recommendation to about one out of forty screenplays. I'll find something I can focus on—a character, a situation, a relationship—because I want to give the executive the opportunity, if he wants, to develop them further. You're not going to find a perfect screenplay.

"Several times I've recommended things," she continues, "where the script was a little less than wonderful because there was a good package attached to the property, or because it was effective in its genre, or would be a cheap enough investment to make its money back."

"In my comments," says Dayle, "I'll focus on what I liked or didn't like. I think the first thing I would say is whether I liked it or not, and then justify the position. If the characters stand out, and I fall in love with them, I'll focus on that.

"If the script is a good idea but poorly executed, I'd comment that this is a really good idea that needs a new story, or another approach, even a new writer. Good ideas, or good premises, come in flashes. A very unusual hook is hard to find. Unique is unique."

"Most writers don't seem to know or understand that if a script comes in that is totally outrageous," Kim says, "the executives are not going to buy it but they're going to remember you because you've written something they haven't seen before. They may think of you for another script, or to rewrite a project they have in development. And they're going to be much more interested in reading your next script. But if you write something mediocre, forget it. You're lost in the Hollywood shuffle."

Part of that "shuffle" is that writers do things that drive readers wild. One time I received a script from someone to read and evaluate. I opened the script and began reading. I saw EXT. HIGH MOUNTAIN RANGE— DAY, and the description read something like "Three riders make their way though the high mountain trails." One of the characters says something, but there was no dialogue. It was simply a scene, with characters, but there was no dialogue, just a blank page. I turned the page; same thing, only this time a different location and description, and then nothing! I went through the entire screenplay and found that this 120-page epic had no dialogue or story line at all.

I was astonished. After showing the script to the people in the office, I called the writer and asked why he wrote the script this particular way. He replied he "wanted to give the actors room enough to improvise their lines."

My boss, needless to say, passed on the project, and gave me the job of writing the pass letter; I simply wrote, "We already have something like this in development." Two people can play the same game.

"Some things drive you crazy," Kim states passionately. "I hate misspelled words. And bad grammar. I mean, I'll overlook it if the idea works, but that's usually so rare, it's like a diamond in the mud. Also, I hate when margins go all over the place. And scripts that are over 120 pages. Some people think it's okay to go to 134 pages. Wrong. Every reader I've ever known goes bananas if they get a script over 120 pages."

The quickest thing that turns Janaki off is "when the script is not in proper screenplay format. I automatically disregard it. If a writer doesn't respect the craft well enough to learn proper screenplay form, I give it very little attention. The same thing if the screenplay comes in loosely bound, that is, not bound with brads. They're so hard to read, I get angry at the writer."

Be selective when you choose a cover for your script. Those stiff plastic covers, where one clamp holds everything together, immediately labels you as unprofessional. The proper way to send in a script is with three-hole punched paper bound together with three brads. A simple title page, or a piece of colored photocopy paper that most copying stores carry in stock, is really all you need for a cover.

Sometimes the reader is in a position to spot certain trends in the screenplays that are submitted. "I see certain things cropping up all the time," says Kim. "Right now I think there's a trend back to the '60s type movies. [As of this writing, several things are currently in development at the studios dealing with the '60s—like *Mississippi Burning* with its civil rights marches, and other events.] Things that have a more tragic ending. Or smaller, personal films that have some kind of dark little twist. I see more and more of that coming in. I don't know if that's going to be a major new trend, but I think the market is more open for that than it's been in some time.

"Also, I'm seeing more romantic love stories," continues Kim. "I think there are more scripts where sex is romantic, as opposed to graphic or titillating. More erotic than anything else.

"It's my understanding that most of the major studios are trying to do a big romance picture. That's different from the scripts I've been seeing which are smaller, and sexier, but from what I've been hearing from a lot of people, the big romance is what everybody is looking for.

"It's certainly understandable. Sex is a very dangerous business these days. So I think there's a need for people to escape into a world where the AIDS virus isn't the main thing you consider when you meet someone you like."

All the readers agreed that writers should avoid certain things. Number one, there should be no list of characters in the front of the screenplay with a note on who they are. Number two, they should not be specific about certain songs or artists; you simply note in your stage directions that a song "*like* 'Candle in the Wind' by Elton John" is heard on the sound track.

"A writer's notes in the beginning are things that should be said in the script," says Kim. "If you can't say it in the script, if you can't justify it in the script, it shouldn't be there. Also, we don't want to hear about your personal hopes and dreams about what your screenplay is going to do for you or the world or whatever.

"The screenwriter's job is to be as unobtrusive as possible. Everybody obviously has their style. If you've been reading for a while you can be given a script that's untitled and have a pretty good idea who's written it.

"He or she shouldn't intrude with his style," Kim comments, "especially in terms of description or editorial comments. I'd rather hear a character say something unusual and funny and intuitive, and have exposition brought out nicely, than read a really funny description of a lizard doing a push-up on a rock. While that's funny, it's not going to translate onto the screen.

"I think something a lot of screenwriters forget is that the screenplay is a very special medium. It's something you read that it not supposed to be read. So if you start getting cute with your style, that's not going to translate to the screen. It may be enjoyable to the reader, but you still have to have an unusual story, unique characters, and good dialogue.

"What a new writer must be aware of is that you can't judge your work by what's out there, by what you see on the screen. You have to push your craft absolutely as far as it can go.

"I've had writers ask me, 'I have this great idea, do you think I should write up a treatment, and go around town and pitch it? Or do you think I should write a really polished first draft?'

"To me, it's obvious you do your best work. You can't expect an executive or a reader to visualize that great idea, or try to pick it out of a badly executed script. Don't ever think somebody will say 'This is a terrible script, but a wonderful idea, and I'm going to buy it.' It doesn't work that way.

"You have to do all the work for the executive. Don't assume he's dying to discover you. Make your script easy to read. Don't include a lot of little side sheets and magazine articles unless you're a producer and you're trying to sell a project.

"If you want feedback on your script, give it to a bunch of people to read, and then make a list of questions to ask them: How did this character make you feel? Did this piece of action grab you? Was it believable? What about this scene? This sequence? Questions like that are going to force them to give you specific feedback. And it forces you to have some kind of objectivity about your work, which I think is very difficult for writers."

If you want to sell your screenplay, the first person you want on your side is the reader. There's only one sure thing you can count on in Hollywood: your script is going to have to climb a ladder of obstacles to the top before it can be sold. And the first step is the reader.

9

Development

"Taking what is to the next step."

More than 750 projects a year are put in development at various studios and independent production companies. Of those 750 potential films, less than 120 movies are actually produced, and of those, only about 20 are developed and put into production by the company that originated the material.

Strictly in terms of dollars and cents, development doesn't seem very economical. But within the film industry, it makes all the sense in the world. If only one of those films in development is produced and becomes a hit, it's a good return on the investment.

But at the cost of what? "In development" means that a studio or producer or production company is paying a writer to write a screenplay based on an idea, concept, novel, play, newspaper story, magazine article, real-life experience, situation, or what have you. You can write a screenplay about anything; like modern art, there's no subject out of reach, nothing that can't be developed into a screenplay.

Some material, of course, translates better into film than other material, and the trick is knowing what you have to work with (the original material), then creating what you need to make it visually dynamic, a story told with pictures.

You can't translate a novel into film, you have to adapt it into a screenplay. You can't take an idea and write a screenplay, you've got to structure it, create characters, develop a story line and chart your direction from beginning to end.

And direction means a line of development. And to develop, as the dictionary will tell you, means to expand or enlarge upon. In geometry, it means to transfer the details from one surface onto another. In Hollywood, that's as good a definition as any. In other words, development is a process.

Every studio, every production company, every supplier of film has someone in charge of development, someone in the story department (usually called v.p. of production, creative affairs executive, or director of development) to read scripts, listen to ideas, track writers, hustle projects, and establish working relationships with writers.

In Hollywood everything is based on relationships. A development person can become a friend, mentor, confidant, lover, supporter, ally, or enemy. The development person's job, says Susan Zachary, formerly head of development for Keith Barish Productions, "is to track a lot of material and find out what's going on around town. It's not just finding a hot script. It's not just finding a hot idea, it's taking what is to the next step. It's taking that idea and fashioning it into something that is ultimately very logical and very tight, very accessible, and very viable."

Historically, the development phenomenon is relatively new. In the '60s and early '70s, studios and production companies bought scripts, novels, plays, or newspaper stories, then hired writers to turn them into screenplays.

Some turned out good, others didn't. As the cost of production skyrocketed, studio executives would sometimes hire as many as eight different writers to rewrite the material so it would be ready to shoot. At a cost of thousands and thousands and thousands of dollars.

Surely, the studio reasoning went, there must be a better way, a *cheaper* way, of getting a shooting script. (A shooting script is simply a completed screenplay approved for production by the studio, production executives, director, and stars.) Maybe they could hire someone, a writer, or someone with a good story sense, someone who knows and understands writers, to work *with* them and develop a screenplay that would be ready to shoot. In this way the company, or producers, would be in control and could pump their input into the script, without the necessity of spending a lot of time with the writer.

"A lot of producers are more comfortable with the business or the social end of their jobs than with the development process," says one film executive. "They may know what they want in terms of movie ideas, but the process of going from idea to finished script is mystifying, even frightening, to them."

It's understandable. Producers work with details, negotiating deals with studios, executives, and agents, focusing on financing and distribution. Writers, on the other hand, work with blank sheets of paper, sketching dreams into ideas, translating experience and feelings into words on paper. They really don't have much in common.

When producers buy scripts, ideas, or any kind of material, they want to make sure the company's investment is covered. They want to know what the writer is *doing,* what progress he or she is making. They can't understand how a writer can disappear for several months and then suddenly reappear with a screenplay.

When I was working as a staff writer for David L. Wolper, he used to wander the halls in slippers and drop in unexpectedly on his writers. When he found me sitting with my feet propped up on the desk staring out the window, he would ask, "How's it going, what's going on, what are you working on?" But what he really meant was, *Why aren't you working?* He didn't understand that I *was* working.

The hardest thing about writing is knowing what to write. Of course, once a producer or studio has a screenplay, the writer becomes expendable. Once they have a script in hand, the producer has a script to produce, the director has a script to direct, the actors have parts to act, the studio has a film to shoot, the camera people, lighting people, electricians, editors, and the rest of the filmmaking crew all have jobs. They have something to work with. A script.

You can't take a blank sheet of paper and film it. In my yearly workshop at the International Film and Television Workshops in Rockport, Maine, there's always a conflict between the lighting students and the screenwriting students. The lighting workshops go from 6 A.M. until midnight. The writers meet every other day, and seem to be writing until all hours of the night. When they room together, there is a conflict. The lighting students want to sleep and the writers want to write. They can't understand what the writers do! It's a different energy. When I talk about screenwriting to the lighting crews, I pass out a blank sheet of paper and tell them, simply as an exercise, to light it, then film it.

As I travel across the country teaching seminars and workshops, I'm amazed at the number of people who don't know that a script is actually written, that stage directions and chase scenes are a detailed part of the screenplay. Everything is written by the writer. There are some people who still think the actors make up their lines as they go along. They don't understand that the story line, the dialogue, the action sequences, the stage directions, are written. In workshop after workshop I get questions from aspiring screenwriters about how much direction they have to write into the script. They think the director, or the camera person, or the film editor is going to design it, stage it, and film it.

The dream of writing often collides with the stark reality of it. No matter what you've heard, prices of screenplays vary. WGA minimum is $54,000 for a production that will cost more than $2.5 million. If someone hires you to write a screenplay for scale, you'll probably be paid $20,000 when you sign the contract, another $20,000 when you deliver the first draft eight to twelve weeks later, another $10,000 upon completion of the next draft and revisions (six weeks), and the remaining $4,000 on delivery of the final draft.

If you write a first-draft screenplay and a studio or producer wants to buy it, it will usually only cost them some option money. Financially, the agent or attorney works out what they call a step deal. Assume you've written a first draft. You'll be paid for the first draft and a set of revisions. They may buy the script for $250,000 but they will option the material for a year to eighteen months, paying you anywhere from $5,000 to $50,000 or more, depending on your track record and stature in the community. They will try to option the material as cheaply as they can. In conversation after conversation I had with producers, studio executives, and development personnel, they unanimously declined to give a specific amount as to how much you can option a screenplay for. The standard answer was from a dollar to $100,000. The rule of thumb used to be that an option price was anywhere from 2 to 5 percent of the budget, but that's not true anymore. In the case of a $250,000 purchase price, most of the monies would be paid to you in stages: so much when a production/distribution agreement is signed, so much when the production is given a green light (a start date), and the balance on the first day of principal photography.

Occasionally a producer will buy a script from the writer for $175,000 or more, and then will turn around and sell that script to the studio for $450,000; the writer usually doesn't know this, and the producer doesn't necessarily say anything about it.

When the script is produced it's possible the writer might get a "production bonus," anywhere from $10,000 on up. Finally, the writer may get a percentage of the producer's profits, usually from 2½ to 5½ percent of the producers *net*. In all probability the writer will never see net profits on a film because the studios and other third-party participants get their profits first, before the writer gets a penny.

The process of development allows a studio, producer, or production company to get the maximum amount of material for the minimum amount of cost. At least in the short run. If just one of those scripts hits—well, it pays for all the rest of the projects in development that didn't pan out.

When I was head of the story department at Cinemobile Systems and Cine Artists, we had no money to develop anything. We had money to buy scripts, money to produce movies, but none for development. It was too high a risk and too low a yield, according to my boss, Fouad Said. Therefore we couldn't compete with anybody who had money to develop material by known writers. Since my job was "to find material," the only way I could access good screenplays was by establishing relationships with new young writers.

That became my job. John Milius, Tom Rickman, David Ward, Bill Kerby, W. D. Richter, and Terry Malick were some of the new "hot" writers on the scene, so I started a relationship with them. It soon became my job to know everything that was going on around town: films in production, films in preproduction, scripts in development, who wrote them, and who was writing what and what other scripts they had; what writers the agents had just signed and what samples of their work they had. I knew who was doing what, where, and for whom.

It got to a point where my boss wanted me in on every meeting. We were getting something like seventy-five script submissions a week because we had a movie production company (Cine Artists), a location facility (Cinemobile Systems), a TV company (Cine TV), and a completion bond company, Cine Guarantors. Our finger was in a lot of pies.

After interviewing several development executives, I realize that development is no different today than it was when I was head of the story department at Cine Artists. Except there's more going on and a lot more opportunities for the writer now than there ever was before.

What does an executive in charge of development do? Judy Boasberg, v.p. of motion pictures at Charles Fries Entertainment, puts it this way: "I'm in charge of finding and developing material for films; that means reading scripts, finding ideas, whether from newspapers, magazines, or writers." Boasberg, who graduated from Yale, then studied in Paris, joined the David Geffen Company when she returned. She was on staff when they did *Risky Business* (Paul Brickman), *After Hours* (Joseph Minion), *Lost in America* (Albert Brooks and Monica Johnson), and *Little Shop of Horrors* (Howard Ashman).

"A lot of my job," she continues, "deals with networking; talking with agents, either on the phone or else meeting them for breakfast, lunch, drinks, or dinner and finding out what's hot, what's sold, what's going on, and who the good writers are. It's important for me to know things; not just what executive is leaving the studio, but who's buying what. So I know what writers are good, and which writers I should investigate further. I also have to know what ideas are out there so I don't go and option a script that may be similar to a script that's already been sold, or slated for production."

The key to success in Hollywood is information; knowing who's doing what before anybody else does. Knowledge is power, the saying goes. Most of the large agencies have books detailing all projects in development at the studios and major production companies. They get this information from their agents talking to people: What's going on? What are you doing? In their weekly or daily meetings, the agents pool their information, and then have key people enter it into the computer so they have access to it at all times. Whenever they need information, they go to these books. As a result, they have a big competitive edge in the marketplace.

The development executive is in charge of finding material and finding writers who can supply them with material. This happens in a variety of ways. One of them is having a specific directive from the person in charge of production: let's do, he or she might say, a romance thriller, like *Fatal Attraction*. Or lets do an action piece, like *Robocop* (Ed Newmeier) or *Lethal Weapon* (Shane Black). Or let's do a comedy like *Baby Boom* (Nancy Meyers and Charles Shyer) or let's do a *Broadcast News* (James Brooks).

The development person takes over from there, "wanting to put the best elements together," as Ilene Kahn, v.p. of HBO Pictures says, "and trusting your instincts for marrying the right writer to the right project. I think that's the thing we have to hone the most acutely as development executives."

That means "balancing your own tastes against the tastes of what the company is looking for," remarks Judy Boasberg.

What happens then?

"You call up the writers you know," says Susan Zachary "and ask, do you have anything like this? You talk to the agents; do your writers have anything like this? Basically, you put out the word and see what comes back."

Jane Kagon, formerly v.p. of production for Michael Douglas and now v.p. of production at the Hendler Company at Tri-Star Pictures and a former entertainment attorney, says, "We interviewed between twenty-five and thirty-five writers for *Romancing the Stone* II [filmed as *Jewel of the Nile*]. We gave them some basic plot points we wanted in the story, plus the setting. They knew the characters, of course, so they came in and pitched their ideas. The one thing I look for is an original voice. A phrase, a new twist on the situation, the way they improvise a solution to a story problem, that's what I respond to.

"When a writer was finally chosen to develop the screenplay," she continues, "we had several meetings to work out a solid concept of beginning, middle, and end; we didn't want any surprises in the story. We made it clear we wanted to see the same animal." It's essential that the writer, producer, development executive, everyone concerned, see the same story line.

When I was actively pursuing a career as a screenwriter, I was given an assignment by a producer-director to develop his idea of motorcycle racers on the racing circuit into a one-hour dramatic TV series. So I came up with characters and a story line for the pilot episode. After we discussed the story I went off to write the series presentation and pilot, and he went off to Europe to direct a movie of the week.

Everything went well during the writing except for one thing: I began to see that the visual elements of motorcycle racers on tour was a limiting concept; there would be more tension, more drama, more visual potential using race cars, either stock cars or formula-one race cars on the racing circuit. I tried to reach the producer-director, but he was unavailable, and there was no one at his office who was any help. I talked to my agent and he told me to do what I thought best.

So I did. I changed the format from motorcycles to race cars, set the pilot on the racing circuit, and turned in the material. When the producer-director returned, he read the presentation and script and was furious. He fired me on the spot.

He was right. I strayed from the original idea. Looking back, I should have written it both ways, but I was lazy, as well as stubborn, and wanted to make him "see" that my way was the "right" way.

I was wrong. I was a writer for hire; he hired me to do a job, and I didn't do it. If there had been a development person to oversee the project, it would never have happened. *Que será, será.*

"Writers naturally want to follow their own lead," says Michael London, now senior vice president of production at Twentieth Century Fox, formerly of Don Simpson/Jerry Bruckheimer Productions, "and often it's the easy way out for a producer or a development executive to give up his or her responsibility. But giving in isn't always the right thing for the screenplay; writers have been known to make mistakes just like everyone else in the process, and a script has to please a lot of people besides the writer before it can get produced and reach an audience.

"The bottom line, though, is that it's the writer who has to face a blank sheet of paper every day. If they don't believe in what they're doing, it won't have any life. In our company, we spend an unusual amount of time making sure the writers share our point of view on the material before we make a hiring decision. If we all agree up front on where we're going, the writer will be much more open to input and in that way it becomes a collaborative process."

The process goes like this: After however many meetings it takes and the story line is agreed on, the writer goes off and writes a treatment, anywhere from four to twenty pages. The treatment (simply a narrative synopsis of the story line) is read by the executives, then presented in a collective meeting. If changes are needed, the writer goes off and makes the changes. If everybody approves, then the writer goes off and writes the first words-on-paper draft.

"During the writing process," London continues, "I'll be actively involved in providing whatever feedback is helpful to the writer. If that means reading pages on a daily basis, fine. If it means waiting until there's a rough draft done in two or three months, that's fine too."

From first meeting to completed first draft usually takes about six to eight months. Here's the way it's broken down: After the meetings and story details are hashed out, the writer turns out a first draft in eight to twelve weeks. The executive needs four to six weeks to read and evaluate the material. That means writing a complete set of notes and changes. These notes are discussed in a meeting and the writer is given about six weeks to make the changes.

The development executive's job is to go through the material looking for continuity of scenes, character development, story development, gaps in logic, anything that needs to be clarified and accentuated. "We'll read the script," says Judy Boasberg, "and isolate the problems. This is what we want to do: we want to up the love story, up the tension and develop this character more fully; the ending doesn't work, it needs to be stronger, more dramatic; the main character needs to be expanded because he has to be stronger, more active."

These changes may be substantial, because most executives don't know, or don't care, that when a writer changes something on page 22, you have to redesign pages 43 and 86 and possibly find another way to make the same incident, or character, work.

Once those pages are turned in, there's another four-week reading period, where company executives read the material and give their comments and suggestions. The writer is given another four weeks to do a rewrite, after which there's another four-week reading period, more notes, more changes, and more revisions, and than a two-week period where the writer does the final polish.

At that point the company and/or producer have a decision to make. Do we bring in another writer, or do we go with the project as is? And more times than not, another writer is brought in, either to punch up the dialogue, make the material more visual, add more dramatic tension, or—hopefully—take the material to the next step.

Sometimes—indeed, many times—the development people will take things in the wrong direction. "It's very easy," Boasberg says, "to get seduced by something in a script that you really like, that you don't want to give up, so you end up letting the tail wag the dog. That happens all the time."

I met a writer at a party one night who told me he had just sold a screenplay to a major production company. And now the development executive and a production executive are having meeting after meeting with him, changing the nature and point of view of the material. They want him to change his original story line, write a new treatment, add new characters, basically write a whole new screenplay.

I asked him why they bought the script in the first place. He shrugged and replied, "For the relationship between the two guys." That's normal.

Whether someone options your screenplay or you sell an idea, once you sign those contracts you don't own the material anymore. They do. You're simply a writer for hire. They can do what they want with it.

The success of any development person in Hollywood depends not only on the talent, ability, and personality of the executive, but on the people they work for. Getting your boss to read a screenplay is sometimes as easy as teaching a cat to swim.

When I was reading scripts and talking with writers, the man I worked for never read anything. Oh, he may have read the first page or two, one or two pages in the middle, and the last page, but he never read the script. He preferred to buy the screenplay based on what the people around him said about it. If everybody agreed a script was worth buying, he acted and obtained the material.

He was always uncomfortable with the process of finding and purchasing screenplays, and he only felt comfortable producing movies. That's what he did the best. He literally supervised the production of 119 films the first year I was working at Cinemobile. Since we provided location facilities, including transportation, equipment, and technicians to movie locations all over the world, the company had a wonderful reputation. But when it came to developing material, or working with writers, he was inaccessible; he never trusted us completely. That's because he never trusted himself.

"No matter how well you do your job, no matter how many agents you meet, no matter how much material you read, no matter how close you are to the writer, if your boss is not accessible, it doesn't make any difference," says Deborah Newmyer of Amblin Entertainment. "Personal rapport is the single most important criterion in a creative development job. You need to be open and articulate in these jobs if you are going to be of any use to your bosses."

As director of development for Steven Spielberg, Newmyer works with Kathleen Kennedy and Frank Marshall. She started out as a ballet dancer, then worked for Alan Pakula on *Rollover,* just prior to *Sophie's Choice.* Paramount asked her to come to L.A. and be a creative executive. Her job at Paramount, she says, consisted of reading twenty scripts a week and writing synopses and script notes. She also previewed the dailies of *48 Hrs.* so that her boss, Jeffrey Katzenberg, now head of production at Disney, could see three hours of the unedited film in an abbreviated, edited version of fifteen minutes. Soon after, she left to work with producer-director Norman Jewison, then joined Jon Peters working on *Vision Quest.*

"He'd only read a script when the project was ready to go into production. If I wanted him to read something, and he wasn't ready to be sold on the project, I would get two actors to read the screenplay and transcribe the script onto a cassette so he could listen to it in his car and see if he was interested."

This is not so unusual; there are many successful executives in Hollywood who never read a script until it's actually in production. "If your boss won't take the time to read the scripts you suggest," Newmyer continues, "if you don't click creatively with him, then you're not doing the job right, and it's not the right job for you.

"I knew when I was interviewed at Amblin," she says, "that I didn't want the job unless I could have an easy flow of dialogue with the person I work for. And that's the key; how much you can get from the person who's going to produce or direct this movie to give his input, his point of view, into the story.

"It's not a job that a lot of people do in this town when they 'do development,' which is basically hustling to get scripts before the next person, or hustling to sell the script to a studio. I don't have to do either of those two jobs."

In terms of finding material, she says, "We run the gamut. We don't read any unsolicited screenplays as submissions; everything we read is a writing sample, and a release form must be signed. So a script could be submitted through an agent or attorney as a writing sample and if we like it—like *Gremlins* (Chris Columbus), or *The Money Pit* (David Giler)—we could make it into a movie.

"If a script comes in written by an unknown, somebody who's not proven, and it's good, I can convince people to read it. It doesn't matter if it will ever get made, or optioned, but so what? It could be a wonderful script from a nonproduced writer. I'm extremely fortunate that the people I work with believe me when I say 'This script must be read.' "

Most of Amblin's projects are developed in-house. "For example," Newmyer says, "Steven might have an idea about a single father, a nice guy, but not particularly a good father, who gets a second chance when he comes back to the family as a ghost. If he wanted to pursue this, he'd say, let's find a writer for this. So I go through my vocabulary of creative talent in town to see who might be best suited to write or direct this particular movie. Therefore, I need to know every single person that's talented in town, whether it's an established Alvin Sargent, a blossoming Phil Joanou, or the current winning Focus Award screenwriter. You have to know all these people, and what they're doing, in order to maintain this vocabulary.

"For instance, we're working on a Georgia O'Keeffe project, dealing with her relationship with Alfred Stieglitz. A young director brought the project to us, and Steven liked it and said, okay, bring me a first draft. So we found a writer. We weren't looking for the most expensive writer, we were looking for the right writer. We found a writer who seemed perfect. He'd written a terrific script about doomed love. And he'd written a wonderful, romantic script about Abelard and Heloise, a period love story between a priest and a nun.

"He did a first draft and handed it in. It needed work, so we worked on it together before we had Steven read it. A lot of it didn't work and no one was really satisfied with this draft.

"He just didn't capture the passion between Georgia O'Keeffe and Alfred Stieglitz. Maybe because he's English, maybe because he's older and didn't understand the passion between a fifty-year-old man and a twenty-five-year-old woman. Whatever it was, it didn't work. Which is always the risk in development, and you've got to be able to roll with a possible creative failure.

"Sometimes, you know, you don't win. He was exactly the right writer, and we'd probably pick him again under the same circumstances. You can't get discouraged if the first step doesn't work. It's so easy to just say it's not there, let's just forget about it. You have to move on. You have to see how this piece will fit into the next step. You can't dwell on it.

"Movies do not get made by themselves. They take a ton of effort and even more passion. The only movies that get made are those where the producer does not give up.

"Since we've had some success with *American Tail,* we hope to do a lot more animation in the future. Especially since there's so much talent coming out of film schools. We're doing another animated film about dinosaurs."

During my interviews I learned that a move is going on in Hollywood where animated films are being penciled into studio production slates. Disney is committed to producing one new animated feature a year. That means, with one film in production, another one is in preproduction, and another one in development.

With Amblin also doing one animated feature a year, there might be a good market in the next few years for animated material, or for scripts utilizing combinations of live action and animation like they had at the 1987 Academy Awards ceremony, and in *Who Framed Roger Rabbit?*

One of the strong markets emerging for the screenwriter is the cable feature market. In development, finding material for pay TV is no different than it is for features. Ilene Kahn, v.p. of HBO Pictures, says, "What I do is as much a selling job as it is a buying job.

"A lot of people don't realize that to be on the 'inside' as a 'buyer,' you have to be a great seller. And once I get something I really want to quarterback through, I have to sell my boss, who is the ultimate yes."

Making movies for cable TV creates special demands. "We look for small-budget films that are somewhat between a feature film and a television film, in the budget range of $3 to 5 million. What we try to serve our subscribers is a well-executed movie—movies that have interesting characters and strong story lines. Movies made for the subscriber. We're not looking to do breakthrough movies. We want to do good movies.

"I don't really think you can sell anything you don't believe in. When I'm looking for material, I have to figure out what's going to spark somebody's interest, and if there are any elements that might be attractive to us.

"We look for strong leads," she continues. "We're somewhat dependent on recognizable names. I look for something that really hooks me, something that strikes an emotional chord, the characters, the setup, the dilemma, the changes the characters have to go through.

"Sometimes you have no control over a script except for your initial spark and your instincts. It's relying on that little voice inside you coming from within and not from without; being able to put blinders on, not listening to what you think is commercial, the 'I should do this,' or the 'I ought to do this' project. It's your belief in the material that guides you, and I rely on my instincts. Sometimes you win, sometimes you lose. But hopefully, you'll at least have the at-bats, the chance to do it.

"We make between eight and ten movies a year, so we maintain about fifty to sixty projects in development.

"I start developing them any number of ways; through ideas pitched to me, from writers or producers. Or we might start with a star who wants to do a certain kind of movie. Sometimes we'll buy the story rights to a newspaper or magazine article. About 25 percent of what we buy are books, and another 25 percent are existing scripts that are in turnaround from the studios that we redevelop and reshape into something more appropriate for us. Another 10 or 15 percent may be original ideas pitched. The rest varies.

"After we put something in development, we have a meeting to kick off the project and get in sync about what the story is. I usually have the writer do a written story outline. It may be as short as three to five pages, or as long as forty pages. I don't like long treatments because it usually takes the juice out of the first draft.

"Basically, we want to know who the characters are, the conflicts, how the scenes are going to work and how the movie is going to end."

When you're in development, you're in a process, and it's always moving, always changing, always in transition, just like life itself. What may be relevant and important today on page 32 may be irrelevant tomorrow on page 36. When you're in development, the executive you're working with today could easily be gone tomorrow.

If you're one of the fortunate writers who has a project in development, or one of the unfortunate ones who has something in development (depending on your point of view), you are a writer for hire. Pure and simple. You have sold your idea, your script, your outline, your *material*, and you have no say in what *they* do with it, no rights unless they're negotiated into your contract.

Even though you created the idea, developed the characters, pounded it onto a blank sheet of paper, when you enter into the process of development, you don't own anything. You develop your idea to fit *their* needs, *their* egos, *their* whims. What's right for the story, or necessary for the integrity of the screenplay, is secondary.

Therefore, you can't be too attached to anything. Especially your story, characters, or some of the essential details of your screenplay. Just do your best to keep the integrity of your story line intact.

I recently met a writer who told me he had just sold a first-draft screenplay and was working with a well-known development executive on the rewrite. He sounded a little perturbed, and when I asked why, he told me that since the contracts were signed, he's had to take meeting after meeting with the development executive and they're going through the screenplay scene by scene, page by page, word by word. Now, he says, he's in the process of writing a new twenty-page outline. As he was writing this new outline, it suddenly dawned on him that the basic relationship between the father and son was being changed into a softer, more mellow story line. What was, in his first draft, a raging fire between the two characters, was slowly being turned into a smoldering ember.

He didn't like it, and he didn't like how he felt writing it, and he didn't know what to do. I asked him if he could afford to buy the material back, and he said no. So I told him there was nothing he could do about it. He had signed a contract and sold his material. They could do whatever they wanted with it. And if he didn't do the job the way they wanted it done, then they'd bring in somebody who would. That's just the way it is.

You can write your first draft and if they don't like it, they'll give it to another writer who will bring in his or her idea of what will make the screenplay work. A new writer brought onto the project comes from a position of pure self-interest; in order to earn a coscreenwriting credit, the new writer must contribute at least 50 percent to the existing material. That means adding new characters, changing names of existing characters, adding new scenes, taking out the best of what you've put in and changing it. A full credit means more money, and if the film is made, a substantial leap in his or her career status. And that, for the Hollywood screenwriter, is where it's at: the credit on the screenplay.

The screenwriter developing a project for someone else is always at risk. He or she must forge and shape the material into something that is arrived at by several people. By committee. And that's really the double-edged sword. On the one hand it's great that you're going to get paid to develop and write your script. On the other hand, what you ultimately end up writing may have no relationship to the script you originally wanted to write.

For many writers, development is something to be pursued and sought after. For others, it's not. If you decide that's the direction that you want to take, that's fine. Just know what goes with the territory. Sometimes the bad news is when they say yes.

10

Pitching the Project

*"It never gets better than the romance
and the blush."*

A good story starts with a good idea. If you have an idea that you want to
develop into a screenplay, the chances are you'd like to get paid to write
it. So you set up a meeting with a development executive to "pitch" the
idea.

Pitching is an art. When you talk about pitching, you're talking about
presentation; your goal, your need, is to convince a production executive
that you should be paid to write your idea into a screenplay.

And when you pitch, you're pitching *story*. Because story is the
foundation of the screenplay. Character and action may be the glue that
holds everything together, but it all starts within the context of story.

Pitching is the blessing and burden of the screenwriter. The agony and
the ecstasy. In order to convince the executive that he should develop this
idea into a script, you, as writer, must have a solid grasp of the material,
yet still be free enough to "wing" it if and when the need arises. A good
pitcher should be a good actor as well as a good writer. Unfortunately, it
doesn't always work out that way.

One of the best "pitchers" in Hollywood was Louis B. Mayer, one of
the founders of Metro-Goldwyn-Mayer Studios. In the '30s, in the heyday
of production, Mayer would face his board of directors, or actors, or
directors, or anyone else he wanted to convince to do something he
wanted them to do, and at the proper moment fall to his knees, clasp his

hands together, and beg and plead to get his way. He would even use tears if necessary. Like Al Jolson singing "Mammy." That's what Mayer would do, and most of the time it got him what he wanted. A movie, a deal, a merger, a star, a script, a loan; whatever it was, he usually got it.

Writers are, by definition, people who are good at putting words on paper. Most of them are not very good at pitching a story. They mumble their words, stare down at the ground, hem and haw about how they see their story and what they want to do. Some writers, depending on their track record and their stature in the community, can get away with it. Most of them can't.

When you set up a pitch meeting, you're preparing a performance. Just like an actor. And you have to be prepared. You've only got twenty minutes to present your idea, so your story line should be structured in order to dramatize key elements from beginning to end. In Hollywood everybody's looking for a new, hot idea, so writers pitching a story are talking to people with willing ears.

A pitch is nothing more than a verbal presentation of a notion, concept, situation, idea, or story. A pitch can be augmented with pictures, casting suggestions, newspaper articles, or anything else that will aid you in "selling" your idea. A pitch is as varied as it is necessary.

If you have a good track record (that is, a number of screenplays to your credit) a pitch can be one line. James Goldman, the playwright and screenwriter, had an idea to do a "love story set against the area of invasion of privacy." So he pitched it to Ilene Kahn, v.p. of HBO Pictures, and she replied, "Well, we're not going to give you a blind script commitment, but we would like to work with James Goldman, so we'll give you a script commitment, but it won't kick in until you come back with a story line we approve of."

That's the way it works with someone like James Goldman. Or his brother, William Goldman. Most of us are not that lucky. We have to go and pitch the entire story. That means *selling* your idea.

You have to present your material with passion, clarity, and confidence. When I would pitch an idea, I worked it out structurally, so I knew the beginning, middle, and end. I had one or two ideas of who should play the leads, a couple of examples of movies currently released that I felt revealed the visual style, or "look," of the film, and a lot of information about the characters.

If you want to walk out of that office with a deal, you have to present your idea clearly and effectively. "I need ammunition to sell something," says Michael Besman, v.p. of production at Guber-Peters, "because I have to sell it to my bosses." Everybody's a buyer and a seller in Hollywood.

One time I had an idea I wanted to develop into a screenplay. I had read an article in the *Los Angeles Times* about a mountain climber who had just accomplished a tremendous climb. I thought it would make a fantastic movie. So I located the mountain climber (I simply called information in the city where she lives; you can also call the newspaper reporter, or any organization that might be mentioned in the article) and talked about a possible movie focusing on her accomplishment. She had her own ideas about what the story should be, and I had mine.

I suggested the following: if she gave me permission to sell her story for a period of three months (ninety days)—that is, a free option—and I was able to get a deal, she would be hired as consultant and technical adviser on the project, as well as doing all the mountain climbing during the shooting of the film. She agreed.

She sent me down a batch of newspaper clippings, several pictures (she's a very attractive woman), and a copy of the map that illustrated the route she forged in a magnificent climb to the top of Half Dome in Yosemite National Park.

I went through the material and chose about six different items I wanted to take in with me to the pitch meetings I was going to set up. Then I went to a bookstore and bought the largest and most elaborate book of landscape photography that pictured Half Dome. I read a biography of Ansel Adams, the man who did the landscape photographs, and found two or three quotes that expressed the wonder of this particular location.

Then I structured the story line: A young woman undertakes to be the first woman to scale a new path to the top of the mountain. It is an amazing and daring feat; it takes several days for her to climb the sheer walls of granite that go straight up. During the climb she gets caught in two blustery windstorms. She slips, almost loses her grip, but manages to hang on, ripping the palm of her left hand open in the process. With one hand basically useless, she continues to the top with courage, faith, and skill.

It took almost two months for me to prepare this pitch. Since I really wanted to do this story, I took the time to prepare it correctly. I also knew that I had to present the story with such drama, and such passion, that the executive would be convinced that this was a film he really wanted to make. To be a good pitcher means you have to be a good actor. For me, that's no problem.

You can't give them a reason to say no. "If your story is strong," says Don Simpson of Don Simpson/Jerry Bruckheimer Productions, and former president of Paramount Pictures, in a *Los Angeles Times* article, "all it takes is a straightforward telling."

A lot of writers don't believe that. They pitch with the notion that more is better. Some writers are "so busy dancing they forget to tell the story," says one executive. "Sparks fly around the room! They're up on the table, they're holding ashtrays on their nose, and they're talking about who should play the part."

Your manner of presentation, your attitude, the clothes you're wearing, everything goes into the package of making a good pitch. When I pitched my mountain-climbing story I was well prepared. I had structured the story on 3x5 cards and knew the basic story points: ending, beginning, plot points I and II, and the midpoint. I knew the mountain climber and had two newspaper pictures of her. I had photographs of the location, quotes about it, and so on.

I walked into the office, chatted for a few minutes, then went into my pitch. The executive was interested, loved the Ansel Adams photographs, and said this seemed to be a perfect vehicle for a very hot director that had just finished a picture for them. Great. I could see she was excited by it, and when I got up to leave she told me she'd get back to me in a few days.

After the meeting, I called my agent, told him my impressions, and then waited. Three days went by. Nothing. On the fourth day, I called, and the executive said she didn't have any news yet but would get back to me as soon as she could. This went on for more than two weeks.

Then I got the call from my agent: it was no. They passed. No reason, no explanation, nothing. That's the way it goes.

Many writers in Hollywood make a very good living pitching ideas, getting deals, and then developing them into mediocre first-draft screenplays. From the company's point of view, it doesn't matter how good or how bad that first draft is; once they have a first-draft screenplay, they can "bring in a name writer for half a million dollars, and that makes it a production deal as opposed to a development deal," says Susan Zachary. "Development is never the end result."

What do executives look for in a pitch? "Something that's interesting, something you'd want to see as a movie," says Zachary. "Something you can turn around and sell. There's only one buyer in this business, and that's the person who puts down six dollars to buy a ticket. I don't care if you're pitching to Barry Diller (CEO of 20th Century Fox), Michael Eisner (CEO Disney), Alan Ladd, Jr. (CEO MGM), or Frank Mancuso (CEO Paramount). What they're thinking about is how they're going to sell that idea to the American public.

"When a writer pitches me," she continues, "I'm always thinking, 'Would I want to see this?' or 'Who *would* want to see it?' What attracts me to a pitch is very visceral, because I don't hear very many good ones."

What makes a good pitch, then? Everybody I interviewed agreed: good story, good characters, good visual background, something well thought out.

"If somebody's coming in with a pitch without any other element [director, star, financing], I look for how well the story is worked out," says Ilene Kahn of HBO. "You've got to know your material cold, and be committed to it. Don't think you're going to sell something you're not committed to, no matter what, because that's when I can smell it. Then I say to myself, if they're not committed to it, how can I be? I look for someone who believes in what they're doing."

I heard this refrain over and over again. The bottom line, as always, is: If you aren't passionate or committed about your idea, who is? "There are a thousand ways to say no," Kahn continues, "and only one to say yes. I have a sell job. I can't sell what I don't believe in. So you better make me believe that you're committed to it. It's never going to get better than the romance and the blush.''

Any writer who's gone through the pitching process and gets a go-ahead on the project knows the feeling of this "romance" period. Everyone is excited about the story, excited you're going to write it, excited by the potential of the project. Your calls are taken immediately or returned quickly; you're invited to screenings and social events; in short, you're one of the family.

But once you start turning in pages, and someone voices a question, or happens to disagree with the way you wrote something, or thought the story was going to be slanted this way and not that way, things change. Phone calls are slow in being returned, or calls are made to check up on how you're doing, how many pages you've done, what scene you're writing, and when can we expect more pages, and did you remember to put this scene in the second act?

At that point, the honeymoon's over. You're still working on the same script, but the executives seem to be more excited about the "new" project they're doing, or the new writer they've found, or the script that was just turned in. That's just the way it is.

Many writers I talk to tell me they don't exactly know how long their pitch meetings should be. We've got to tell the story. But how long should it take?

"Fifteen or twenty minutes," replies Jane Kagon. "That's the longest. I have writers come in who are wonderful, great personalities, with a great sense of humor, and they go on and on for forty-five minutes. So much of pitching is style; you have to win someone over with the energy and theatrics of it.

"My constant refrain is 'Well, what's it about?' And not on a superficial level. Over and over again I find people don't really know what their story is about. They have some kind of a vague notion, but the thematic content is usually missing. For me, that's the place you start.''

When you're pitching, it's the writer's job to convince the executive in the shortest period of time that he or she has something to say, and simply the way you present yourself is going to determine whether you can say it on paper. It's very hard to tell from a pitch if somebody can actually write.

"Some writers are not very articulate verbally but are eloquent on paper. It's the rare ones who can do both," says one executive.

In a *Los Angeles Times* article Ron Shelton, screenwriter of the powerful *Under Fire* (with Clayton Frohman), *The Best of Times,* and *Bull Durham*, says when you pitch your idea for a development deal "there's too much baggage attached. Too many committees. Too many complicated turnaround deals. Too many changing executives. It's better to spend six months writing your script on spec because then you own it."

Some people spend most of their careers pitching ideas. I know writers who have spent over a year pitching their idea before they got anyone interested in it. Personally, I couldn't do that. But everybody has to make that decision for himself.

Nobody is immune from the pitching process. Everybody in Hollywood pitches. Writers to executives. Executives to the head of production. The head of production to the CEO. And so on.

Since pitching is so variable, there are no clear-cut rules to follow. So, I started looking at it from the point of view of the executive.

What does an executive look for in a pitch meeting? The first thing the executive looks for is a "great idea," says Michael Besman, of Guber-Peters. "The process usually begins with finding a new writer you're excited about.

"For example, I read a script a few weeks ago that I liked. It wasn't something the company would be interested in buying, but I read it as a writing sample, and I liked it. So I wanted to meet the writer.

"The writer came in and we talked about idea and areas of interest. One of her ideas was a movie about a Japanese internment camp during the early days of World War II."

(After the bombing of Pearl Harbor, many Japanese-Americans were interned in prison camps and their property and valuables confiscated by the government. There has never really been a film done about this subject, although people have been trying to do it for years. When I was at Cinemobile in the mid '70s, we had a Japanese internment camp project we were working on, but we could never get it off the ground.)

"I wondered about who or what was behind this imprisonment and what happened to the confiscated property," Besman continues. "I thought it could be the seed of a very good movie.

"The internment project is more a great movie story as compared to an easy-to-sell high concept idea. It's a great arena for a movie.

"So I called her agent and conveyed my enthusiasm, and wanted to set up another meeting. She had to do some research first, and when she was ready, she came back in.

"At this second meeting, I was looking for the bones of the story line, not a scene-by-scene breakdown. I wanted to get an idea of the studio's reaction, so I called an executive I felt would respond favorably and said, 'What do you think of this idea?' and I got a positive response, but she wanted to hear the whole pitch.

"A few days later I was at a meeting with my boss and the subject of internment was brought up, and I mentioned that's something we might be interested in, and he said, 'That's good, but it better be something you're interested in.' "

In other words, if Besman wasn't interested in the project, then for sure, his boss wasn't going to be interested. That's the way it works. Everybody pitches everybody. If you understand where everybody is coming from, you can prepare your pitch appropriately, whether you're a writer or an executive.

What's going to sell your project is an interesting idea, yes, but almost as important is the passion and the manner of presentation. Your writing ability comes in second. You've got to remember that everybody's a buyer and seller in Hollywood. It is the Town of Sell, built on a foundation of hype, fear, greed, insecurity, and ego. You can't afford to offend anybody.

"Somebody who writes a bad script today," Besman says, "may write a great script tomorrow, so you leave the door open.

"If somebody pitches me a story and I see it another way, I'll try to give them my point of view, some feedback, food for thought. Sometimes it works, and sometimes it doesn't. You try to be constructive about passing because writers are putting themselves on the line.

"The most important thing in pitching is to emotionally involve the listener; you just don't throw out a laundry list.

"If you don't bring a sense of personal excitement and personal passion to what you're doing, it's going to be flat," says Michael London, formerly of Don Simpson/Jerry Bruckheimer Productions. "Pitching something just because it's commercial is a trap. The trick is to find a commercial idea that you really want to write; not because it's commercial, but because you love the idea.

"What we look for in our company are stories that take us behind closed doors into an unfamiliar, hopefully exciting world. And that means two things: one, you've got to choose a world that people want to be in for ninety minutes or two hours; and two, you better render it convincingly. You better not try to fake it.

"The one mistake I see a lot of first-time writers make is writing things they think will please other people instead of themselves. In this business you have to please yourself first and hope your instincts reflect what audiences want to see. That's why Don Simpson and Jerry Bruckheimer are so successful."

When you examine the track record of Don Simpson and Jerry Bruckheimer, you have to agree. *Flashdance, Beverly Hills Cop, Beverly Hills Cop II, Thief of Hearts, Top Gun* are films that forged a new look and a new, contemporary cinematic style in background and subject matter. You have to go back to the films of the '30s and '40s for comparison. That's what development executives are looking for.

Barbara Corday has been a writer (cocreator, with Barbara Avedon, of the TV hit series *Cagney and Lacey*), a network executive (v.p. of comedy development at ABC for three years), an independent producer (under contract to Columbia), and a studio executive (president, Columbia Pictures Television), and is now Executive V.P. of Prime Time Programming for CBS. She is bright, articulate, outspoken, and knows what she's talking about. Though her expertise is television, what she says is applicable to both film and television.

"When I was at ABC," she begins, "I would have two or three pitch meetings in the morning, and two or three in the afternoon. Figure five pitches a day, twenty-five a week, and if you multiply that over a period of eight months, that's almost eight hundred pitches a year."

One of those rare executives who's been on both sides of the pitch, she describes the ideal pitch as being "five minutes of schmooze, twenty minutes of pitch, and five minutes of good-bye.

"When a writer comes in for a pitching session, what strikes me the most is his or her attitude," she says. "I think presentation of self is very important. Somebody who's a slob, or who hangs out of their chair and defies you to like their idea, is not somebody you're going to warm to as much as somebody who's friendly and open—someone who looks you in the eye and feels good about what they're doing there and about what they have to say; someone who wants to engage you in their endeavor.

"Unfortunately, some people come in and pitch five different projects in a meeting, and from a buyer's point of view there's nothing worse than a writer who brings in a bunch of ideas to pitch. You should never pitch more than one, maybe two projects at a time. Never, never, never pitch more than that.

"First of all," she continues, "the attention span of the executive you're pitching to cannot handle it. There's not a buyer in this world you can convince that you have the same passion for five individual projects. What you're selling is your passion. You're rarely selling the idea. You are selling you. You are selling your commitment, your point of view, your execution of that idea. And if you tell me that you feel the same way about five different ideas, I'm not going to buy anything from you because I don't believe you. So you come in with one thing that makes you jump up and down and pace back and forth in my office and tell me it's keeping you up nights because you can't wait to do it. When you do that you've got a much better chance of selling it to me than sitting there with some treatments or 3x5 cards saying, 'Oh, you don't like this, well, what about a guy in college who does . . .'

"I can't stress how important enthusiasm and passion and belief in your project are to the executive you're pitching to."

When I was pitching a project, I would prepare two things I wanted to do. One of them, my first pitch, would be what I set up the meeting for, and I had it worked out clearly and cleanly. I knew my characters, my beginning, middle, and end, and the key structural points of the story line: ending, beginning, plot points I and II, and the midpoint. In case the executive didn't like the idea, and asked me if I had anything else I was interested in doing, I went into my second idea. I never prepared the second idea as much as the first. I knew my characters vaguely, my story line vaguely, and I purposefully left enough room in the story line so I could improvise whatever I needed. I could see what the executive responded to, and went from there.

A typical pitch meeting, says Barbara Corday, is one where "you'll schmooze for a few minutes and you'll be looking for an opportunity to say, I'd like to tell you about my idea. When you've said enough hellos, carefully choose the moment and then you can plunge right in.

"Introduce the idea by telling a few lines about the overview of the story. It takes place in an inn in Connecticut. It's two hundred years old and it was left to this guy who used to be an advertising executive in New York and now he's running this little inn. That's what it's about. Now I'll tell you a little bit about who's there. This former advertising executive is married to a younger woman and they've inherited the handyman who worked for the people who formerly owned it, and he's been there for a hundred years, and this is what their relationship is like with him. And this is what his wife's relationship is to him. There's a woman who lives next door and this is what their relationship is to her, and this is what some of their conflicts are. I'm thinking of doing character-related stories dealing with relatives who come to visit, guests who stay at the inn, and the townspeople they know."

That's the start point of almost every pitch, a brief overview of the idea so the executive can understand the idea and character relationships within the premise. At this point the executive can raise some basic questions about the idea or characters and you can become more specific about the elements of the story line.

"A great pitch," she continues, "is where you're prepared, you have the answers to questions raised, you have enthusiasm, you know where you're going, you have some ideas about the kinds of people you see in the parts. You have an idea for the pilot episode, you have an idea for a couple of stories later on so that it gives the buyer a sense of direction as to where you're going with it. You have an idea what town it takes place in, what it looks like, what style you see it in. Is it a one-camera film show, like *thirtysomething,* or is it a four-camera film show like *Designing Women*? If it's a drama, is it a multicharacter show with continuing stories, like *L.A. Law*?

"You have to come in prepared and know how you see this show progressing. If you walk in the door of a network or a studio for a meeting you've been waiting three weeks for, you're supposed to be a professional person who knows how to do what you're there to do. And if you pitch a few lines and the executive asks you two or three questions and you can't answer them, you really aren't ready to be in that room.

"If you're talking about the first pitch of an idea for a TV series, nobody cares that much about the story line at the first meeting. If you sell the idea, the second meeting will be the story meeting. That's when you'll have to answer all the questions about how the characters relate to each other; why they are together, what are they doing in this office or apartment or wherever they are, and how they relate to each other and how they know each other. You need to know those characters because what you're selling in a television series is the characters.

"If you're selling a TV movie, then the first meeting is where you pitch the story idea. It isn't totally worked out, act by act, necessarily, but you better know what the beginning, middle, and end are and what it's about.

"If you're going to a studio or a production company, you prepare your pitch a little differently than if you're going to a network, because the studio or production company is not usually going to buy what you're pitching as much as they're going to say, yes, we like the idea and we want to be in business with you, so let's go pitch it to the network together. You may get a small amount of option money from a studio or production company but it's not really what you're after. What you want is their help and expertise and clout to go with you to the network.

"When you pitch to a production company, you may want to openly discuss with the production executive what the problems are. For example, you might say I'm thinking there are two ways to do this and I was thinking about doing it this way or this way. What do you think? Maybe this character could be a teenager because of this situation, but it could also be a younger child. You really have to have a working meeting with this executive, but if you're going to the network you should pitch it as though you know exactly what it is you want to do.

"You see, when you pitch to a production company or a producer you're asking them to be your partner. You're not asking them so much to buy it. They're not putting their million dollars on the line by what you say in that room. They're going to go with you and try and sell this thing.

"It's almost like the defense attorney and the client versus the judge. You need to be honest with the defense attorney, you need to discuss everything openly. You need to talk about the problems you're having, like I feel strongly about this but I don't feel as strongly about that. What are your feelings about it? But when you go to court, you go as a unit, a team, working together. So you've got to feel strongly about what you're doing."

That's the real key to pitching your project: how strongly you feel about what you want to write about. That means you've got to prepare your material. You've got to put in the time and structure your idea, outlining the action and building the character into a narrative story line with beginning, middle, and end. As discussed in *Screenplay* and *The Screenwriter's Workbook,* your story line always begins with a subject, an action, and a character. Define it. Articulate it. "A plainclothes cop, the character, falls in love with the woman he's assigned to follow. The action." That's *Stakeout* (Jim Kouf).

Once you've worked out the subject, go into your character. Do a character biography. Where was your character born? What was his or her life like growing up? Was it a good, happy childhood, or a bad one? Define your character's dramatic need, what your character wants to win, gain, get, or achieve during the course of the story. Define two or three obstacles your character has to overcome to achieve his or her dramatic need. All drama is conflict; without conflict you have no character; without character, no action; without action, no story; without story, no screenplay. So define the obstacles your character has to overcome to achieve his or her dramatic need. It's a good start point for your pitch. Actors and actresses do this when they prepare to read for a part. In fact, many actors take my screenwriting workshops because it gives them a new set of tools to build their characters. It is a process that forms the foundation of character.

Once you have a brief three-sentence story line, you can establish the beginning, middle, and end. Design your story line. What is the resolution of your story? Not the specific scene or shot, but the solution; does your character live or die, succeed or fail, win the race or not, get married or not? If you don't know how to end your story, how would you like it to end? Use that as your start point for the time being. It can always change later.

Once you've determined the resolution, go back to the beginning and structure the story on the *paradigm*. What happens in Act I, the Setup? Describe the action briefly. Determine plot point I, the incident, episode, or event that hooks into the action and spins it around into another direction, in this case, Act II. Then determine the plot point at the end of Act II. Once you know these four elements—ending, beginning, plot point I and plot point II—determine the midpoint, that incident or episode on page 60 that breaks Act II into first half and second half. (If you need more information on building and structuring Act II, read Chapters 11–14 in *The Screenwriter's Workbook*.)

This is only one of several ways in which you can you prepare your pitch. It's an effective method because you have enough story information so you can probably answer any questions the executive might ask. You know the structure of your story and a little bit about the characters; you certainly don't know all the details but at least you have a story line, with direction. And direction, remember, is a line of development. That's what the production, studio, or network executive wants to hear when you set up that pitch meeting.

"The fact is," Barbara Corday says, "a good pitch is something that gets bought. Because to walk out of that room and say, that was a great meeting, and then they pass on your project, what does that do?"

Nothing at all. You're right back where you started from. With an idea, nothing else.

11

Television

*"Television is an advertising medium that
exists to sell products, and the shows
only fill up the time between commercials."*

That's how one top-ranking executive described the nature of television. Television is an advertising medium that deals more in quantity than quality. Very simply, commercial television exists to sell soap. One show, no matter how bad it may be, still has the potential of reaching more than 50 million people; and that's a lot of soap.

Television appeals to numbers, and that's why ratings and demographics play such an important part in the determination of which shows stay on the air and which ones don't.

Year after year, we bear witness to the cancellation of some of the best shows on the air because "the numbers aren't there." Not enough people are watching the show. Why?

There could be any number of reasons: the inability of the networks to find the right time slot for that particular show; the tendency of the network to compete *mano a mano* against each other; the decline of network viewing due to the rise of cable programing and the rental of videocassettes. And more.

The process of writing for television has changed over the years, the same way writing and selling screenplays has changed; since I haven't written for television is many years, I decided to explore and define that buying process from the point of view of the production executive.

That's what I had in mind when I interviewed Barbara Corday, cocreator of *Cagney and Lacey* (with Barbara Avedon) and now vice president of programing for CBS; Scott Kaufer, head of comedy programing at Warner Bros.; and Ron Osborn, one of my former students, a senior producer and staff writer, with his partner Jeff Reno, of *Moonlighting*.

To me, selling material to television is harder than writing and selling an original screenplay. How do you explain that? First, take a look at the obvious. A screenplay is a story told in pictures, in dialogue and description, and placed within the context of dramatic structure. That doesn't work in television. Why not?

Number one, the size of the screen is smaller; second, there's a forced commercial break every seven to nine minutes; third, the distractions are much more pronounced: phones ringing, babies crying, dogs barking, cars going by outside; fourth, it's a passive medium—we "watch" television, and "go" to the movies; and fifth, television is a talking medium, a radio show with pictures.

To understand the basic nature of the medium as a seller, you have to understand the *business* of television. Looking back, it took Barbara Corday a long time to understand that. Corday began her career working in publicity, then started writing comedy with her partner, Barbara Avedon, gradually moving into dramatic series, like *The Doctors*, with George Peppard; *Lucas Tanner*, with David Hartman; and *Medical Center*, with Chad Everett. Soon Corday and Avedon were staff writers, because, Corday says, "as a free-lance writer, if you do a good job and write for one or two shows that like your work, ultimately you are asked to be on staff."

At this time, in the mid-seventies, Molly Haskell's provocative book *From Reverence to Rape* came out, and pointed out some very obvious facts; for example, that while men had "buddy shows," women did not. Corday and Avedon took that information and wrote "this wild, exaggerated female buddy movie about the first women police officers to make detective in the oldest precinct in New York and how they were treated." The script was called *Cagney and Lacey*.

So much has been written about this hit television series that everything else becomes redundant. Before the series evolved from the screenplay, "I realized I wanted to move on," says Corday, "and Barbara realized she wanted to be free to write what she just wanted to write."

Corday went to ABC as an executive in their comedy development department, and one of the most important things she learned, she says, was that "(a) television is a very personal business, and (b) very often the best script that comes in isn't the one that gets made, because it doesn't happen to be what they need for a certain time period. The ultimate goal of television is to be an advertising medium, and it's foolish for any of us to think that because we've written a great script, it's going to get on the air. If they need an eight o'clock comedy and you've written a ten o'clock drama, that's it."

She left ABC after three years and became an independent producer, forming her own company, Can't Sing, Can't Dance Productions. ("My mother was a singer," she explains, "and my father a songwriter; my grandparents were vaudeville performers and when I was a child they were concerned about what I would do in life because I couldn't sing and I couldn't dance.") After making two pilots, a TV movie, and six episodes of a series, she was asked to be president of Columbia Television. Her job, she says, "was to be the person ultimately responsible for bringing talent to the studio. It was my job to convince a writer, producer, actor, director, whoever it is you're going after, that your company is the company they really want to be in business with."

Corday was president of Columbia TV for three and a half years, and was abruptly let go when Columbia and Tri-Star merged. She is now Executive Vice President, Prime Time Programming, for CBS.

In television, "as a writer, even as a producer," she explains, "you're outside the decision of what shows get selected, developed, and produced. You're a seller, they're a buyer, and you never know how or why those decisions get made."

Why? I asked.

She answered that "first of all you have to know the difference between a series and an idea.

"An idea usually says something about the characters, explains the main theme or premise, and how they work together. But what an executive looks for," she continues, "is something that has a lasting quality. Too often you see shows produced because somebody gets excited about a good premise that doesn't go anywhere. By the time you've done your eighth episode you've said everything there is to say.

"The best premise for a series has to do with locking the characters together. They use the old Sergeant Bilko show [*You'll Never Get Rich*], starring Phil Silvers, as the best example. These guys were in the army and there was no way for them to get out; nobody could say, I'm leaving now. They were stuck together because they had no choice about who they were in the barracks with. The same with *M*A*S*H*." That basic situation led to the humor and longevity of the series.

But if "you have a show about two roommates who hate each other, why doesn't he or she move out? A lot of times people come in to pitch a series and all they have is an idea; they simply don't understand what it needs to work."

What does a series need to work? Scott Kaufer, head of comedy development for Warner Bros. Television, and formerly editor of *California* magazine, explains: "We don't want to sell scripts to the networks unless (a) those scripts have a good chance to be made into pilots, (b) the pilots have a good chance to be ordered by the networks for a series, and (c), most important of all, the series stands a good chance of staying on the air.

"A studio in television," he goes on, "makes its money from syndication. We incur a deficit when we supply programs to the networks. We don't enter into profit until the show has lasted a sufficient period of time on the air to give us enough negatives to sell into syndication, which usually takes four or five years.

"From the studio's perspective, we want to make sure it's more than just a show that'll be great for six episodes; we want to make sure it will increase its holding power over an audience season after season. We're looking for ideas that have strength and imagination, characters with enough depth and dimension that you want to see them week after week, literally for years."

I asked him how a studio solicits ideas to develop into series. "We generate ideas in three ways," he begins. "One would be from the writers, producers, and actors we have under contract who come in and pitch us ideas; since we've spent money for their exclusive services, we tend to give their ideas careful thought.

"The second kind of idea comes in from outside writers, producers, directors, or actors, anyone in the creative community who is not under contract to Warner Bros. In those cases, the most important question we ask is, Who's bringing us the idea? We have to know it's somebody we think has the ability to execute that idea.''

I asked him to elaborate.

''The idea isn't enough by itself,'' he says. ''The idea is simply a starting point, a blueprint; you wouldn't ask somebody to build a house if you liked the blueprint but didn't know whether they had the ability and experience to do the job. In the same way, we're not going to commit to going into business with someone who has a good idea but lacks the talent and experience to bring it to fruition week after week.

''The third way we get ideas is by coming up with them ourselves; we sometimes get an idea for a character, or a situation, or a concept. Sometimes we'll only have a fragment, and then we'll turn around and share those thoughts with those writers and producers in whom we have confidence.''

I asked what attracts him to an idea he might possibly pursue as a series. Without any hesitation he replied, ''Characters. That's the first thing I look for. Who are these people? What is their life about? Why do we care about them? What will we see them do every week? Why do we want to see them do that every week? How will they grow and change as characters week after week, potentially for years?''

He paused briefly, then went on. ''Unfortunately, it seems a lot of writers and producers make the mistake of ignoring or giving short shrift to their characters, so they come in and pitch us trends or venues.

''They call and say, 'Are you interested in a show set in a beauty parlor?' Or 'Are you interested in a show set in an airport lounge?' Or 'Are you interested in shows about Latinos?' or 'men with peg legs?' And I answer, 'Who the hell knows? We're interested in a show about compelling characters, and if you present us with compelling characters, we'll worry about the location later.' ''

''The two things that make any good television show are the characters and what happens to them,'' says Stu Erwin of GTG Entertainment, Grant Tinker's new company. ''That's simply good drama.''

If you think you have a good idea for a television series, you've got to build and expand your characters so they become integrated into the fabric of the idea. (If you need guidance, or exercises to do, read the chapters on character in *Screenplay* and *The Screenwriter's Workbook*.)

"If we like the characters, and the premise of the idea," Kaufer continues, "we'll ask the writer questions. If a character moves back in with his parents, for example, we'll ask the writer to tell us about his parents, about his relationship with them. Tell us why he moved out in the first place. Tell us why he's moving back in, what his attitude is about moving back in. Is he embarrassed? Unconcerned? How long does he think it will last? Two weeks? Two years? How do his parents feel about it? Are they happy to see him? Do they dread his return?

"You'd be astonished how many writers don't have a clue about the answers to those questions. The answers tell me a lot about whether the writer has thought about his or her characters enough to have a workable idea for a show.

"For us," he goes on, "the ideal meeting is where the idea is a good one, the writer has the talent to execute it, and has done the necessary homework to explain his characters convincingly to others.

"At that point," he continues, "we'll offer our suggestions to the writer, then he or she will select what works and what doesn't.

"When we feel the writer is ready to present the idea, we'll take the next step and set up a pitch meeting at the network. When we go into that meeting, usually we're asking the network for a script commitment.

"If the network approves the idea, they will fund the writing of the script. The writer then goes home and writes a first draft. We expect that to take anywhere from four to eight weeks.

"When we get the first draft, we'll offer comments and suggestions on the material, and the writer will then make the changes that he or she sees fit. When the rewrite's done, we'll give it to the network. They'll read it, give us their notes and suggestions on the material, and the writer will make the necessary changes. When that rewrite is done, we hope the network will like it enough to order it shot as a pilot.

"We usually give the network our pilot scripts around Thanksgiving or Christmas, and they'll generally let us know sometime after the first of the year if they want to go ahead and shoot the pilot. March or April is the time we'll produce these pilots, delivering them to the network in time for their April and May meetings, when they come up with their fall schedule.

"We then travel to New York and sit with every extremity crossed during the first few weeks in May, hoping to get a phone call saying our show is on the fall schedule. Then we get to produce it; a glorious burden."

That's the process of turning an idea into a series as seen from the studio or production company's point of view. In turn, "the networks will develop between sixty-five and eighty-five pilot scripts each season in comedy and drama," adds Barbara Corday. "Sometimes as many as a hundred if they feel they're in great need.

"And they'll make about twenty-five pilots from that hundred scripts," she continues, "and they'll buy fewer than ten shows.

"That means that out of the 9000-plus members of the Writers Guild, you have to be one of those people that gets the assignment of writing one of those hundred scripts. Let's say it's one hundred scripts at each network, which it isn't, so that's three hundred scripts. Then, you have to be one of the twenty-five that gets their pilot picked up. Then you have to be one of the ten at each network that gets their series picked up. So you're dealing in numbers that are very small."

The other thing you have to remember, Corday goes on, "is that when the network decides somebody is a star this particular year, flavors of the month we call them, they put them under contract for several years, so the current group of executives at the network are stuck with the deals made by the last group of executives. That means the studios and production companies are constantly fighting for those few spots that are left after all those prior commitments have been used up.

"So if you're not one of the people with a commitment, if you're not one of the people in business with an actor the networks want, if you're not one of the people in business with a heavy-duty producer or a company that already has some commitments, if all you have is a terrific script, sometimes it's not enough.

"Now, sometimes the reason it's not enough," she continues, "is because they just don't need that project. That's the hardest thing for a writer to understand. If you've written a show that takes place in 2010 and it's a ten o'clock adult drama, and the particular network you've written it for has all their dramas at ten o'clock working well, or they've already got a futuristic show at eight o'clock Tuesday, and they don't want two futuristic shows on their network, you're just out of luck.

"It has nothing to do with the quality of work you did. The good news is that if it's a terrific script they'll probably ask you to do another one. But it won't get made.

"The second hardest thing to deal with is when you're told that you were one of the next two or three pilots that were going to get picked up but they tell you they've already got so many commitments they just can't make another one. And you've just spent the last four months of your life sitting in your office, doing everything they asked you to do; you've taken their notes, taken their meetings, and then they tell you you would have been the next one picked if they didn't have those previous commitments. That's heartbreaking.

"But it's the nature of the business. The network executive has to think there's five years in that series, that they can cast it with somebody hot, that there's a terrific producer behind it, and that they'll be the first ones on the air with that kind of a show, and it fills an eight o'clock Saturday time slot they haven't been able to figure out how to fill. It has a lot to do with about twenty-five other things than whether it's a terrific script or not."

That's the business side of selling your material to a studio, production company, or network. And that brings us right back to the question at the beginning of this chapter: What's the difference between writing for film and writing for TV?

A lot. Here's the way it works in film. Suppose you're a studio executive, and your mailman comes to you one day and says he's written a screenplay. Would you read it? (This happens to me all the time.) And you say yes, because you want to get your mail delivered intact.

So you have some free time one day and you sit down and read it. And surprise of surprises, it's great. Interesting. Different. Marketable. What do you do?

You ask the mailman if anyone else has read it, and he says no, so you ask if you can send it to somebody to read. Of course, he replies. So you send it to a few other executives for feedback, and they all agree; it's great. You're going to buy this script.

You get an agent to represent the mailman, then your company buys the script, it's greenlighted for production, and the mailman begins his pursuit of a new career. Everybody's fantasy come true, right? That can and does happen with original screenplays.

But you take the same situation and apply it to television. It's entirely different. Why? Because, as Scott Kaufer says, the mailman's script "would be limited by the nature of the television business, which demands not that you execute a script just once, but that you do it on a weekly basis, potentially for years."

You don't just sell the show, or the idea for the show; you also have to be able to execute the idea according to *their* standards. "I need to know a few things about this script," says Kaufer. "Since this is a first script, it's unlikely I could get the network to approve this mailman as being part of the creative element for the show, even if he wrote a great pilot script. He's had no background in TV, so that means he's never produced, he doesn't know how to cast, he's never run a table reading, he's never done any of those things an experienced writer or producer often must do.

"The best I could do for this mailman is to get that script, with his permission, to a writer who would take over for him. Which is why creating TV shows is such a unique animal, because the networks usually insist on dealing with people they've worked with before. And that's not entirely unreasonable. Unlike the movie business, simply having a great script isn't enough. When you commission a television script, what you're buying is the ability to produce *a good script each week for years.*"

Television companies, unlike movie companies, do not buy scripts they're not going to make. That's tough for a writer to digest. Occasionally there are exceptions, and ideas are bought from people outside the industry.

Such was the case with the TV series *China Beach.*

William Broyles, Jr., a former editor-in-chief at *Newsweek* and *California* magazine, author of *Brothers in Arms,* a book about returning to Vietnam after the war, came to Scott Kaufer with an idea. What about a TV series dealing with a traveling women's rock band during the Vietnam War? he asked. It would be the story of war as told through the eyes of women.

Kaufer liked it. It was a different, unusual approach. "I felt it would give us the chance to put a women's steam room inside a men's locker room," he says. Gradually the idea evolved into dealing with women who had different occupations during the war. One could be a rock singer, another a nurse, another, perhaps, a Doughnut Dolly, a Red Cross volunteer who gives doughnuts to soldiers and helps them send messages home. There would be other characters as well, both male and female. Harvey Shepard, president of Warner Bros. Television, suggested the pilot be written by John Sacret Young, whose *China Beach* script would later win an Emmy nomination.

William Broyles became a consultant to the project, writing the first episode after the pilot had been written, produced, and picked up, then stayed on with the series helping produce it. It's important to remember that this is the exception, not the rule, because Broyles had the background and credentials to make this happen; he just didn't have the experience.

What's the best way for a writer to break into television? And what should the writer know about writing for television? That was my next question.

So I went to see one of my former students, Ron Osborn, who, with his partner, Jeff Reno, were senior producers and writers for *Moonlighting,* one of the most unique television series to be on the air in the last several years.

Osborn started out as an advertising illustration major at Art Center College of Design, but soon became interested in film. That's when I first met him. He wrote a script called *Dime Novel Sunset,* which had been optioned by William Holden shortly before he died.

Osborn and Reno joined forces and wrote a *M*A*S*H* episode on spec. "*M*A*S*H* had been on for seven seasons," Osborn explains, "so we watched as many reruns as we could. Then we went to the library and looked up old *TV Guide*s and got one-liners of every episode they ever did, then wrote a spec script we truly believed they hadn't seen.

"Of course, we couldn't get the people at *M*A*S*H* to read the script," he says, shrugging his shoulders. But the people at *Mork and Mindy* did read it, liked it, and put Reno and Osborn on staff.

It happened that fast. But as Osborn explains, going "from a part-time typist who gave plasma and wrote screenplays in my spare time, to being a staff writer on *Mork and Mindy,* starring Robin Williams and Pam Dawber, was a tremendous challenge.

"We worked six and seven days a week, twelve-hour days, sometimes doing rewrites between the afternoon and evening filmings on Friday. I remember getting up in the morning, having breakfast, and then losing it because there was so much pressure."

What's the difference between writing thirty-minute sitcoms and screenwriting? "First of all," he explains, "the form is completely different. The half-hour structure flies in the face of everything you know about good structure. But it works with a twenty-two-minute format. Instead of a three-act structure you have two acts with an interruption, the act break, the cliff-hanger. In the first act you have to set up the conflict, and over the course of the act bring that conflict to a head. That's the act break, the commercial break which you use as a cliff-hanger. Then you save the block comedy scene for the second act, which is the big payola, after which you wrap everything up.

"The first directive we got from the producer on *Mork and Mindy* was 'We like our stories reality-based.' Now what does that mean? A man comes down in an egg in Boulder, Colorado, and they want reality-based stories!

"What he meant, I later learned, was the emotion in the stories had to be based in identifiable situations. Every week we got to examine the human condition in a different perspective. The things we take for granted, for example, are the very things Mork would react to and want to explore; like jealousy. What's jealousy? So he asks around and is told that you're jealous when you love someone; it's thought to be a normal reaction. So, because he loves Mindy, he becomes maniacally jealous. The show was a wonderful mirror to hold up to ourselves.

"We did an episode called 'Twelve Angry Appliances,' where Mork learns about consumerism and standing up for your rights. The basic idea had to do with Mindy having something repaired that repeatedly keeps breaking down. And Mork can't understand why humans don't take more pride in their work. When Mindy finally gathers up enough courage to confront the repairman, he turns around and runs them out of the shop. Their humiliation was our act break.

"In the second act, Mork comes back late at night and brings all the appliances to life and they put the store owner on trial for negligence to their owners. Which was the block comedy scene. And out of that grew the resolution in the next scene, where the repairman, having the stuffing scared out of him, comes over to make amends."

Osborn says that people submit spec scripts to him all the time, and he finds "the most common problem people make when they write a half-hour spec script is that when they get to the act break they simply stop the story then pick it up in the second act. That's the worst sin you can do. You have to think of the act break as a cliff-hanger. You have to build the problem to a peak, so the audience is hopefully wondering how you're going to resolve it.

"The other thing writers have to remember is that the second act has to be better than the first. You've got to have the block comedy scene in the second act. You always bring out the big guns in Act Two. In a show like *Mork and Mindy* the challenge was to be as good as Robin Williams."

Osborn and Reno next joined the staff on *Too Close for Comfort*, then took a year off to "reinvent ourselves," as Osborn says. "It was hard; after working for two years straight we realized if we wanted to start getting more quality material we'd better present more quality calling cards.

"So we wrote a spec script for *Cheers*. Now, writing a spec script for episodic television is a very special animal. For one thing, you have to walk a fine line between being true to the situation and characters, yet still be refreshing and illuminating. Second, you should never write a spec script that changes the course of the series.

"The spec *Cheers* we wrote, for example, was based on a situation that was established in the show that had never been capitalized on before. The attitude of Norm [George Wendt] toward his wife was well established, so we wrote a spec *Cheers* where Norm suddenly thinks his wife is having an affair with the fumigator. What's his attitude toward his wife now? That's something we hadn't seen. It doesn't compromise any of the characters. It simply illuminates. And we were able to get across the fact that Norm, despite everything he says about her, loves his wife.

"That was a fresh approach.

"Ironically, *Cheers* wouldn't read it. [Take note: this was after they had been staff writers for two years on two hit shows.] Two years later, believe it or not, it somehow came across Glen and Les Charles's desk; they read it, called it the best spec *Cheers* they had ever read, and offered us a job to go on staff. We thought carefully about it, but chose to leave for the unknown, which was a brand-new one-hour series called *Moonlighting*."

Glenn Caron, the talented creator and guiding hand of the series, gave them only one instruction: "Release yourselves from the old formulas, and develop characters that the audience has an emotional investment in."

When *Moonlighting* first aired, it had such a sparkling wit and unique approach that it quickly soared to the top of the ratings. *Moonlighting,* says Osborn, "is a placebo detective show. It looked like one, it smelled like one, it tasted like one, but it was, in fact, a romantic comedy.

"Acknowledging it to be a romantic comedy, the mystery is always secondary to the characters. Each show focuses on illuminating an aspect of the characters, or their relationship, because that's really all that matters. The case that comes in is always a case with strong emotional undercurrents, and always presents an interesting twist on the human condition.

"One of my favorites," continues Osborn, "was written by Roger Director. A woman comes in wearing a veil, having been disfigured by a jealous lover who had thrown acid on her some ten years earlier, and she wants to find the man who did it. But it wasn't for revenge, it was because she wanted to marry him! That gives you a wonderful arena to talk about possessive love, and the lengths people will go to for it.

"Jeff and I did a show where a man comes in and says, find my perfect mate. You people are hired to find people based on characteristics; here are all the characteristics, now you go and find someone who matches them. So that became an arena for David and Maddie talking about what men look for in women and what women look for in men, the subtext being what they look for in each other.

"So the case always becomes an arena for Maddie and David to discuss and illuminate aspects of themselves. For example, a writer came to us with the story of a woman coming in, saying, 'My husband is a magician who died on stage last night. I want you to guard his body. But only until he's cremated. I've been unfaithful, and we stayed together just for the act, but he always said if he died before I did he was going to come back and kill me.'

"What got to us emotionally was talking about an afterlife, which leads right into the question, does God exist? Do you believe in God? And the neat little revelation that David does and Maddie doesn't.

"That was really what that particular show was about. The case itself was thick and convoluted, but we didn't care. What we cared about was the way David and Maddie were illuminated."

Interesting. Henry James, the great American novelist, had a theory of fiction he called the Theory of Illumination. What James believed was that your main character occupies the center of a circle. Around him or her, in a circle, are the characters he or she interacts with. James felt that every time the main character comes in contact with another character, the interchange should "illuminate" certain aspects of the main character, just the way you walk into a darkened room, and turn on various lamps around the room. You "illuminate" the room, just the way the other characters illuminate the main character. It's a wonderful tool to use when you're writing a script.

I asked Osborn about people sending in spec scripts of *Moonlighting* and he replied that they "usually come in with a very straightforward case that had no subtext to it: find my missing daughter, or the missing jewels. Or they would come in with a silly case. Basically, though, our cases are always serious and weirdly human. Once we resolve the particular issue we're dealing with, *then* we get silly.

"The kinds of cases we looked for were ones that affected David and Maddie, or their relationship; cases that gave them an emotional arena to explore, discuss, or argue about, so by the time we got to the end of the hour, we discovered something new about them, or managed to advance their relationship, even a little bit, in a new direction. Generally speaking, I think this approach, of advancing the characters emotionally, is the best way to approach any script on any show.

"The pressure on *Moonlighting* was so intense," Osborn continues, "we would sometimes be writing a day ahead of the camera, or even on the day it was being shot.

"Jeff and I did an episode where David confronts the villain in the fourth act and says, 'Here's everything you've done; here's how you did it, here's why you did it,' and then he checks them off one by one. Maddie, who's been along for the entire ride, reflects what the audience has to be thinking at this point—which is, when did you figure all this out, David? And he replies, 'During the commercial.' As we were writing, we ourselves didn't know how David could know all this, but in order for the story to progress, he had to have this information. Why? Because the scene was shooting the next day. And we were stuck.

"Because it's a romantic comedy masquerading as a detective show, we could get away with it. It was born out of having our backs against the wall, and in this case, it just happened to work.

"We had to do the same thing in another episode," Osborn goes on. "We had to finish this particular show in a grand way, and we didn't have a clue as to how we were going to do it. And it was the day before it was supposed to be shot. We finally came up with the idea of having a bizarre chase sequence during a funeral procession where the villain takes off in the limo, and David and Maddie give chase in the hearse, and the entire funeral procession, thinking they're being left behind, fall in and chase the hearse. As we were writing it, we loved it, but we didn't know whether they could do this kind of complicated chase sequence on such short notice.

"The next morning, after a sleepless night, as I drove on the lot, I had to pass stage 20 and I saw a hearse parked outside. That's when I knew they were going to do it. I was never so happy to see a hearse."

I asked Osborn what a writer should do when he or she wants to write a spec script for a current show, like *Moonlighting, thirtysomething*, or *Cheers*.

"The thing most writers do," Osborn replies, "is watch an episode of the show and say, 'I can do that.' That's the worst thing a writer can do. If we're looking for new writers, we're not looking for someone to imitate what we've already done, we're looking for someone to do better, someone who's going to take a fresh approach. Basically, TV has done it all. But if your approach makes it appear fresh and new, we're going to sit up and take notice.

"The second thing you should not do in a spec script is write a script that creates a series decision, because that decision is made only by the producers. For example, we get a lot of spec scripts of *Moonlighting* where David and Maddie get married. And I'm sure *Cheers* gets a lot of spec scripts where Sam and Diane got married. I guarantee you the producers have thought about this a lot longer and a lot harder than you did, and they probably have a better way to do it. If, in fact, they want to do it at all.

"Another thing the writer should not do is introduce an outside character to resolve the story dilemma. It's okay to bring an outside character in to establish the problem, but not to resolve it.

"Plus, it's not good writing. The audience has an emotional investment in the ongoing characters, and that's who they want to see.

"By the same token, you shouldn't try to establish a new ongoing series character. That's the producer's decision, and not something an outside writer should do. I find a lot of writers who seem to think that spec scripts can bring in and develop new characters to enhance the series, when they don't know what the series really needs, or if it needs any new characters at all. Many new writers think creating a new character becomes a solution to the story line, when in fact it's the major problem."

I asked him how an outside writer should prepare writing a spec script for an existing series.

First of all, you have to define what kind of show you're writing for.

If it's a half-hour, what kind of show is it? "There are three kinds of half-hour scripts," says Osborn. "There's a half-hour one-camera show, there's a half-hour three-camera show, and there's a half-hour three-camera tape show. A half-hour one-camera show is similar to a screenplay in that the rule of thumb is that a one-camera page in television runs about 50 seconds. [In a screenplay, one page of screenplay equals one minute of screen time.] A half-hour script tends to be between 30 and 35 pages.

"A half-hour three-camera film show, like *Mork and Mindy,* or a four-camera show, like *Designing Women,* has a different configuration; that is, the dialogue on the written page is double-spaced; those scripts tend to run about 45 to 50 pages.

"A one-hour show is always written in a one-camera format and runs in the area of 55 to 60 pages, although in *Moonlighting* the banter is so fast and furious it's not unusual for a script to run 90 or 95 pages.

"If you're submitting a spec script to an existing show, you have to know what form they use. If it's a three-camera tape show, and most sitcoms are that now," Osborn says, "try to get hold of one of their scripts, because if a person submitted a script to us for a three-camera tape show that was written in one-camera form, it was hard to gauge how it played itself out in terms of real time. Invariably, it's too long.''

If you don't know where to find one of these scripts, try the local library, or the film school library at a university. You might even call the show, explain to the secretary that you are writing a sample script and ask what kind of show it is—one-camera film, three-camera film, or three-camera tape. The secretary is always your best friend, and most of the time they'll give you the information you need.

''I know television form is a superficial thing to harp on,'' he goes on, ''but the presentation of your script can hurt the read, and you don't want to hurt the read.

''In terms of structure,'' he says, ''the general approach is that act breaks have to escalate the action in terms of tension and suspense, or heighten what's at stake emotionally. In an hour-episodic series format it's a four-act structure. The first act establishes what's going on, the second act develops it, the third act starts to explain it, and the fourth act pays it off.''

This will vary depending on whether you're writing an open or a closed mystery. A closed mystery is where you don't know who did it, like *Murder, She Wrote*. An open mystery is where the audience knows who did it, and it's a question of how the main character is going to solve it. *Columbo* is always the example used. We see the crime committed and know who did it, so we get to watch Columbo working through all the steps to find the murderer.

How does the Osborn-Reno collaboration work? ''We outline the script together, then divide it into parts,'' explains Osborn. ''The fun parts versus the expositional parts. And then we trade off who does what. Then we exchange pages and rewrite each other, then get together for bloodletting sessions where we give each other notes that always come from a healthy mutual respect.'' (For more on collaboration see Chapter 15 in *Screenplay*).

What's important about writing for television is knowing the show you're writing for. And as Barbara Corday says, you have to understand that which script sells has nothing to do with quality of the material.

And who decides that?

The networks.

12

The Networks

*"I want the audience to throw a shoe at
the television and say, Goddamn it, I
have to cancel my dinner plans tomorrow
night because I want to see how
this turns out."*

At a time when television viewing is being eroded by the growth of cable, independent TV stations, and the explosion of the videocassette market, the average audience share for network programing is dropping at the startling rate of 10 percent a year.

Why? Because network television is an advertising medium that exists to sell products; it aims at the largest possible audience and therefore must cater to the lowest common denominator.

Is it the networks' fault their audience is slowly decreasing?

Maybe. Networks don't buy scripts; they buy *ideas*. Then they develop those ideas into scripts, hire producers to produce them, then turn around and sell advertising space to advertisers who want their products seen.

That's how the networks make their money. It's the American way.

Producers come to them with books, either published or unpublished, as well as ideas, concepts, notions, scripts, songs, whatever, and if the networks like the project, they join forces with the producer, who will deliver a script and oversee the actual production.

There are different types of network programing. There is series television, which includes half-hour episodic series, news, and sporting events.

Then there is long-form television, which includes the miniseries and movies of the week. That's what this chapter is about.

To understand the networks' point of view, I interviewed two network executives in charge of long-form television, along with the national programing director of KCET, the PBS station in Los Angeles.

The miniseries is a form unto itself. Spread out over two or more nights (*War and Remembrance* was thirty hours long and spanned some fourteen nights), the miniseries really began with *Roots* (from the Alex Haley novel, produced by David L. Wolper), and since then has grown into a sophisticated form of television programing.

Some ideas just need more than two hours to tell the story; they need to be spread out over a week or two. The function of the miniseries is to "show you things you can't see elsewhere on television," says Susan Baerwald, vice president of miniseries and novels for television at NBC. "It's the only adaptive form that allows you to choose the length according to what your material dictates."

Baerwald began as production assistant in tape television, then moved to the story department at NBC "reading books, or stories taken from magazine articles; any kind of preexisting material on which a script will be based."

Baerwald's job consists of working "from beginning to end with miniseries. From the original pitch to working with the writer and producer on the first draft, then doing notes for each draft.

"When we start out we'll agree on a story line," she says, "then the writer goes off and writes. If it's an original, or if it's a huge book, we'll go through a 'bible' stage, where a long outline, or presentation, is prepared so we know what the length and breadth of the piece is."

Baerwald says she'd rather read the first draft of the entire show, rather than just the first night, because "it's hard to read two hours of a four-hour script and know where it's going.

"When the script is ready, I submit it to Brandon Tartikoff, president of network programing at NBC, who will either say yes or no to a film commitment. Then I work with the producer to select the director, and ollow the project all the way through, seeing dailies every day, the rough cut, the first-answer print. The average miniseries usually takes about two years to complete, sometimes longer.

"When it's delivered, I'm the point person in selling it. I coordinate all the promotion, press, and advertising within the various departments at NBC on the project."

I asked her to explain the network's role in developing the miniseries, from idea through completion. "What we do is develop scripts," she says. "We don't buy them. A producer, or a producer-writer, will come in and say, 'Would you like to do the new book by Randy Shilts called *And the Band Played On*?' I'll say yes, can you get the rights; or maybe the producer has already negotiated for the rights. At that point the producer and I will discuss who the best writer is for the project based on the material, and an available list will be drawn up."

Sometimes the network will develop a book proposal. Joe McGinnis, author of *Fatal Vision,* proposed a new book which NBC prebought to develop into a miniseries. "A well-known book," Baerwald says, "brings us a presold audience."

I asked if there's anything special the network looks for in terms of subject matter. "I get asked all the time 'What are you looking for?' " Baerwald replies. "I say I don't know what I'm looking for. My major priority is a good story, and I don't care whether it's a period piece or a contemporary piece.

"The form has special needs. Certain stories work better than others. Spy thrillers, for example, usually don't work because they're hard to break up into successive nights; there are so many red herrings thrown in that are essential to the plot that if you don't start and finish in one sitting you're apt to be very confused.

"Biography usually doesn't work because it's episodic by nature. First she did this, then she did that, then she did this, and it's this progression that drives the story forward. Unless there's a major punch at the end, you don't know whether or not the audience is going to come back and tune in the next night.

"There are exceptions, of course. In the case of *Peter the Great* a man is on the path to destruction, so it becomes larger than just a biography. It's really the story of a man who sets out to modernize and change his country so after he's gone his son will have a modern nation to rule. It was Russia, the great bear, a country we in the West didn't know anything about, and he opened it up to us.

"But it became a path of destruction for Peter because the son did not want what his father wanted to give him. That merited a story treatment longer than a single night.

"In the miniseries," she goes on, "the most important story element is the break. There's an ability to create a cliff-hanger. I always cite *Murder in Texas* as an early miniseries that has a great break point. At the end of the first two hours the character Dr. John Hill [Sam Elliott] has murdered Joan Robinson Hill, or else she has mysteriously died; we don't really know what happened to her. Then he marries someone else. Is he going to kill her too?

"That's the break. So the audience has to tune in the next night to find out what's going to happen.

"*Anastasia* works the same way. At the end of *Anastasia, Part I,* Anastasia gets on a train and looks around at the faces who have been with her while she was growing up. And the question is, are they going to recognize her if and when she returns? Is she going to recognize them? It's a natural break point."

What do you do if you have an idea for a miniseries? "Go to a production company, or producer, who has experience in the miniseries area," Baerwald says, "and ask if we can present this as a potential miniseries. A writer going directly to the network is not the way to get things done," she says, "because we feel a qualified production company should be behind the project.

"Sometimes a screenplay written as a feature can be developed into a miniseries. We did that with *Dress Gray,* the Gore Vidal script that had been written as a feature several years earlier. *On Wings of Eagles* was also originally written as a feature, so we expanded the screenplay into a five-hour miniseries.

"At present we're redeveloping a wonderful story based on a book called *Time and Again,* by Jack Finney, which had been bought years ago by Universal and never made it to the screen. We have adapted it into a four-hour script."

The network operates on deficit financing, a system where the producer or production company produces the program and the network licenses, or leases, that program for two runs. The network pays for those two runs with a license fee. The average license fee is about $1.5 million per hour, so it is the producer or production company who is always taking the biggest risk.

"There aren't many miniseries," Baerwald emphasizes, "that can be made for $1.5 million an hour. The producer is called upon to deficit anywhere from $500,000 to $4 million on a miniseries. Now, why would a producer or production company want to do that?" Baerwald asks rhetorically. Where does their profit come from?

"Well, they own the product," she says, answering her own question. "So they have worldwide television rights to cable, cassette, and everything else. After the network runs, they get a chance to recoup their investment and make a substantial profit.

"Also, production companies may have a string of TV movies or a series on the shelf, and it's possible they can put them together with a high-profile miniseries and sell them as a package in syndication. They'll say, 'We'll give you *Poor Little Rich Girl* if you'll take these three series and these five TV movies.' "

I once believed that a writer for television should forget the act break and simply tell the story. The placement of the commercial, I thought, is a film decision, not the writer's decision.

I was wrong. The act break in television, especially the long form, is an important element in the script. It's the writer's responsibility to design the act break and make it into a real cliff-hanger. The writer must make sure the audience stays tuned to watch the next portion of the show. If I'm watching television and something doesn't hold my interest, I'm gone; I'm zipping and zapping around the tube until I find something else.

Writing movies for television requires different skills than writing a screenplay; instead of the normal three-act structure the television movie of the week has a seven-act structure (there are seven commercial breaks), "even though the two-hour form with seven acts is creatively a very poor structure," says Nancy Bein, formerly vice president of motion pictures for television at CBS.

Bein was selected to intern at NBC while still in the UCLA Film School, and stayed there nine months working in Dramatic Series and

Dramatic Series Development. Then CBS hired her, first as a trainee, then in TV Movies, and she stayed there for eight years. CBS had made a strong commitment to movies of the week, and Bein worked her way up to head the Motion Pictures for Television Division. Recently, she left her position at CBS and is now an independent producer; she has just completed her first movie of the week, *Liberace: Behind the Music*.

"The seven-act form makes up the network movie of the week," she begins, "with the first act setting up the story and covering a lot of ground, so frequently you find writers who have a good, solid beginning and end, but the middle, Acts II through VI, almost always have a problem. Surprisingly, there are many writers who choose to ignore the seven-act structure. Garson Kanin, one of Hollywood's most gifted writers [*Adam's Rib* is one of my favorites], once said he was continually amazed at how many writers wanted to believe there were not seven curtains in the MOW. Personally, I wish we didn't have commercials; but we have them and therefore you need seven curtains. As bizarre as the form is, it needs to be dealt with. Writers who write in a three-act structure and pretend these commercials aren't going to be there haven't learned the craft of writing a movie for television.

"Act breaks," she emphasizes, "are the writer's decision, not an editing decision. They should not be an editing decision. If the act breaks aren't clearly designed and spelled out by the writer, then the director or editor or producer has to try and create them, and it becomes a haphazard approach. It works much better if everyone knows where the act breaks are.

"Outlines, or treatments, are often a necessary evil," she continues, "because many times when you've pitched a story verbally, you have the illusion the story is fulfilled. But when you read the script, you may be in for a big surprise. There may only be two acts; the rest is simply a recap, with no plot or story progression.

"Which is why step outlines can be so effective. If you tackle the story in a step outline you see immediately if you've got problems; then everybody can talk about it and help find the solutions and it makes for a much faster, less painful, process.

"Everybody writes step outlines differently. Some are sparse, seven pages for seven acts, and in the story meeting the writer talks everyone through it, so it's there to refer to as a skeleton to be fleshed out verbally. Some writers hate step outlines, and won't do them. That's fine when they're established writers and you know they won't hand in a poor script.

"In terms of form, we know, for example, that a certain style often works better than others; it's better going with a long first act, for instance, about twenty-two minutes long, in order to set up the story as much as possible. By the end of Act I, the first commercial break, the audience should know what the movie's going to be about. Some writers then make the subsequent acts shorter and shorter, so Act II will be the next longest, Act III the next, and so on until Act VII.

"As for subject matter," Bein goes on, "at CBS we made about fifty MOWs a year, so we stockpiled as best we could. We were material-oriented, so we made good scripts when they came in. Most of the time we didn't make them for any particular air date, because we didn't know which nights on the schedule would be movie nights.

"If you knew, for example, that you would be making the Sunday Night Movie, that's one set of guidelines. If you knew you were making the Tuesday Night Movie against *Moonlighting*, that's something else.

"So we made a big mix, which was what everybody wanted to do anyway. We made male-oriented films, action films, comedies, and socially committed films; we tried to do the whole spectrum. Plus, we had an enormous backlog of scripts to choose from, in case there was ever a sudden need.

"There are times, for example, when a new series might be failing, and they're dropped from the schedule, then movies are used to hold the audience—and ratings—until another series can take its place. Every network season begins with the optimism that most new series will succeed, and thus the television movie will be at a one- or two-night minimum. But if ratings fall, movies are used to pull a good rating and thus hold down the competition."

When I was at Cinemobile and Cine Artists I'd have meeting after meeting with agents, writers, or producers and they always asked the same question: What are you looking for? The truth was I didn't know what I was looking for. All I knew was that I wanted to find scripts that "hit 'em where they ain't." That means I always wanted to go against the grain; if buddy films were popular, I was looking for a love story. If cop films were big, I was looking for a personal-relationship story; if thrillers were big, I was looking for comedies.

F. Scott Fitzgerald once said, "When you create an individual, you create a type." The vamp (Theda Bara) was a type; the dumb blonde (Jean Harlow, Marilyn Monroe) was a type; the Beatles created a type; Madonna created a type; Bob Dylan created a type. Be original, be innovative, and "hit 'em where they ain't."

I asked Bein what she thinks makes a good script for a movie of the week. What does she look for? "When people asked what I was looking for, I told them I was looking for something special. Something that was not predictable; not a one-liner you saw in *TV Guide* and knew what the entire movie was about.

"It was always amazing to me the numbers of writers who wanted to write TV movies who didn't watch TV movies. So they didn't know, for example, that ABC did this same kind of movie six weeks ago, or NBC did this three months or a year ago, and you just can't do another story that's almost identical.

"In most cases, pitches came in through the eight executives who worked for me, and every two weeks I'd meet individually with each of them to discuss whatever submissions they felt were worth talking about. We always responded to material that was fresh and original and special," she says.

"In terms of deadlines, we made an effort not to push a writer before he or she was ready, as each situation and person was different, and racing to get a bad script defeats the whole purpose. But there are exceptions; for example, if you're running out of movies because of an unexpected depletion, or if a star suddenly becomes available. If we found a promising script that had a star attached, and we could work out the timing, we would go forward with the project, even though the script might not be in satisfactory shape. In that instance, we would give the writer a deadline that was governed by the production schedule."

That brings up something that every writer must deal with in Hollywood. As a professional writer, you're always given deadlines. It's part of the process. Usually it's "We need this yesterday." So you go home, stay up for days and nights living on sugar and caffeine and anything else you think will help you with your "creativity," and deliver the script as quickly as possible.

Then the producer, or network, will sit on the script and not read it for weeks. I used to go crazy waiting for a response, mumbling to myself if I'd only had that extra couple of weeks, I could have made it so much better.

There's a lot of mythology in this business that says if you're late or delayed delivering a script, the network hates you, and you'll be black-listed for life and never work again. But that's not the way it works.

"The way it works," says Nancy Bein, "is that producers frequently give the writers deadlines, not the networks. A smart writer will always ask the question before he walks out of the network: 'When do you need this?' And we'd say we'd rather it be good than quick. That way, they knew when the producer started beating up on them they didn't have to panic.

"The producer is usually the one who needs the script as quickly as possible," Bein says. "Most producers live from overall deal to overall deal. [An overall deal is an arrangement with a production company or network, where the producer or writer has a yearly contract, so they receive their fees in advance. That means they get a weekly paycheck. The most recent example of an overall is when ABC gave Stephen Bochco, creator of *Hill Street Blues* and *L.A. Law,* a ten-series $10 million deal.]

"Once a producer gets an idea approved, which may take several months," Bein says, "you need a writer. And the writer needs network approval. In some cases you get your A list of approved writers and find they're all busy. So you either wait for a writer or try to find someone else. You're lucky if you find someone six months into your deal. So, as producer, you're frantic to get that script into the network because you want your deal renewed, or you want visibility as a producer who gets projects made, as opposed to a producer who can't get a project out of development.

"It's not uncommon for a writer to call up directly, or have their agent call, to ask the network executive if it's all right to take an extra week or so. And it could be a script we never even thought about in the six weeks it was being written. When the script is turned in, sometimes the concern is that writer needs to expand, or rethink, the material. After a few passes, if it seems the writer has gone as far as he or she can go on the project, another writer will come in and do a rewrite. If the script goes forward to film, the writers go to Writers Guild Arbitration and the Guild determines the credit. Sometimes a writer is hired to come in and do a rewrite and won't get credit, or chooses not to take the credit. In that case the credited writer will sometimes turn around and get jobs on the basis of somebody else's work. [That's common.]

"That's why people in Hollywood talk to each other all the time," says Bein; "people are constantly calling to find out what really happened." That's how commercial television works.

PBS, the Public Broadcasting Service, although not really a network, is included in this chapter because some 360 independent stations around the country are affiliated with it. "We're affiliated, but we're not affiliates," says Ellen Geiger, in charge of national program development for KCET Los Angeles, one of the largest PBS stations in the system. "The stations take programming from the Public Broadcasting Service," she explains, "as well as other sources. It's more like the U.N. than a commercial network. PBS programs the prime-time segment of our broadcast day with a core schedule, from 8 to 11 P.M. Other kinds of program blocks are on the air, as each station programs its own local shows.

"KCET," Geiger says, "is a member of several different consortia. There's the *American Playhouse* consortium, composed of KCET (Los Angeles), WNET (New York), WGBH (Boston), and South Carolina's ETV. Together these stations form the artistic committee of *American Playhouse, the* American dramatic anthology series on public television. *Wonder Works,* the other consortium, is a family show for kids.

"As far as *American Playhouse* goes, the operative word is 'American.' Either it's material by an American author, or it somehow concerns America, either an American experience of the last century, the present, or the future, or Americans abroad. Currently we're developing a miniseries about Gerald and Sara Murphy, American expatriates who lived in France in the 1920s and knew everybody: Hemingway, Fitzgerald, Gertrude Stein, Picasso, James Joyce; they coined the phrase 'living well is the best revenge.'

"If it doesn't examine the American experience, it's not an appropriate project for the series. We do teleplays, features, and a few plays. We do entertainment specials like *Liza Remembers Vincente and His Films,* which received four Emmy nominations, and *Sentimental Swing,* a salute to Tommy Dorsey, and we're hoping to do a Harold Arlen tribute called *Over the Rainbow.* We'll also do a documentary series for national airing.

"There's a lot of drama on public television, but half of it consists of acquisitions from Britain, like *Masterpiece Theatre, Mystery,* and *Great Performances.*

"What we're looking for at KCET," she goes on, "is quality programming; not the disease of the week, but important social issues or humanitarian values. For example, we did a *Wonder Works* called *Maricella,* about a little Salvadoran girl whose mother goes to work as a maid for a rich lady in L.A., who has a daughter the same age as Maricella. The rich lady thinks the two girls can be friends. But it's not easy, because one of them is a political refugee and the other is a typical L.A. kid.

"We try to have a lot in development because it's so hard to find funding. We're working on about twenty to twenty-five projects at any one time, and we only commit to a project with the expectation that it will be funded.

"We put our projects through a rigid scrutiny because our funding is so limited we have to be sure we can get our project made. If the commercial networks would put up 1 percent of their advertising revenues, public television would have something like $2.7 billion dollars a year. Then you'd see some great public television. Then we could be as daring and inventive as the British. They are really the standard bearers for television around the world."

It's something to be hoped for. Unless we take care of our needs for quality broadcasting and support PBS programming, our cultural heritage in the next decade will be based on sitcoms, cop shows and TV movies. That's not a very optimistic thought.

For writers wanting to break into the television movie market, it's better to write a movie script to use as a writing sample than an episodic script, says Nancy Bein, "because the lead characters are already created, and the formula is already set. Plus, if the script has been produced, there's no way to tell what a story editor or writer-producer added or refined. There were times at CBS when we bought 150 scripts a year, three scripts for every one made. We constantly tried to get the right writer the first time, but sometimes that didn't work out. Most of the scripts needed to be rewritten. The monetary guidelines for TV movie scripts are such that you're not able to afford an established writer to rewrite someone else. Under the Writers Guild rules, you can replace the writer twice. So the first writer's fees would determine whether other writers would be hired or not, and for how much. So we were always looking for new writers to do rewrites for us.

"If you're writing a script on spec as a writing sample, I'd write what you really care about and believe in. You want to show how good you are and you also want to learn how good you are yourself. If you're concerned about getting this script made as a television movie, I'd write for a woman in the age bracket of thirty-five to forty-five, because there are so many actresses who fit that range they may respond to your script and want to get attached; that will help you sell it.

"When you get right down to it, television movies are really a producers' medium. Most the time it's the producers who bring in ideas. It's a simple and logical way to do it. For a long time TV movies were based on true stories. Several years ago we used to say that the typical television movie concept was if you had one leg, you skied. It was a great rush of one genre, the disease-of-the-week story.

"When we stopped doing them, the suppliers couldn't believe it and they continued pitching us those stories. This is a story about courage, they would say, not affliction. What was unfortunate was that they became formula. It's so easy to do a formula of an idea that was fresh yesterday. The tendency now is to shy away from the docudrama, but some incidents in a true story can be so unpredictable, so bizarre, you'd never believe it, so there will always be a place for the true story, although they're not the mainstay they once were.

"I think the three networks overused the true story for a long time, and now if CBS does one it has to be special; we can't keep remaking the story of a noble judge who fights back in a corrupt system. Or the good cop who, even though his department has given up on crime, spends his off hours tracking down a killer, jeopardizing his marriage and family relationships.

"We want writers to find some new element that would make it a better movie. This happened on the T. S. Cook script called *Out of Darkness,* the true story of the cop in New York who solved the 'Son of Sam' killings.

"The way it was pitched was interesting because it wasn't just the story of a cop who tracked down a killer. It was the story of a man whose wife—his childhood sweetheart and best friend—had just died because of a doctor's error. Working on the case helps bring him out of mourning, and keeps him from dwelling on his loss. When he finally catches the killer, it becomes a release and helps him accept his wife's death. It was an unusual way of looking at the story and showing how people's lives aren't divided into two separate compartments, their jobs and their personal lives."

This is how you, as writer, should approach your subject matter. You can see how this twist in the personal life of the main character makes it into a more appealing and universal story line.

Over and over again in my screenwriting workshops, people come in with ideas that are too direct, too right on the nose, too "predictable." I tell them that's only the start point. Take that story line and examine it from all sides to find an unusual approach, an indirect approach, like using the Henry James Theory of Illumination as start point for your subject matter. It's something to keep in mind.

"Sometimes a current event will not merit a television movie simply on concept alone," Bein explains. "For example, a few years ago a lot of students at college were submitting to sexual harassment by professors in order to get good grades. We must have gotten at least ten pitches along those lines, from true stories to fictional stories with young actresses attached.

"What we found was that the episodic shows picked it up immediately, and rightfully so. A lot of episodic writers comb the papers looking for ideas. Besides, it was no longer fresh subject matter, so there's not too much to say about a movie like that. It's very easy to see who the bad guy is, and who the good guy is, and you basically know the whole movie from the first sentence. It's predictable."

Is there anything that would be interesting in today's market? I asked. Bein replied, "There's been a lack of female-oriented stories in TV movies, but the fact is that the woman's audience is a very important audience. So the stories we might be interested in, for example, might be a look at a woman married to a man in the stock market who's been involved in a white-collar crime. They've been popular, they've been wealthy, they've been successful. And her husband gets caught. Maybe she knew what was going on, maybe she didn't. How does she react to this? Going from a certain social station to now being on her own for however long he's going to be in jail. How does she react? How does she live?

"Those are the kinds of stories we think could fill a two-hour movie, and be worth doing. Even if an episodic show, like *L.A. Law,* picked it up, it would be a different story because you'd have your lead character handle it differently.

"Movies on television," she goes on, "have to stretch the genre as far as it can go. If there's anything that's a trend, it's to do things that are unusual. The material is the cornerstone and foundation of the movie. If the material isn't good, it's not worth doing. Some people feel if you can get the right one-liner in *TV Guide,* you can get people to watch your show.

"I don't believe that. Audiences are film-literate today. I watch those one-liner movies, and after two or three times I get disappointed, and reject the Friday Night Movie, or whatever. Television movies, for the most part, are regarded as an anthology series, so you must keep a standard every time out to attract a repeat audience. They play every Tuesday, Wednesday, Saturday, and Sunday. And each night provides a different kind of movie."

During 1988 there were 8,000 to 10,000 pitches at CBS for movies of the week, and fifty movies made, slightly less than the year before. When you go in to pitch a movie for television, it would be effective if you left behind a page the network executive could refer to, even though it's against Writers Guild regulations. (It's considered speculative writing.) Usually, in a pitch meeting, the executive has a secretary or assistant take notes, then type them up for later reference.

"At the network," says Bein, "you don't sit down at the end of the day and reflect on what you've been pitched. You don't look at those pitches for maybe two weeks because you're so busy with the other parts of the job. When you do go back and look at what you've got to present to your boss, you may have forgotten a lot of the pitch. And if you don't have something written up that hits the right notes, it may not sound so good anymore. You don't quite remember why it stood out at the moment.

"You need something that will trigger your initial response to the story. It could simply be statistics; in 1989 an *x* number of people had this problem. And it's reported in such and such a magazine that by 1990 it will be this many, and a lot of people are talking about it, and this is the story we want to tell.

"If you want to break in as a television-movie writer you have to have some prior writing experience. So many new writers say, look, I have a great treatment, I have a great idea, why can't I write the script? What do I have to do to get a deal? And the networks say unless you have a script that shows you can write, why should we give you a deal?

"It's important to learn your craft. People learn from their mistakes. I knew a man in school, a Vietnam vet, who wrote screenplays. He used to work as a security guard in an apartment building, and night after night he would sit in his little booth, writing screenplays.

"One time a television executive came to speak at UCLA. During the class he said he wouldn't read any scripts. But after class this man followed the executive to his car and asked him to read one of his scripts. And the executive said, I'll read the script because of your determination. The moral isn't that he liked the script; he didn't, but he liked the writer's persistence. The writer didn't quit, or feel rejected, or criticize the executive's 'bad taste.'

"He kept writing and improved and soon got a break and started writing for episodic television. He worked his way up to become a successful writer earning a lot of money.

"He was totally determined. It was a dry ten years; that's a long time to believe in yourself and have nobody else really believe in you."

It's a lesson that bears repeating. For all of us.

Part Two

The Writers

13

Oliver Stone

On patience: *"There are so many heartbreaks
and disappointments in this business
that pain and joy go hand in hand."*

Oliver Stone represents everything this book is about. Stone is the
screenwriter of *Midnight Express, Salvador, Scarface, Platoon,* and *Wall
Street* (co-written with Stanley Weiser). Stone's epic journey of selling
Platoon is inspirational.

We met for our interview in his office, located in a large guest house
next to his garage. We shook hands and he explained that the very first
exhibitor screenings of *Wall Street* were in progress at that very moment.
He looked tired, and he sounded tired, his voice rough and hoarse.

I had originally attempted to interview him in mid-February, just
prior to the announcement of the Academy Award nominations and a
few days before he was scheduled to leave for New York to shoot
Wall Street. It was raining hard when I got to his house to do that
February interview, and when I got inside he said there had been a
mistake: he had an important casting session now, and could we do the
interview the next day, Saturday. I had to decline because I had a
previous commitment. Secretly I was glad to postpone the interview. He
had been working very hard preparing the production of *Wall Street,* and
his mind would have been filled with so many details that it would have
been hard for him to concentrate on anything else. We agreed to do the
interview when he got back from New York, some time in July, but it

was not until November, a few days before Thanksgiving, that we finally connected.

Again he looked tired. He explained he'd been up since three o'clock in the morning. A few days earlier he had decided to change the end-credit music on *Wall Street* and was in the process of changing the exhibitor prints so he could leave within the next few days for a promotional tour of Dallas, Toronto, New York, and San Francisco.

When I arrived, workmen were all over the place doing some remodeling, and the kitchen was filled with people supervised by Stone's wife, Elizabeth, preparing a dinner for the more than twenty film editors who had worked on the picture.

When we sat down, he said, "I've turned off the phone, but I'm waiting for two calls that I have to take." So with his golden retriever sitting next to me, I turned on the tape recorder. We had no sooner started than one of the phone calls came in. It was a report from the exhibitor screening. Concerned, he repeated over and over, "Did they laugh?" *Wall Street,* though a serious subject, especially after the recent October 19 crash, has much more humor in it than did his other work: *Midnight Express, The Hand, Scarface, Year of the Dragon, Platoon,* and *Salvador.* Oliver Stone is not known for his comedy writing.

When he hung up, I asked if he had previewed the film in front of an audience, before the exhibitor screenings, and he replied he doesn't believe in that. He gives the film to the studio just the way he wants it. So he's still a little unsure about how the audiences will accept it.

It's the same way you feel when you've completed the screenplay you've been writing for several months and preparing to send it out into the marketplace. At that point you can't see anything; you have no objectivity at all, only a gut feeling that it's working. And there's always that little doubt at the back of your mind. Does it work? Did I fix everything? Is it good?

As we started talking I began to see he had been asked the same questions over and over again, and the more he spoke the more I could hear the fatigue in his voice. He had been through a tremendous ordeal and this was the final moment. But there is no rest, at least not now. The second call comes in, from the postproduction supervisor for the studio.

Stone constantly checks on whether the prints will be ready; the supervisor assures him he'll do the best he can.

That may not be good enough. The publicity tour begins in a few days.

Oliver Stone's life has been dramatically shaped by the tides of war. His father, an American GI, met his mother, a French citizen, in Paris during the Second World War. Stone grew up in an affluent part of New York, but his father "never owned a single thing; everything was rented, right down to the cars, the apartments, and if it had been possible, the furniture." He enrolled at Yale but dropped out after a year. He traveled to Southeast Asia, where he spent two years in the Chinese district of Saigon teaching English to Vietnamese-Chinese students.

Then, like Eugene O'Neill, Stephen Crane, and Jack London, Stone went to sea. He worked as a wiper on an American merchant ship, then settled in Guadalajara, where he finished his first novel, *A Child's Night Dreams* (still unpublished), based loosely on his experiences in the Far East.

Two years later, at the age of twenty-one, he enlisted in the army and found himself back in Vietnam. He stayed there for a year and a half and completed his tour of duty in 1968. He arrived home with a Purple Heart (with an oak leaf cluster) and a Bronze Star for combat gallantry and a head full of memories.

It wasn't long before he enrolled in the NYU Film School. "Vietnam was a demarcation point," he begins, "in the sense that I started to see the world less in a cerebral way and began to see it more visually. In Vietnam you dealt with six inches right in front of your face. You dealt with the jungle, the smells, the senses, with your peripheral vision, just to survive. You have to see, *S-E-E*, in the jungle. That's the way you make it. So by that act of seeing I think I awakened some impulse in me which I hadn't as yet been aware of.

"The last few months I was in Vietnam, I was carrying a still camera into the field to take pictures," he goes on, "and took hundreds of pictures which literally opened my eyes to color and composition. So when I got back to the States I got a super 8mm camera and continued to shoot everything I could, documentary style. When I enrolled at NYU I moved from 8mm films to 16mm films. I made three short films while I was there, from twenty to thirty minutes in length."

After his graduation from NYU, "I couldn't get anywhere as a writer-director," he says, "because nobody was reading scripts. There was no market at that point in time [the early '70s] for young screenwriters. It was a desert. The studios were drying up and only doing six to eight big films a year on the order of *Planet of the Apes, Patton,* or *Papillon.* There was no room for young people, except for Scorsese and Coppola and a few others; for the rest of us it was an old man's business.

"So I begged for jobs as a production assistant, but they were hard jobs to get. I was married so I drove a cab, was a Xerox messenger, and my wife helped support me. It was temporary employment here and there, unemployment here and there. I worked for a year at a sports film company and got paid pretty well literally doing nothing for a year. It was all a scam. From 1968 to 1976 [the year he wrote *Platoon*] I wrote eleven screenplays and several treatments; it was very hard getting anyone to read the scripts, and many of them were returned unopened. I got turned down everywhere; it was all very depressing, and I must have had a thousand rejection letters.

"New York's a much tougher town to start out in the film business, because it's very small, and there's not a lot of employment and it's somewhat clique-ish. I got a divorce in 1976, so I moved to L.A.

"When I came back from Vietnam in 1968, I wrote one of my first screenplays, *Break,* where I used many of the same characters that were to crop up later in *Platoon.* But my reaction to war was totally surreal. I was doing enormous amounts of grass and was actually numbed out by the war, anesthetized. I couldn't deal with it on a realistic level, so that screenplay was a very dreamlike, very bizarre piece. It was a period when they started to make films like that; Fellini was very popular with *8½* and *Juliet of the Spirits.*

"My earliest attempts at screenwriting were certainly in the area of fantasy," he recalls, "and my short films were pretty far out, very much in the style of Jean-Luc Godard. But by 1976, after much failure, I became more and more realistic and decided to go with a more naturalistic style.

"*Platoon* was based on my own experiences in Vietnam. It was the summation of my feelings, my reaction to what I had seen over there. I wanted to write it before it was forgotten, because in 1976, after eight years, it was beginning to fade from memory,'' he explains.

"Everybody in that platoon was based on somebody that existed. Barnes [Tom Berenger] existed; Elias [Willem Dafoe] existed; since I was in three different units I made a composite platoon and put all the archetypes I saw over there into one platoon.

"Now, how I was going to tell this story took a long time to lay out, but once I thought it through, the actual writing went pretty fast. I wrote it in about six to eight weeks in December of '76, then revised it a couple of times and sent it out.

"I used the *Iliad* as the model when I started working on the script, in the sense of the personalities that stood out. The Trojan War was a barren war fought for many years on the bloody shores of Troy and nobody could solve anything; the Greeks were always fighting among themselves. I certainly thought there was a reflection of that in Vietnam. That America was fighting this war was completely wrong; there was no moral purpose and no moral intent. It was a bad war in every sense of the word. And the resulting dissent that I showed, the so-called civil war that was being fought inside the American lines, was symbolic of what was going on in the country as a whole, between left and right, between student protestors and people in the establishment. America was split and it was one of the few times we woke up to the fact that the establishment was a fraud and we did something about it. Vietnam was the front line of that battle, and it was fought in a very ugly way. Very quietly, very secretly. The bombings did go on, as much as the Department of Defense denied it.

"From my point of view I wanted to make these two sergeants the mythic heroes I thought they were; I looked up to those two guys as leaders. As one kid says in the movie, 'I was a child born of those two fathers.'

"In the end, after all the hardship and misery, I felt it was important to find hope for these boys. They were going back to another war in the United States. One far worse than they had ever imagined. I think it's important for vets to put that war behind them and start building and teaching the U.S. what they know and learned—to be a cadre of political consciousness in this country to prevent another war.

"I used narration because it nails down what has to be said and cannot be shown. I narrated the movement of the infantry, without showing the process.

"The letters home showed the increasing sense of despair: 'Six inches in front of my face was all I could deal with.' That's literally quite true. I culled all this from my letters and others. I went to the interior feelings that people don't usually talk about. The only way to accomplish this was with the letters.

"After I finished *Platoon,* Stan Kamen, then head of the William Morris Agency [Stone had signed with the Morris office the year before when Robert Bolt, the great English screenwriter of *Lawrence of Arabia,* had taken an interest in an earlier script and recommended the agency sign him], loved the piece and got it everywhere. He really wanted to see it made.

"But when he sent it out everybody thought it was too realistic, that it had too downbeat an ending, and too many characters. Sometimes there's twenty-five characters on a page. I knew what each character represented, but on a page it's much more difficult to see the differentiation. So I guess everybody read it and didn't know who was who.

"Everybody liked the writing, but nobody wanted to make the movie. I never fit the screenplay to the fashion of the time. I had offers from producers to change the script, or change the title, even send the Charlie Sheen character to R&R in Bangkok; some of them wanted to throw some women in the movie, and have a happy ending. Total Hollywood bullshit. There was a lot of that.

"I did come close with a few directors. Mark Rydell, who directed *On Golden Pond* [Ernest Thompson] and *The Rose* [Bill Kerby and Bo Goldman], to name a few, really wanted to make it at one point, but nobody would finance it. Michael Schultz also wanted to do it. But you have to understand that Vietnam, at that time, was a downer subject. Francis Ford Coppola was doing *Apocalypse Now* but he literally had to mortgage his house so he could take on the project. We had lost the war and people didn't want to be reminded of it.

"The script worked for me insofar as the people who read it, liked it. They wouldn't buy it, or make it, but they liked the writing and it allowed me to get a foothold in Hollywood. On the basis of *Platoon*

Columbia hired me to write *Midnight Express,* a book they owned. So I went to England and worked with Alan Parker that winter.

"There's a lot of me in *Midnight Express,*" he continues, "and I was criticized for it. The character in the book is not the way he's portrayed in the film. The real Billy Hayes is quite different. I romanticized him. I used my own experiences in jail. I'd been thrown into jail when I came back from Vietnam. It was a feeling of terror. I used my experience and met the character halfway. [Stone won an Academy Award for his screenplay.]

"When I came back, *Platoon* kept circulating for a couple of years, but there was no interest at all; the juice was gone. Nobody wanted to do it. So I shelved it. I never showed it around anymore.

"So it sat there for about four or five years. After the success of *The Deer Hunter* and *Apocalypse Now,* I simply shrugged and said nobody's really interested in the real experience of Vietnam, so forget it. It's just not going to happen in my lifetime.

"Then, in 1984, Michael Cimino [writer-director of the *The Deer Hunter*] approached me to do *Year of the Dragon*, which I wasn't keen on doing, and he finally convinced me to do it by saying he would produce *Platoon* after he completed *Year of the Dragon*. He had a deal with Dino De Laurentiis, and I knew he could get it made.

"So I said, 'Don't you think Vietnam is spent as subject matter? I mean, who really cares?' And he said, 'No, it's coming back. You're wrong. It's coming back.' And he was right.

"The Vietnam War Memorial had come through that year; Stanley Kubrick had announced his plans to do *Full Metal Jacket,* and Vietnam books were doing very well in sales.

"But I had a hard time even then. I did some rewriting once it was revived, and really tried like hell to get it made with Dino De Laurentiis. I did a lot of preliminary work. I cast the movie. I went to locations and I went to Mexico and the Philippines. Organized the production design.

"And then nobody wanted to make the movie. They thought it was a downer. Dino De Laurentiis was willing to finance the movie but nobody in America was willing to distribute it, which was the key to Dino's financing. That was very disheartening for me.

"Eventually I got the screenplay back from De Laurentiis through legal channels, and it rebounded immediately toward Hemdale, a British company. And they said, 'Let's do it.' Which amazed me because I really didn't believe it would get done. That's why I did *Salvador* first, because I felt *Platoon* was cursed. And *Salvador* became my training ground to do *Platoon*.

"I have to give John Daly credit, because he plunked down all his money on *Platoon*. He's a boxer, and that's what the project needed, because it had been rejected outright by all the American studios.

"There are so many heartbreaks and disappointments that occur in this business that the pain goes hand in hand with the joy. I think the only way you can be productive or fertile in producing things is to forget. Or at least wash the slate clean so you can go on. You can't be too attached to it."

This is the lesson that occurs in the *Bhagavad-Gita* over and over again: you cannot be attached to the fruits of your actions. Once you complete your screenplay, and send it into the marketplace, you've got to let it go. When studios, producers, or directors pass on your material, it's not a personal rejection, it just means they (whoever "they" are) wanted to choose something else. If you take it personally—"They didn't like my script, and therefore they must not like me"—you're emotionally plugged in, attached to whether they like it or don't like it.

I used to do a lot of that.

It's a no-win situation.

"I still have some other screenplays like that," Stone continues, "still unproduced. For example, I spent a year and a half writing *Born on the Fourth of July* in 1978, and Al Pacino was going to star in it. He was great in rehearsal, and then the money fell through during the last three days before shooting. That was a real setback and really disillusioned me about Hollywood and the whole system here. That was a killer. I put that on the shelf emotionally. [The picture is now shooting with Tom Cruise starring.

"I wrote a piece about Russia called *Defiance,* which is a beautiful love story. One day it will get made. But it was shelved in a very brutal fashion by a very brutal producer, and it hurt me for quite a while. All these things hurt, but you can't walk around bitter about it. The more bitter you are, the more you hurt yourself."

He leaned back in his chair, stared out the window, and paused for several moments. "When I look for something, it's very intuitive and comes from the gut out. I wanted to do the story about a journalist, and whether it was set in Afghanistan, Nicaragua, or El Salvador really didn't matter. It was the character I was interested in. He sucked me in, and the more I found out about the background, the more I became interested in that.

"*Salvador* is the story of the soul of Richard Boyle [James Woods] trying to redeem himself, trying to find his salvation in this screwed-up backcountry where all of a sudden things matter, and he begins to care for somebody, Maria. And this leads him to a broader understanding of the forces at work in the country of El Salvador and just how evil the evil is he's fighting. In the beginning, he's a scumbag who's got absolutely no morality. And in the end he's preaching to the American advisers about the moral state of the world in Salvador. I find that good.

"Basically, *Salvador* is a sad story became Richard never really found his soul. He's still wandering in the purgatory of ghosts, looking for it.

"*Scarface* was written for Al Pacino [based on the 1932 film classic *Scarface* with Paul Muni, from a story by Ben Hecht, based on the novel by Armitage Trail] I knew him from *Born on the Fourth of July*, and I was fascinated by his ability. I believed in him as an actor and I believed this was the right vehicle for him and it grew from there. The background of Miami was fascinating at the time because in 1980 the homicide and cocaine trade was at a maximum.

"While I was writing, I thought its get-rich-quick Miami mentality had certain parallels with New York, where an acquaintance of mine was making a fortune in the market. He was like some crazed coke dealer, nervously on the phone nights trading with Hong King and London, checking the telex, talking about enormous sums of money to be won or lost on a daily basis. His life-style was "Scarface" North. He had two huge Gatsby-like houses on the beach in Long Island, several dune buggies, cars, Jeeps, a private seaplane company, an art collection, and a town house in Manhattan.

"Then he took a giant fall; his empire came crashing down around him. He was suspended from trading; he lost millions and spent millions more in legal fees clearing his name, which he finally did. It made him a different, stronger person as a result.

"In *Wall Street,* the Michael Douglas character is on the side of Barnes in *Platoon* in terms of pulling the boy toward the darker view of the world, the darker view of life. And the father, Martin Sheen, is on Elias's side of the spectrum in pulling the son toward the light. And there's that pull, because they're both fighting for the soul of the young man.

"I'm interested in that period of time between eighteen and twenty-one," he reflects, "when you are an adolescent and you're exposed to the world for the first time and those forces hit you with maximum brutality and ferocity.

"*Wall Street* basically grew out of the characters; the whole composite picture of the yuppies in the '80s that I saw in New York of people making easy money, living easy lives; it was literally something out of *The Great Gatsby.* Having beach houses, apartments, vacations, and not really knowing the value of a dollar earned, because it's all stolen money on Wall Street. It's all unearned money, it's all speculation.

"I would see these guys and be fascinated by them, and that led to my deciding to cast this character of Bud Fox [Charlie Sheen] in the middle of this as a character out of a Dreiser sort of novel; he would most resemble Hurstwood in *Sister Carrie* and the temptations of that world. It was partly this tale of seduction, corruption, loss, and ultimate redemption that intrigued me and became the basis for Bud Fox.

"It's not all black and white, it's a very gray area; I wanted to concentrate on the ethics of the characters and see where they lose their way, where they lose their sense of values, where net worth starts to equal self-worth.

"Insider trading has not been defined legally, it's a complicated definition of the law. The film deals more with the concept of paper wealth. Of what John Maynard Keynes called 'the renter class' as opposed to the entrepreneur, the worker class. The film takes a stand against the people that own and don't do anything; people that don't earn income and make unearned income off their stocks and bonds. Their stock and real estate speculation is fueled by profit and greed, and it takes a position about that. It seems we've gotten away from a world where Wall Street existed fundamentally to capitalize American business, to provide research and jobs and launch new companies. That was the place to get the capital. Now it's really about something else. It's about huge sums of money that get split up among brokerage houses and lawyers, legal fees, green mail, and corporate debt and takeovers. And that's very confusing, because a lot of times nothing constructive happens from these takeovers. It's a breakup or reassessment of assets; it's simply rearranging the deck chairs on the *Titanic*."

He paused for a long moment and I could hear the fatigue in his voice, so I decided to wrap it up and asked him what he thought a new writer should do when he or she is writing a screenplay.

"Write it from your gut," he replied. "Write it the way you feel. The one thing I notice about the writer's first or second screenplay is that they tend to write it with an image of what it should be. The idea always creeps in that this is a movie. It has to have this twist here, it has to have this chase here, and it has to have this peak here. When you get into the mimetic quality of paralleling what you think is a Hollywood movie, you somehow lose the essence of yourself. True there is a basic structure common to most successful screenplays, but you really have to write from your gut and if you do that you'll do okay.

"Write it fast," he continues, "and don't waste a year or two of your life on a screenplay, because sometimes it's just going to miss completely and your heart's going to get broken. Be fertile, be productive, write two or three things a year if you can. Keep circulating, be humble, and be grateful enough to take no for an answer, because you're going to get a lot of nos.

"Tenacity is very important, sometimes more important than talent, because luck strikes as a result of tenacity." Which can lead to success, as it has with Oliver Stone. And that's another set of problems to deal with, because "it can be a liability in a way," he concludes. "Success often corrupts because Hollywood always makes something bigger. Once you do a $6 million movie, then you drift into a $15 million movie. Before you know it, you can only work with Paul Newman or Tom Cruise because somehow you need the best for everything. You get fatter and fatter until you're this giant blimp and you're no longer yourself. That's where the corruption occurs. You lose yourself. The challenge for me is to stay lean and tight and make good films."

"The only sin in life," said D. H. Lawrence, "is going against your own integrity."

14

Dan Petrie, Jr.

On choosing a subject: *"Boring never works."*

Dan Petrie, Jr., is an excellent example of the contemporary screenwriter in Hollywood. Bright, articulate, outspoken, his screenplays for *Beverly Hills Cop, The Big Easy,* as well as a shared credit on *Shoot to Kill,* a picture he also coproduced, are perfect examples of "the good read." Clean, lean, and tight, they offer an individual insight and perspective to writing the contemporary screenplay.

Interestingly enough, Dan Petrie, Jr., comes from a motion picture family. His father, Daniel Petrie, Sr., is a well-known television and film director who directed such notable productions as *Eleanor and Franklin* and *Sybil* for television, as well as acclaimed feature films like *Raisin in the Sun* and *Fort Apache, the Bronx,* to name a few.

His mother, Dorthea Petrie, decided to build a career as a producer and produced the highly acclaimed production of *Foxfire* for the Hallmark Hall of Fame, starring Hume Cronyn and Jessica Tandy.

His brother, Donald Petrie, is a director, and has just completed his first feature film, *Mystic Pizza* (Amy Jones, Perry Howze, Randy Howze, and Alfred Uhry) for the Samuel Goldwyn Company. His sister June is a development executive for Bob Swain, the stylish director of *La Balance*. His other sister, Mary, is an actress. Quite a family.

But coming from a theatrical family is both a blessing and a burden. You can always get your foot in the door, but it's up to you to stay there and get the job done. And other people's expectations of your talent and abilities are always higher than for someone who has a different name.

So, like many others in a theatrical family, he was not really encouraged to pursue a career in the motion picture business, but "when it became clear that I was going to do it anyway, they were very encouraging," he says.

After graduating from the University of Redlands, he started writing, and "fortunately, there are no copies of those scripts floating around anywhere. In about two years I made a grand total of $3,500.

"I wanted to write," he continues, "but I also wanted a day job so I could keep a roof over my head. So I got a job at ICM, the talent agency, in the mailroom. They were paying $115 a week, and I thought I'd be able to save half my money and by the end of six months I'd quit and start writing.

"That's essentially what happened, except I didn't save anywhere close to half the money, and it didn't take six months, it took five years. And it was rather more involved than just being in the mailroom. I was so naive when I started that I didn't realize the big agencies like ICM, or William Morris and CAA, had a training program. You may start in the mailroom, but your ultimate goal is to become an agent.

"I knew this, but I didn't fully comprehend what it meant. What it meant was that you worked all day in the mailroom and then you read and synopsized scripts at night. If you did this diligently, in a short time they would make you a reader, so you could read scripts full-time. But as a reader, you hung out in the agents' offices all day and tried to help them in whatever way you could, and you *still* did your reading and synopsizing at night.

"So I worked in the mailroom, and shortly thereafter moved up to being a reader, then became an assistant to Jack Gilardi [one of the top agents there], and finally became an agent.

"All this time I wasn't writing, at least I wasn't putting words down on paper, but I was intensely interested in it. As a reader, and then as an agent, you continue to read scripts, but you also market them to the industry, and that means you're always trying to imagine how they could be better, so it's a tremendous training ground.

"It teaches you some obvious things—like don't submit a screenplay with a drawing, or any kind of illustration, on the cover. And don't ignore the budgetary considerations of what you're writing. One time I read a screenplay about Napoleon that had a scene calling for a quarter of a million extras coming over a hill. That's how it read: 'A quarter of a million men scale a hill.'

"I also learned that there are many successful, working writers who just abandon the idea of using any stylistic grace, or elegance of expression, in their writing. They're just telling the story; they figure they're going to be rewritten anyway so they'll just throw words down on paper and forget about it. And they've made a lot of money doing that.

"That made me take a certain amount of pride in my craft. Believe it or not, I was inspired by the enormous numbers of bad screenplays. Inspired because I knew that I could be competitive in the area of those writers who are taken seriously by readers: only about 10 percent. So I knew that if I wrote a screenplay that was well executed, and had interesting components, a reader would say that this is a real screenplay, and then they would put me in the 10 percent category of writers they would consider for an assignment.

"At the same time I was enjoying being an agent and working with writers, some of whom are my best friends now. David Greenwalt and Jim Kouf, for example. They cowrote *Class, American Dreamer,* and *Secret Admirer,* which David also directed. Jim went on to write *Stakeout,* and now both he and David are writer-directors.

"I represented Jim Kouf when I was still in the mailroom. He became my first client. I'd sneak him into the mailroom on Saturdays and we'd Xerox all his scripts, put them in the agency's ICM covers, and then I'd write letters to producers: 'Enclosed is the new script which we're all very excited about by Jim Kouf, called such and such. Please let me know what you think. Best Regards, Jack Gilardi.' I would type these in the mailroom, then watch Jack's incoming mail for the script, or letter, from the producer I had sent the script to.

"Jack knew what I was doing. He didn't know how often I was doing it, but that's how you learn. We were all told to open everybody's mail and read it. If you're not doing that, then you're not doing your job. Sometimes, at night, I would go to the agents' offices and look through all their deal memos.

"It was *the* way to learn the business.

"At the end of five years at ICM, I was very unhappy. I had been wanting to leave for a year. My mother had given me her old office in the Writers and Artists building in Beverly Hills, but somehow I just couldn't leave. Eventually I got fired, because it was obvious my heart wasn't in it. And they were right. I was too conscientious to deliberately try to get myself fired, but by the same token it was clear I didn't want to be there.

"I knew I wanted to write, but things were different than they were before. I was married, and if I started writing it meant my wife would have to go back to work full-time, so we both had to be prepared for that.

"So I left ICM on a Friday afternoon, and on Monday morning I went to my little office to become a writer. When I started I knew exactly the kind of script I should write, but I didn't write it. The first thing I did was get in touch with being a writer. So I wrote several treatments, which I knew from my agency experience were absolutely worthless. They're only useful as a tool for you, the writer, and even then, an outline is much more useful. A treatment has absolutely no effect on a sale at all.

"Then I wrote a couple of outlines for a television series. Again, precisely the thing you shouldn't do, because television series are a completely closed shop. The networks pick who they want to write their pilots from the list of people who have already written for them. It's very difficult for a writer to break into that. It's much easier to break in as a feature film writer than a television pilot writer.

"Nevertheless, knowing full well I was making a mistake, I went ahead and did it anyway; I had the ideas and it was a good way to be at the typewriter every day, establishing discipline and sharpening my skills.

"I spent a couple of months working on these, then wrote a science fiction script. Again, a science fiction script is not the kind of script you want to use as a writing sample, much less a first screenplay. You don't want to be labeled a science fiction writer. And if that's what you show the readers, agents, executives, and producers, they'll only consider you to write science fiction screenplays. They're not going to say you would be perfect to write our love story set in Africa.

"But believe it or not, the script, called *Fire Star,* came close to being sold. It also got me an agent, Robert Wunsch, who had been an agent, then became a producer, doing *Slap Shot* [Nancy Dowd], and then vice president of production at UA, and later senior v.p. of CBS Films, before he went back into the agency business.

"He told me what I already knew: to start a career I needed a writing sample, a script that would not necessarily sell or get made but which would show what I could do. I thought about that.

"What would be a good writing sample? First of all, I reasoned, it should be a contemporary story. It should have genre elements, but not necessarily be of a genre. It should not necessarily be in the cop or detective genre for example, but it could have those elements.

"A writing sample should have a strong male leading role. It should have a strong female role. And having those two roles implies that it's got to be a love story, or a romantic comedy, or at least something that makes use of the male-female dynamic.

"It's important to establish that you can write terrific male characters as well as terrific female characters. There should be some action in the piece, but it should not be an action movie. There should be humor in it if it's a drama, and if it is a comedy, there should be strong dramatic moments.

"In other words, the script should reveal a broad range of writing talent. But it needs more—it has to have a good story. It's of no use to showcase good writing in a dull story. Boring never works.

"If I was going to do this I needed a story. I knew this was what I *should* write, but I wasn't ready to write it. Good stories don't grow on trees. And if they do they don't necessarily fall into a category that has a good male lead, a good female lead, comedy, drama, action, but not too much action, all the elements I was looking for. So I started thinking about a script called *Windy City,* which later became *The Big Easy.*

"The first thing I considered was the love story. What does a love story imply? A love story about two people who are alike doesn't really work, so it's got to be about two people who are unalike. So who are two people who are the least likely to fall in love? And I wanted to set it against something that would have genre elements in it, but would not necessarily be in the genre.

"Like a cop story. Well, what cop haven't we seen? We haven't seen a corrupt cop as a hero. Now, who's the best person—in the sense of the least likely person—for him to fall in love with, and her to fall in love with him? How about the D.A. who's investigating his corruption? Now a story's beginning to emerge.

"What is it that keeps them together? Why don't they just have one encounter and then drift their own separate ways? Because you've got to set up a situation in a love story where people aren't likely to love each other. Otherwise, there's no drama, no conflict. You got to have your story throwing them together many times in order for them to have the opportunity to fall in love.

"It seemed to me in this case that the way to do that was to create a larger investigation, a murder investigation, something that's larger than the original corruption she's investigating him for, something they're both interested in solving.

"Which led me to the idea that she should have some piece of vital evidence she's withholding from him because he's one of the suspects. And he knows she's got it. So they're glued to each other by this circumstance.

"So the whole story laid itself out. Now, I don't think this is the best way to come up with a screenplay. It would be better in general to come up with it by contemplating a character or a situation. But remember, this was thought of as a writing sample.

"It took about four or five months to write the first draft. Originally I set it in Chicago, and I didn't go there to research the first draft because I didn't have the money. So I contented myself with secondary research about Chicago. After the first draft, I went there to look around and meet with some cops there, and I was able to revise the script to accommodate what I found.

"I never thought *Windy City* [*The Big Easy*] would sell. I thought it would be something my agent could send to producers and say, look, you have an assignment open and it's an action movie, and I have a writer who could do it and here's a sample of his writing. It's not really an action movie, but it's got some good action scenes. And if producer B has a love story, he could say, well, this really isn't a love story, it's a cop story, but it's got some love story elements in it." (The love scene between Dennis Quaid and Ellen Barkin, with their clothes on, is one of the most erotic scenes ever put on film.)

"When I gave it to Bob Wunsch, he said he felt it was not only a good writing sample, but also a script he thought he could sell, and sell, moreover, for a lot of money.

"So he showed it to Steve Friedman [of Kings Road Productions, and formerly Robert Wunsch's coproducer on *Slap Shot*] on Friday, and the following Monday Steve called up, made an offer, and bought it.

"This was about two years after I left ICM. Now, you may say that's a relatively short time. But if you look at those first two years I was writing, and the five years I spent at ICM, and then the two years after that, I actually spent nine years writing my first screenplay that *sold*.

"What happened after that was wonderful. Because *The Big Easy* sold for a lot of money on its first submission, it became kind of a celebrity screenplay. Now, executives pride themselves on the ability to get screenplays that no on else can get. A week prior to that no one particularly wanted to read the script. They might have been willing to read it, but it would not have been a question of them calling up and making an effort to get it.

"My agent kept saying, 'No, I can't get you a copy because the script's been sold,' which meant of course that it got read all over town, and in the very best of circumstances.

"That's the way Don Simpson and Jerry Bruckheimer got hold of it.

"*The Big Easy* was the perfect writing sample for me to get the job, because their idea was about a cop, a tough character, who comes to Beverly Hills from Detroit. So they hired me to do the rewrite.

"Everybody's rewritten in Hollywood, and sometimes you rewrite the person that rewrites you. And it stems from the fact that a director or studio or producer feels they want additional imput from another writer. Sometimes they need the budget cut, sometimes they want six more jokes, or the female star has too many good lines and the male star wants more; whatever the reason, being rewritten in Hollywood is an accepted practice. That doesn't make it any less painful.

"I've seen more scripts ruined by writers trying to fix something that isn't broken in the first place. You know, they just change something to be changing it. [Under the Writers Guild of America rules a screenwriter must change 50 percent or more of an existing script to qualify for a co-screenwriting credit.]

"Many people—even some writers—think dialogue is the screenplay.

Well, that's actually the easiest part to change and the least important aspect of the screenplay. The most important aspect is the story, followed by structure and characters. These are the linchpins of a screenplay. And it's amazing how you'll see the story, the structure, the characters remain the same. Everything else gets changed, the names, the locations, the dialogue, and people think, oh, I changed everything. Even though the three most important things have not changed at all. I've been on both sides of the street and have felt that when I've rewritten things I've really changed it all. But then, on further examination, I realized I haven't.

"It's actually harder to keep the existing good things in the script because it's much easier to change everything. Then you don't have to worry about how your great scene fits in with everything else. You're changing everything so you'll make it fit. But in order to get your great scene in you may have to put in six or seven mediocre scenes, whereas if you had subjugated your own ego a little bit you can keep the eight terrific scenes that are already there and make your contribution by cleverly figuring out how you can put in that great scene of yours.

"With *Beverly Hills Cop* they wanted a greater departure.

"We spent a lot of time working out the story. Finally, I wrote a 35-page outline that was approved. Then I started working on the script. I turned in the first draft, they liked it, and after I did a second draft, the studio made it a 'go' picture.

Last year Petrie was brought in to rewrite—again by Ricardo Mestres—and co-produce *Shoot to Kill*, starring Sidney Poitier and Tom Berenger, at Touchstone/Disney. He wound up sharing credit with Harv Zimmel and Michael Burton.

"I had a wonderful experience. Harv Zimmel, who wrote the original story and first faced the blank page, and Michael Burton, who worked out the structure, had the tough writing jobs, and Ron Silverman, the co-producer who was in charge of the physical production, had the tough producing job. I had the fun of working closely with Roger Spottiswoode [director of the highly acclaimed *Under Fire* with Nick Nolte and Gene Hackman, written by Clayton Frohman and Ron Shelton] and the challenge of working with him to solve problems as they arose in preproduction or on the set."

One difficult choice the filmmakers faced in preproduction involved the film's mystery subplot. The story is about a city detective (Sidney Poitier) who must team up with a wilderness guide (Tom Berenger) to apprehend a vicious killer. The killer is one of the people on Kirstie Alley's fishing trip, but we don't know who it is.

Any time you confront this kind of creative decision, the choice you make will always affect the story line. Dramatically, there are two ways to solve this kind of a problem. One is to create a sense of dramatic tension with a *Ten Little Indians* approach, in which the reader and audience are kept in suspense about which person is the killer. This is a closed-mystery approach. (*See* Chapter 11). The other choice would be to reveal the killer immediately, then proceed with the story.

This particular question had to be answered, both on paper and on location. Originally the studio favored the idea of creating a sense of dramatic tension by stretching out the period where we don't know who the killer is; the closed-mystery way. But after Dan Petrie, Jr., and Roger Spottiswoode carefully weighed the consequences of each choice, they decided to do it differently.

Good screenwriting always follows the focus of the main character, so the first question that has to be asked, says Petrie, is, "What is this movie about? Is it about Kirstie Alley and the fishing party, one of whom is a killer? Or is it about Sidney Poitier and Tom Berenger chasing them? Obviously, the fishing party is an important subplot, but it's not *the* plot. If we had followed that line we would have lost sight of the real story, which is the chase. So that's what we decided to concentrate on. Once we made that point to the studio, they agreed.

"There was another choice we made, for which we got hit critically," Petrie continues. "Very often you make those creative decisions with your eyes open, and you know you're going to take a hit from somebody.

"The question we anticipated was this: Why doesn't the killer simply kill Kirstie Alley at the border? Why does he keep her in Vancouver? We thought of all kinds of explanations for this. The explanation we finally settled on, and wrote several scenes about, was that the killer was now sexually engaged by Kirstie Alley. But his survival came first and he knew it was too dangerous for him to rape her while they're still on the trek. He wanted to keep her alive so that at a moment of leisure he could seduce her, feeling she'd appreciate his sterling qualities by that time. If that didn't work, he'd rape her. We didn't know what sacrifices we would have to make in order to answer that question. It certainly would have left a gaping hole in the Sidney Poitier and Tom Berenger story. How did they find out, the audience would ask, where the killer is going to be next? The difficulty with the screenplay is that there's only a finite amount of time. You only have 120 pages to tell your story.

"Even though it was a complicated thing to get across," Petrie goes on, "we tried it; we wrote some scenes, filmed them, then took them all out because it wasn't what the movie was about. This is not a movie about a killer and his hostage. Instead, we chose to tell our story, the chase, and spend the time with Poitier and Berenger getting to the killer. In terms of good storytelling, I think that was the right decision."

Screenwriting is a craft that occasionally rises to the level of art. And on those occasions, the process of writing a screenplay becomes one of those magic moments where the writer and subject matter "connect," and the screenwriting process becomes a voyage of discovery rather than an invention of plot and characters in a prescribed, contrived story line. And if that happens, all you have to do is follow the guidance of your creative self and the story will virtually write itself.

Jorge Semprum, a Brazilian screenwriter, once told me that when he sits down to write a screenplay he knows the script is already written. All he has to do is find it.

15

Alvin Sargent

On adaptation: *"Writing a screenplay is like going
to the movies. . . . It's about doing
something that nobody expects you to
do; I think people go to the
movies to see something they can't
see on the street."*

When I was teaching at the Sherwood Oaks Experimental College in the
mid '70s, I moderated an evening panel of celebrated writers and producers. The panelists included Charles Joffe, Woody Allen's producer; Richard
Roth, the producer of *Julia;* screenwriters Edward Anhalt (*The Young Lions*)
and Alvin Sargent, the screenwriter who had written the screenplay for *Julia,*
adapted from a story in Lillian Hellman's *Pentimento: A Book of Portraits.*

Most of the evening was spent talking about adapting novels and plays
into movies, and what it's like working with Woody Allen. *Julia* had just
been released, and while receiving a great deal of critical acclaim, most
of the audience had not yet seen it.

Only a few questions were directed to Alvin Sargent. He appeared
uncomfortable, somewhat ill at ease, because, as he explained, he doesn't
like to talk in front of a large group of people, and that day there were
well over three hundred people attending the seminar. But what he did
say impressed me greatly; his insights and observations about screenwriting
brushed against the walls of my own experience and he put into words
what I felt but couldn't articulate.

Bruce Springsteen once said in an interview that his job, as a song-writer, is really "pretty simple. I search for the human things in myself," he said, "and then I turn them into notes and words, and then in some fashion I help people hold on to their own humanity—if I'm doing my job right."

The same thing can be said of Alvin Sargent. When you look at the screenplays he's written, from *The Sterile Cuckoo,* with Liza Minnelli, to *Paper Moon,* with Ryan and Tatum O'Neal (for which he received his first Academy Award nomination), to adapting Paul Zindel's Pulitzer prize-winning play, *The Effects of Gamma Rays on Man-in-the-Moon Marigolds,* to *Julia,* to the forceful, often brilliant *Straight Time,* with Dustin Hoffman, to *Ordinary People*, directed by Robert Redford, for which he won an Academy Award, Alvin Sargent is a screenwriter of cinematic brilliance, who, if he does his job right, might say he "searches for the human things" in himself, so he can help people "hold on to their own humanity."

Asked about the craft of writing, Sargent replied, "I believe in blind writing. I believe the conscious thought is more about denial than is the unawareness of free association. To be unaware is the best answer to writing block. Turn out the lights and close your eyes. Write what your fingers want to say. Be free, as free as you can be. To make no sense is to find sense. Sense will always appear. Trust it to arrive. It is the core of nonsense. It is not about anything but about everything. The glitter gets lost and the truth comes through. And then, when the lights are up, you will sift through it as would a sifter of gold. The mud will be gone and you will find at least a golden kernel or two has been stirred up. The characters speak from their own darkness. It is the darkness we have to invade. Close your eyes. Then write. Preferably in the middle of the night. More preferably, unclothed. When everyone is asleep. When nobody gives a damn what you're doing anyway."

I first became aware of his work when I read his script *The Sterile Cuckoo,* which had been submitted to Cinemobile for partial financing and a completion bond, a sum of money held in escrow to guarantee the completion of the film. I was impressed with the script's cinematic dynamics, as well as the emotional honesty in the characters, all set against the backdrop of a college-age love story.

When I first saw *Julia*, I responded immediately to its mood, and the evocative stirrings of time and memory. The opening, a brooding, haunting image of Jane Fonda as an older Lillian Hellman in a rowboat fishing, reflecting on her relationship to Julia, sets up the story line immediately. In voice-over, we hear an explanation of the word *pentimento*. As Fonda explains, it is a process, used in art study: peeling away the many-colored coats of paint on a canvas often reveals the first sketches of the artist's vision. It is very much like the writing process, where the first words on paper will hardly be recognized in the final draft. As a visual experience, it hooked me immediately.

There are other moments in the film as well. The way Sargent overlaps the last line of dialogue from one scene into the next gives a clean and interesting transition, stirring the heart as well as moving the story forward. Or the way the relationship between Julia (Vanessa Redgrave) and Lillian Hellman (Jane Fonda) evolves as they are growing up, where one of them starts a story and we listen as it unfolds, Fonda offering one line, followed by Redgrave adding a line, then Fonda adding a line and so on, until we have a personal and poignant glimpse of their relationship.

The many wonderful moments in *Julia* are a testament to the artistry of Alvin Sargent; like some of the music of Bruce Springsteen, what he has written lingers in the memory long after we have left the theater.

The first time I made a list of writers that I wanted to interview for this book, Sargent was included, but I held little hope of actually getting him to sit down with me. I thought he would be too busy, or simply not want to do it. So I didn't contact him, and wove an elaborate rationale in my mind justifying my failure to call him.

A few months later I was talking with my cousin, who manages a doctor's office. She asked me if I had ever heard of a screenwriter named Alvin Sargent.

Does the sun shine? Does day turn into night? Does Bruce play music? I said, of course I knew him; everyone knows Alvin Sargent. She was surprised at my reaction. He's such a nice man, she explained, and went on to tell me she had just talked with him the day before; it turns out he's a patient of the doctor she works for. Trying to be cool, I told her I would like to interview him for the book, and left it at that.

A few weeks later she called and told me she had seen him again and that he would be glad to sit down and do an interview. Needless to say, I was elated. I called him and we met for about an hour.

Alvin Sargent is lean, trim, healthy, and looks a lot younger than he is. "I don't do well in interviews," he began.

"How many have you given?" I asked.

"One," he replied. "Twenty years ago." Ironically, he went on to explain, the man had just called that morning. I didn't know exactly what to ask, so I suggested we just turn on the tape recorder and see what would happen. Little did I know that's the way he works.

First of all, he told me he didn't start writing until he was thirty-five years old. What did he do before that? "I was in the navy," he began. "That's where I learned how to type. I spent a year in college, then went east to work as an actor. Unsuccessfully. Although, when I came back to Los Angeles and had given up acting, I landed a part in *From Here to Eternity,* directed by Fred Zinnemann, in which I had the pleasure of appearing in a scene with Montgomery Clift; later I was gunned down by a Japanese Zero. That was 1953. End of acting career. [Twenty-five years later Fred Zinnemann directed *Julia.* Anything can happen.]

"I was not a writer at that time and had no aspirations to be one. As a matter of fact, I was just in my first year of a nine-year gig as an ad salesman at *Daily Variety* [Hollywood's trade paper].

"While at *Variety* I wrote a half-hour television script, sold it to an independent TV company, and remained a salesman for seven more years.

"And then, through a friend of mine, I met Sam Adams of the Triad Agency [his agent now for twenty-six years]. Sam read a few sketches I had written and somehow got me a job as a story editor on a television series called *Bus Stop.* I'd only written that one script, and knew almost nothing about writing. But Sam is a great salesman. So after nine years on the newspaper, married, with two children, I quit.

"I knew nothing about being a story editor. I had to ask around what they did. I didn't have time to learn, but it didn't matter because I was fired eight weeks later. I hadn't even met the boss [Roy Huggins, executive producer of *The Fugitive* and later, *Run for Your Life,* among others]. I didn't have a strong urge to write, I wanted only to make a living for my family. I didn't know quite what to do with my life.

"Months went by and then Sam called again and said, 'I got you a job rewriting a *Ben Casey*, a TV drama. Can you do it?' No, I thought. 'Yes,' I said. And that was the start of about five years of television work. *Route 66, Naked City, Alfred Hitchcock Presents, The Nurses*— shows that allowed me to write character.

"After years of television, Sam called again. He got me a job rewriting a movie called *Gambit*, my first feature film. After that Alan Pakula asked me to adapt *The Sterile Cuckoo*, his first film as a director."

I wanted to find out how he worked, so I asked him about *Julia*. He paused for a long moment. "I used to believe that character was everything. I used to start with characters and I would find my story through them. Now I believe that story is everything. I think that's what screenplays are all about, telling a story. Right now I'm concentrating more on trying to think in terms of stories as opposed to characters.

"*Julia* was a short, fragmented 25-page story in Lillian Hellman's *Pentimento*. It was the reality of the story that appealed to me and seemed like a strong dramatic situation. At first I didn't want to do it; I didn't know how to do it.

"There was something about these two women, these girlfriends; they mattered to me. So I would begin to write about them, little exercises; I wasn't sure where to start, I needed to stir up my own people. Sometimes it's necessary to read between the lines of the writer, and pull out a hidden meaning, something's that not said. I remember I played with them by having them tell romantic stories to one another. That started something for me. I decided to have them make a little game out of it, each offering a line; one, then the other, building a romantic tale. It allowed the friendship to develop. Their characters developed. It began only as an exercise, but I came to use it in the film. It's necessary to be playful, to doodle, in order to see things blossom.

"So I developed the girls (my girls) and then I began finding the people around them. All, of course, based on real people, but with a touch of me added. I took the incidents in the novella, played with them, created whole scenes, and then, slowly, the form began to appear. Pieces began to fit together. When you have enough material in front of you then you can begin to see the outline. For me, the outline comes about halfway though the screenplay. As it grows, so does my confidence. In

Julia I began without any sense of what the structure was going to be in this very disorganized piece.

"With *Ordinary People*," he continues, "it was the same process. First I had to own it, make the people mine. I read the book a few times, thought about it for a while. I had to find the essence of what was happening. What was at stake in the relationships. I began by writing a scene that was not in the book. Again an exercise. I had Calvin, the husband [played by Donald Sutherland], come home, park his car in the garage, remain in the car, and just wait. He waited, and I waited. Finally Beth [Mary Tyler Moore] came out of the kitchen. She asks what's wrong, she tells him to come inside. And then out of the blue, Calvin says, "When I went to Buck's [their dead son's] funeral, how come you were worried about what shoes I was wearing that day?" He surprises her with that memory of how she behaved with him on that day. The scene grew. My favorite scene in the movie. It was unpredictable. A surprise to Beth, a surprise to me.

"It was the first scene I wrote. I liked it. I didn't know whether I could use it or not, but it was something I knew I had to have down. It came easily, unexpectedly. It gave me an energy. I could always refer to it when I felt that dreaded sense of deadness in the work. I could go back to a lively core.

"Then I knew I needed a scene between the doctor and the boy, Conrad [Timothy Hutton]; the boy talks about how he reacted when his brother drowned, and I played around with this notion from *The Waltons* [the hit television series created by Earl Hamner, staring Richard Thomas] and found the character wondering what John Boy would say if he had to say something about his brother's death. He related to John Boy. I liked the speech. It was off center and exactly right for the piece. I had another reference point. Now I had two pieces, and knew I could always refer to them for fuel. For truth.

"The way I work would be to take a line, or an interesting piece of dialogue, and then write little pieces, or little scenes around them, so it becomes like a crazy quilt, where I have all these little pieces piled up in a basket next to my desk. When I get a lot of pieces, I say, let's see how I can make some kind of a whole piece out of it, and I begin to lay them out. And pretty soon they begin to take some shape.

"I also know there has to be that one unifying idea the entire film relates to. That's something in your soul, I guess; where you can write a scene and say, does this ring true to whatever this story is about? If it doesn't, you have to let it go, discard it [file it, don't throw it away]. Always there is a core. Everything must relate to it. Always.

"The writing process is about trusting your own instincts. About allowing your imagination to take you places you might be afraid to go; you have to go over the line, allow for the outrageous, nonsense. Sense comes out of nonsense. Good writing, I think, is about doing something nobody expects you to do; people go to the movies to see something they can't see on the street.

"The act of writing a screenplay is exactly like the act of seeing a movie; there must be no more written on the page than what you see or hear on the screen. As soon as it becomes more than that it becomes your prose or your poetry and has nothing to do with writing the screenplay form.

"If you go deep into somebody's mind or heart, then you're going to interest people, make them a little uncomfortable. Make them as uncomfortable and as curious as possible with the truth."

I thought about that for a while. I remember when I first started thinking about writing screenplays; I had just graduated from UC Berkeley, and under Jean Renoir's direction, was at the UCLA Film School (I left after a year because I felt it was too academic). Coming from an English literature background at Berkeley in the '60s, being influenced by Eugene O'Neill, Henrik Ibsen, and James Joyce, and involved in the revolution going on in this country at the time, I wanted the theater seats to be like an electric chair, wired to jolt and jar the complacency of the audience and engage them in an uncomfortable manner; to make them think and respond and react. I understood what Sargent was talking about.

"But that raises another question," he continues. "How do you know it works? What works for you might not work for me. It's all about what you want it to be and what your perception of something is. If what you put down on that paper connects to what you feel, you know that's the truth. Now, you may have to dramatize it a little more effectively, play with it a little more in a nice way, or an exciting way, really make love to it to make it yours. Don't just make it neat and clean. When a producer says to me, 'We need a little "polish" on this material,' I cringe. It's the worst thing he can want because he wants you to take that script you have in your hand and make it nice, safe, and flawless, unlike life.

"In other words, boring and predictable.

"It's always the rough edges that make something work," he goes on. "Everything is flawed. Flawed lives. Flawed romances. Flawed plans. Pity the flawless. When you see the flaws in anybody's character, even the way a story's going, there's something to be said for not making everything so damned right.

"So you write something, then read it; you know it's wrong, but you like it; it feels right. So you keep it. And then somebody will say, well, we don't need that scene. I say, I know you don't need it, but that's the very line that sparked you to get this whole project off the ground, the line that made you really love it. That's what you responded to; it's like meeting someone new and it's this little scar here, or a birthmark there, or the way she walks, that really makes you want to see her again.

"And when you put it on screen people love it."

It's so true. Jean Renoir used to say over and over again, "Perfection exists only in the mind, not in reality." We always want everything we do to be perfect; the way we look, the way we dress, the impression we create. But that's not revealing the truth about ourselves; it's simply presenting an "image" of what we want somebody to see. We are "perfect the way we are" say the teachers of the eastern philosophies; in other words, we are perfect in our imperfection.

This point of view is what makes Sargent's work singular and distinctive. Nowhere is this more clear than in his screenplay of *Ordinary People*. Adapted from the novel by Judith Guest, *Ordinary People* is the story of a young man (Timothy Hutton) struggling to free himself from a blanket of guilt after the death of his older brother, and his relationship with his parents; it is a moving and eloquent portrayal of a family under crisis.

The screenplay is a wonderful reading experience. Everything is there for a purpose. Whether it be the way the contents of the refrigerator are described, "orderly, and neat as a pin," reflecting Beth's (Mary Tyler Moore's) character, or the question the English teacher asks Timothy

Hutton about Thomas Hardy's classic novel, *Jude the Obscure*: "Is Jude powerless in the grip of circumstances, or could he have helped himself?"

"I guess he thought he was," Conrad replies, thus illuminating his own dilemma. At this moment in his life (he has just been released from a mental hospital where he tried to "off" himself by slitting his wrists), Conrad feels powerless, caught in the grip of circumstances. His answer forecasts his own journey to mental health, and sets up the relationship with Dr. Berger, played by Judd Hirsch.

"There was a lot of the doctor in the book," Sargent goes on, "and I was fortunate to know a doctor I could draw upon who was very much like that. I related to the boy but I related more to the doctor. The relationship between the doctor and the boy allowed Conrad to open up more, so I could explore areas that I enjoy writing about.

"More than anyone I related to Calvin, the father, and what was going on in his head. I understood the mother perfectly. It seems each viewer focuses strongly on one specific character in that film. Mostly the mother."

Conrad has a hard time expressing himself. "Sometimes I lose it," he confides to Dr. Berger. "I just can't figure out what I'm supposed to do. What I'm supposed to wear in the morning. And that scares me."

When he quits the swimming team, his self-image is so low that he's afraid to tell his parents about it because there's a "tradition" of swimming in the family. He appears to be on a collision course with that self-destructive attitude that led to his suicide attempt.

If you go into *Ordinary People* and examine the relationships that are woven throughout the script, you find strong, intimate portrayals that are emotionally moving and insightful. For example, the mother-son relationship between Conrad and Beth is wonderful. A screenplay is a story told in pictures, and nowhere is this better illustrated than in the scenes that reveal the dynamics of this relationship.

In one scene, Conrad has come home early and surprises his mother, who is sitting alone in Buck's room, still kept the same as it was when he was alive. "It was just an exercise scene," Sargent says. "I just asked myself what would happen if Conrad suddenly walked in and surprised her. It told me something about Beth. Another reference point. Finally, every scene is a reference point."

The result is a lesson in screenwriting. First, she's startled, then cold and angry that Conrad walked in on her like that. He tries to "talk" to her, to connect with her, but she shuts down and moves to her own room, leaving Conrad isolated and alone. He goes to his room and "sits on the side of the bed. He doubles over, arms crossed, pressed against his waist. He falls back on the bed, stares at the ceiling. Closes his eyes, not allowing himself to cry."

"For every action, there is an equal and opposite reaction," states Newton's third law of motion. The subtext, what's not said in the scene, shows us more about this relationship than dialogue ever could: Conrad, desperately reaching out to his mother for help and support, while she suffers silently. Conrad is alive, but Buck, her favorite son, is not. It's a wonderful display of cinematic subtext.

The scene I personally like the best, however, is where Conrad, Beth, and Calvin are visiting her parents for dinner on a Sunday afternoon. They are taking pictures, and Calvin wants to take a picture of Beth and Conrad together. Conrad is willing, but Beth is reluctant. As Calvin fiddles with the camera Beth grits her teeth and says, "Do it." When Calvin can't get it together, Beth breaks the pose and tries to wrestle the camera away from him. He resists, trying to get a picture of mother and son. But she wants the camera. Finally, Conrad shouts angrily, "Give her the goddamn camera!"

Silence. Everything stops.

"Calvin is still," the script reads. "Beth hesitates a moment; then, as if it had never happened, takes the camera away from him. Calvin looks at Conrad, standing alone, then at Beth, now setting the camera. Calvin looks at Beth, disturbed."

Calvin sees Beth with new eyes, and his insight will affect their entire relationship. In that one scene we have visually dramatized the emotional "portrait" of the family: Beth, angry that Conrad is alive; Calvin, placating, trying to keep the family together; and Conrad, angry at himself because he's alive and Buck is dead. Mother and son are very much alike. It is a great scene.

Alvin Sargent still types on a manual typewriter, and "then I make marks and arrows on the page until there's some kind of life on the paper. There's more life on a piece of paper when you do it that way than there is on the screen sometimes. I think if you can take the energy that's on the paper and put that on the screen, I think you just might have a more exciting screenplay. If a director can pick up the writer's energy, then there is pure collaboration.

"I'm finding some pages now that are so marked up, they fascinate me just to look at them. You can hardly read them, but it's not about what you read, it's about what you see. I framed one of these pages. It's really rather startling just to look at. I'm going to frame a series of these pages to hopefully illuminate the process of writing before the word processor eliminates all memories of this process, where you can see what is actually going through the writer's mind. All the anxiety is there; all the doodling and crossed-out words have something to do with what you're trying to make happen, or allow to happen. Strange, but all of that mess appears to represent resistance, when all it's intended to do is break down resistance.

"It's a very organic process."

At present, Sargent is adapting a novel called *Anywhere But Here,* by Mona Simpson, about a mother-daughter relationship. "I think screenplays are like dreams, or jokes," Sargent says. "The structure of a screenplay is edited the same way a joke is. If you tell a joke, you say: a guy walked in the door and a lady was behind the counter, and he walks up to her and says, there's a parade down the street, or whatever; you tell it quickly, and it's beautifully edited. No deadwood. When you retell your dreams they're all edited and visual, the perfect display of what a screenplay is. If you have the freedom in a screenplay that you have in a dream, with all the confusion and interest, if you think of a screenplay like that, you can dig as deep as you want, and be as outrageous as you want.

"When I'm writing, as I go to bed, I'll ask myself where are my characters tonight as I sleep? Where are they? Forget the script, but what are they really doing? Where are they sleeping tonight? Who's with them? When I wrote *Paper Moon,* I always wondered, Where is Mose tonight? Is he out with a woman? What's she doing? Where are they eating dinner? Where are they sleeping? Is Addie out of cigarettes? So I'll go to bed, and when I wake up, they'll wake up with me.

"I wonder all day long where they are and what they're doing. I'll drive down the street and see somebody sitting on a bench or waiting for a bus and I'll wonder about my own people; maybe they'll be on the bus. Any number of things could be going on with them.

"When the work is succeeding, the process has you always in touch. When you've touched the heart, the truth, then everything relates to your work.

"Screenwriting is a process that's larger than you are; it must need you as much as you need it."

16

James L. Brooks

On research: *"Mama's always right.*

When *The Mary Tyler Moore Show* first appeared on television in the early '70s, it revolutionized the half-hour situation comedy. Starring Mary Tyler Moore, Ed Asner, Valerie Harper, Cloris Leachman, and Ted Knight (as the lovable, inept TV anchorman), *The Mary Tyler Moore Show* was television at its ultimate, wackiest best.

Created by James L. Brooks and Allan Burns, *The Mary Tyler Moore Show* graced our screens for seven years and spawned a style of television comedy that was new, refreshing, and novel. The characters were so strong and vivid, so memorable, that new series were created around them; Valerie Harper went on to *Rhoda,* Ed Asner to *Lou Grant,* and Cloris Leachman to *Phyllis*.

What James Brooks does best is create characters, real people in real situations; people with feelings, emotions, and fears, people who are brave, vulnerable, and funny, people who linger in our memory with warmth and affection.

When *Terms of Endearment* opened in movie theaters across the country, its effect was immediate. Winning five Academy Awards, the film catapulted James L. Brooks into the national spotlight.

A few years later came *Broadcast News*. Besides being a critical and financial success, *Broadcast News* was splashed across the covers of *Newsweek* and other national magazines, sparking waves of controversy within the television news industry.

Terms of Endearment and *Broadcast News* illuminate different aspects of American society. *Terms of Endearment,* adapted from the novel by Larry McMurtry, explored the wonderful relationship between a mother and daughter (Shirley MacLaine and Debra Winger) and was an insightful, emotionally rewarding film. *Broadcast News,* a triangle story with a difference, examined a contemporary woman of the '80s, a new kind of heroine in American life.

James L. Brooks began his career as a page boy–usher, moved up to copy boy, then became a newswriter at CBS in New York. In 1965 he moved to L.A. and began working for David L. Wolper. That's when I first met him, and we worked on several shows together. But his dream was always to write comedy.

In his spare time he wrote a spec script for a TV series called *My Mother the Car* starring Jerry Van Dyke. He showed me his first draft and I still remember thinking how original and bizarre it was. Like so many others before and after him, he didn't sell that spec script, but the experience led him to Allan Burns, and a short time later they became collaborators.

It was during this time his series idea, *Room 222,* was picked up by Gene Reynolds, the producer-writer of the TV series *M*A*S*H,* and Brooks entered the world of series television. Then came *The Mary Tyler Moore Show*, which ran for seven years and earned Brooks four Emmys. This was followed by *Taxi* (cocreated with David Davis, Ed. Weinberger, and Stan Daniels) which ran for five years and won him three Emmys.

His first feature, *Thursday's Game,* a TV movie he wrote and produced, starred Gene Wilder, Bob Newhart, Ellen Burstyn, and Cloris Leachman.

In the mid-seventies, Brooks, going through a divorce, adapted Dan Wakefield's scathing, humorous novel *Starting Over;* it starred Burt Reynolds, Jill Clayburgh, and Candice Bergen. As he was writing the script, he says, "I got the first feeling in my life of wanting to direct. I had always been definite about not wanting to direct before that."

It was also about this time that he started thinking about a mother-daughter relationship. A short time later Jennifer Jones sent him a novel by Larry McMurtry; it was called *Terms of Endearment.* It was one of the few times, Brooks says, "that I cried reading something." He was referring to Emma's (Debra Winger's) speech to one of her sons in the hospital before she died. The speech reveals a masterful insight into the state of mind of a child whose mother is going to die. Emma's trying to give him something to remember:

> I know you like me, I know it. The last year or two you've been pretending like you hate me. I love you as I love myself, and in a few years, when I haven't been around to be on your tail about something, or irritating you, you're going to remember. . . . You're going to remember the time I bought you the baseball glove when you thought we were too broke; or when I read you those stories; or when I let you goof off instead of mowing the lawn, lots of things like that. And you're going to realize that you love me; and maybe you're going to feel badly because you never told me, but don't. I know that you love me, so don't ever do that to yourself.

The first time I saw *Terms of Endearment*, that particular scene brought up a childhood memory of my own; I was twelve, visiting my father in the hospital, and suddenly understood that he was going to die. I responded to Emma's words immediately, wishing my father could have said something like that to me. But he couldn't.

This speech is what Jim Brooks initially responded to when he read the book. It's that kind of feeling, or reaction, that sparks filmmakers [and all other artists for that matter] to make a full-time commitment to see their vision realized.

But there's a natural law about that kind of commitment; the first thing that usually happens is that the universe tests you on it. With *Terms of Endearment* the first obstacle was acquiring the rights to the book. It was a long and involved process because Brooks knew the only way he could be true to himself and his vision was to gain complete control of the material. When you adapt a novel into a screenplay, you must approach it as an original screenplay *based* on other material. And sometimes the novelist doesn't agree with the screenwriter's approach.

In this case, ''Larry McMurtry and I spent about three hours together,'' Brooks says, ''and basically all he said was 'I already wrote my book, now you go and do your movie.'

"It was very liberating, because I wanted to make *Terms of Endearment* a comedy; otherwise it wouldn't work for me. What I had to do in order to give it a narrative drive was generate a romance with a beginning, middle, and end. That gave it a structure, and if I didn't do that the story would have just been about two people who are together and then one of them gets ill."

The second obstacle was that *Terms of Endearment* was a hard sell. After a lengthy legal process to obtain the rights, Paramount finally committed to the project with one stipulation: the movie's budget was not to exceed $7.5 million. That created a problem because "in order to truly do the picture right," Brooks says, "it would have to go on location in Houston, and that meant it would cost $8.5 million. And Paramount was absolutely unwilling to put up that extra million."

Most people in Hollywood would shrug their shoulders, accept the studio's terms, and end up compromising. But that's not the way James L. Brooks works. If you do something, you better do it right; you don't spend two years of your life making a movie you don't want to make. That's not what it's about. He began to raise the extra million.

And that took him two years. "Asking people for money is an awful thing to do," he recalls, "and to do it for two years constantly, day in and day out, and keep on getting rejected, is rough. At a certain point it's not that different from asking for it personally. It's not like 'Will you invest in my movie?' It's 'Will you loan me the money?' That's what it feels like."

I asked him how he managed to keep his perspective while he was trying to raise the money. Rejection is a difficult emotion to deal with, but common with any creative endeavor. How did Brooks do it?

"I was good at serving the work," he states. "I was good at swallowing whatever doubts and feelings I had, and then simply asking in every way I could. For example, I used to go to the agent's office before anybody came in so nobody could avoid me. I was good at doing whatever was necessary.

"It was during this time that Paramount let the project go. UA was interested for a time, but there was a big shake-up in the organization and all the executives were replaced, so I was back out on the street again.

"Finally, MTM Productions came forward with a million dollars and

NBC came forward to guarantee they would buy it for TV. And with those two events, Paramount went forward."

There were other obstacles as well. "During the writing—actually about ninety pages into the first draft," he recalls, "there was a moment when I knew it wasn't working and I couldn't go forward, and it was too late to back out. Paramount had done this terrific thing when they optioned the book for me, but when the option ran out they either had to buy the book or let it go.

"I asked them to buy the book without letting them read any of my pages, because I wasn't ready to show anything. And once they did I no longer believed I had the option of abandoning it. But at the same time I couldn't go forward with it either.

"I was stuck. It was a period in my life that seems to be four lifetimes in hell, one of those miserable periods we all go through at one time or another. And during that time I suddenly started blushing. I'd just turn beet red for half an hour and I'd never know when or where it was going to happen; it just came out of nowhere.

"One day I was talking to a very gifted pianist, and he mentioned that before he played in front of a large audience he, too, experienced the blushing. He even had a name for it: he called it "a state of shame." For some strange reason the fact that there was a name for the condition made me feel a little better. He said he didn't feel worthy enough to have so many people paying so much money to hear *him* play. As soon as he said that I realized I was simply embarrassed by my inability to figure out how to go forward with this material.

"That's when I had my first major breakthrough; it was a rule, really, one of those little rules you follow that nobody ever notices, but really helps in the writing. And that was 'Mama's always right.' No matter what Aurora [Shirley MacLaine] says, no matter how horrendous or how awful it is, Mama's always right. And that did it; that rule freed me from the block, and the blushing stopped immediately.

"Once I achieved that insight, I dug a little deeper and found the real problem. What was the nature of Emma's [Debra Winger's] heroism? It seemed silly to do a picture that declares somebody a hero simply because they get sick. That's not the nature of heroism.

"What finally clicked and seemed to be the basis of her character was when I realized Emma was the least judgmental person I'd ever experienced. She made no judgments about anything. She was heroic in her acceptance of people as they were, her mother, husband, lover, friends, children; she never manipulated or attempted to force anyone to change their ways. She knew her feelings, was aware of her judgments and opinions, but she never judged anybody else.

"I even wondered, in terms of my relationship with her, whether Emma would like me or not. If anything, she'd probably think I made too big a deal about everything, and had a tendency to overdramatize and become too intense.

"That was something that was hard for me to accept, but it helped me enormously in my relationship to her character. To this day, I'll quote Emma; for example, just the other day I was having a conversation with someone and they started criticizing another person, taking cheap shots at them, and I found myself saying, 'Anybody can do that to anyone, about anything.' That's one of Emma's lines.

"When you're adapting a book you're in an incredible void. I used to feel Larry McMurtry as a presence, and whenever I was stuck I would pick up the novel and read it and try and have my thoughts jangled."

I asked him, since this was his first directorial effort, how he prepared for the filming.

"I watched *The Best Years of Our Lives* a lot [William Wyler's masterful film about veterans returning home after World War II, starring Fredric March, Myrna Loy, and Teresa Wright, adapted by Robert E. Sherwood from MacKinlay Kantor's *Glory for Me*], and when you see that picture everybody on screen is delivered. Everybody. Virginia Mayo is the best she's ever been, extraordinary. I think one of the most important questions you ask yourself when you're preparing is 'What do I want my movie to do?' As I sat watching *The Best Years of Our Lives* I knew my answer: I wanted to be able to deliver characters that linger in your memory.

"That was my start point. Then I had to deal with the fact that I was adapting a book by one of the great Texas writers and I had never even been in Houston, never even been in the state.

"I come from a journalism background, and I remember when we first started working on *Taxi,* we owed everything to the research we did during this one forty-eight-hour stretch at a taxi garage. All these great things happened right in front of us.

"Originally, Gene Reynolds had driven me crazy in *Room 222* getting me to do research, forever hanging out at this high school, so research is a big deal with me. What it can do is give you certain specifics outside yourself to serve.

"When I went to Houston and began to spend time there, the feeling grew that it was as much Middle America as Texas. It was all my fantasies about those Mickey Rooney and Judy Garland movies. And that's where the boy next door comes from, the Jack Nicholson character.

"I spent a long time interviewing a lot of women, just to get ideas about Emma and Aurora. For some reason the feeling of family seemed important in Texas, important in a way I'd never experienced before.

"For example, I was interviewing a woman of fifty at the end of the day when the house was empty, and I could actually feel the loneliness; it was palpable. Somebody could say that the problem of a woman living alone in her fifties is loneliness. But that's a meaningless phrase. If you're actually in the room, you feel it as a force; it humbles you, and gives you something that's profoundly human. You've got to respect that and not abuse it in the writing. It just doesn't give you a fact; it gives you a sense of mission. And that's what research is all about.

"From Houston I went to Nebraska," he continues, "also for the first time in my life. Here I was, wanting to interview young academics, staying at this preposterous place; it was so noisy, I couldn't work and I couldn't think. There were video games downstairs, people swimming right outside my door; the noise was everywhere. I got angry. 'Why am I staying here?' I asked myself. I can't get any work done because it's so noisy, and suddenly it hit me; this is where Aurora would stay if she were visiting Emma. And that became our location. It only happened out of research.

"When I interviewed an academic in Nebraska, I tried to get an idea of what his house would be like. If you're sitting in someone's house and know what it looks like, you're not going to accept something less when it comes time to shoot.

"You have to feel the air, feel what your characters feel. That's the whole reason for shooting on location.

"That's why research is so important."

The key to all research is patience and persistence and keeping an open mind so your expectations about what you would like to find don't distort the information you do find. You have to be a sponge, absorbing everything.

When I was working for David Wolper, I did both film and text research. One time I was working on a network special about Grace Kelly. Not much had been written about her at that time, and early footage on her was nonexistent. I called her publicist, and during our conversation he casually mentioned the name of a fashion photographer in New York she had modeled for. So I called the photographer, and he referred me to another photographer, who referred me to someone else, and so on. I filled up two pages of a legal-sized pad with names and phone numbers, and I just kept calling and calling and calling.

And then, when I least expected it, a photographer in New York told me he had some early stills of her. He sent proofs of what he had, and they turned out to be the very first modeling shots she had ever taken. She was seventeen years old and had just come from Philadelphia to New York seeking a career as a model. It was quite a find.

The only way I got those pictures was to keep on asking questions, because everybody knows somebody, who knows somebody, who knows somebody, and that's always your start point.

"With *Broadcast News* I did more research than I've ever done in my life," Brooks continues. "I knew I wanted to do a romantic comedy, and I thought we should look for a new kind of heroine, the kind of person you could only track through her work, the end product of a social movement, yet not part of any movement.

"Her age became very specific, because I wanted to write about change; everything's changing; it's happening in motion pictures, in the media, in music, and everywhere else. In relationships, especially."

The first thing he had to do was find his main character. "I had come from the broadcast industry, and things there had changed so much that I was totally ignorant of the current state, so I spent two years doing research. Then I spent a year writing. But during those two years of research there's always some writing you're doing; you're taking notes, you're thinking up scenes, you're writing bits and pieces of dialogue.

"One of the things I decided to do was make sure the picture would not declare a hero. I wanted to do each character fully and leave the question of who was or was not a hero totally to subjective opinion. I wasn't going to make that call. Nor would I make a call about what the news business should be about.

"That was my frame of reference when I started writing. And then I found I didn't like any of the characters. Here I was, halfway through the script, writing for more than six months, and I didn't like the people I'm writing. At that point, I had to decide whether to go back and make them more likable, lovable, vulnerable, or accessible; all the things they weren't.

"But as a writer you have to ask yourself, 'Should I be truthful? Or should I respect the fact that I'm in the writing process, and perhaps not liking the character is a legitimate part of that process because of the juncture I am at in the story?'

"With *Broadcast News* I decided to stay with it, and endured not liking Tom, Jane, and Aaron. And by the time I got to the end, I had gotten all my own confusion and ambivalence into the screenplay without realizing it.

"That was especially true with the ending. I knew the characters fully; there are people I met doing this research that I spoke to a couple of times a week for two years. And during the filming I felt if we all did our jobs as honestly as we could, and we all worked very hard, we could absolutely be true to each moment and not worry about where we were headed. I write in continuity and I film in continuity, and both William Hurt and Albert Brooks knew all along that Jane might end up with either one of them, so that gave a certain abandon to every scene we did; there was no wrong way for it to go from the story's point of view.

"From the writing point of view, when I saw one of the relationships start to rise head and shoulders above the other, or when a character started to dominate the screenplay, I'd try to push that character back and bring the other two forward, to keep it as even as I could.

"If you're going to do a triangle story, then do it. Keep it even. Keep every line and corner the same. That made it very difficult, but at the same time I think it gave a certain atmosphere to our work. If Aaron [Albert Brooks] and Jane [Holly Hunter] seemed wonderful together, you weren't in trouble. And you weren't in trouble if Tom [William Hurt] and

Jane seemed wonderful together. Because there was no specific end we were trying to reach, no finish line we were trying to manipulate towards. Whatever happened, happened.

"Of course, what I hoped would happen is that Jane would end up with one of them. That the picture would dictate the ending. When I got to that point, and had to create an ending, I could not write a scene that seemed honest with Jane ending up with either one of them. I tried. In the filming, I shot half a scene, looked at it, and knew it didn't work. At one point I had Jane run and get on the plane with Tom. I didn't even have to look at the footage; it just looked preposterous to me when it happened. I filmed a scene with Tom when he came back and got in her cab. It didn't work. It seemed to be what it was, simply a device to end the movie in a way people were likely to approve of."

When I saw the film I was moved and saddened by the ending. I had wanted so much for Jane to get together with either Tom or Aaron, and when that didn't happen, I felt sad. I didn't know why.

But when I thought about it, I remembered the water fights we used to have when I was working for David Wolper; or staying in the editing room for seventy-two hours straight in order to deliver a show to the network on time; or the times when our narrator was recording downstairs, and we had less than an hour to write the entire second act. All those moments we enjoyed brought us into a community of shared emotion. At that moment, at that place and time, we were family. When the experience was over, the show complete, we all went our separate ways, and often did not see each other for years.

I hadn't seen Jim Brooks for several years when I ran into him at a basketball game one night. Yet there was a time we had worked closely together. I remember after I had left Wolper, writing my first screenplay on assignment (under deadline naturally), he called and "persuaded" me to leave the script and toss a football around. Reluctantly, I went (I was stuck on a scene and was absolutely relieved to get away); we went to the park and got into a touch football game with some kids, and I ended up tearing the cartilage in my knee. I wound up in the hospital, and wearing a leg cast for six weeks. Memories.

I thought back about those times, and realized that's the way it is in Hollywood. People work together in an intense situation, for weeks, months, sometimes years, and when it's all over, everyone goes their separate ways, and it may be years before you see them again. It is shared experience.

I recognized that feeling when I saw the end of *Broadcast News;* it was sad, yes, because I wanted Jane to end up with one of those characters, but she didn't.

Everybody went their separate ways. Like life, the big L. That made it very real for me, and that's why I responded on an emotional level.

Is that what he was striving for? "What I hoped would come out of all this is that the picture would inform the participants," says Brooks. "That the picture would say something to us we didn't know when we started, say something about whether the concept of romance had changed or not.

"I don't know whether it did. I think we show that there are practical considerations when it comes to love and romance, and that a career makes romance a narrower and more difficult experience.

"A few weeks before the picture came out," Brooks continues, "I looked at it and realized it was a picture about three people who miss the last chance of their lives at real intimacy with another human being.

"I didn't set out to write that, but I think that's what the picture ended up being about. You know, it might all be some kind of romantic illusion that life is full of choices.

"Everything wonderful in the picture was in and out in postproduction," Brooks goes on, "because that's how crazy it was. I knew the picture couldn't succeed without Aaron's flop [sweat] scene but I couldn't make it work, so I took it out for a day. And I knew it was so important that I couldn't take it out. I can't tell you the kind of energy and work that went into that scene. Finally, I separated it from the rest of the picture and just had one editing room devoted to the sweat scene simply to make it work. I finally moved one piece within the scene, and everything just fell together.

"It was the same with Jane's crying. There were three or four times in my research when women brought up the fact that they cry at work. And if you hear something that many times, you assume it's accurate. Nobody told me they scheduled a time for crying, but it just seemed like a smart thing for her to do. I became very attached to it. Before *Broadcast News* came out I was afraid that somebody would come out with the observation that a contemporary woman spends a fair amount of time crying; I was so afraid someone would do that before me. You become possessive about this kind of thing.

"It also was in and out of the picture. During the main titles, the audience is confused and in the dark because they have no understanding about how they're supposed to feel about this woman who unexpectedly breaks into tears and then goes on as if nothing has taken place. Should you feel sorry for her or not? It's not funny and it's not sad, yet she seems sad.

"The second time she cries it became more intriguing because it revealed an aspect of character rather than story. The third time she cries the audience laughs with her; that key laugh finally happened in the third preview and we celebrated because we knew the audience understood and accepted Jane Craig. They may not have loved her, but they understood her.

"When you're writing something, everything becomes subjective, and at some point you really don't know what's working or what's not working. It sounds easy, and it's such a great illusion to say to yourself, 'All I have to do is write three pages a day and in 40 days I'll have 120 pages.'

"But then you have these traps you fall into. I'd hole up, write five pages, and call friends to read the pages to see whether they were working or not. I got a lot of encouragement from friends."

What struck me about *Broadcast News* is the way the media can "sell" a person, a product, or an event to the American public. Just look at our presidential campaigns. Everything, it seems, is a sell job; we're more interested in the image of something than what's underneath it.

Whether it be a screenplay, a bar of soap, a new car, the American Dream, or the notion of romance, everything we do is designed to sell; to convince someone that what we're offering them will make them feel good, help them make a lot of money, or lead to fame and fortune.

It's the same with the television news industry. What is news? Jim Brooks seems to ask. Is it those little snippets of information we receive each night, glossed over with a slick narration, or a detailed examination into the cause and effect of an event?

Take your pick. "The world is as we see it," says the *Yoga Vasistha*. And things are changing every day.

17

Anna Hamilton Phelan

On development: "Just like manna from heaven."

In 1984, the noted primatologist Dian Fossey sold the rights to her book *Gorillas in the Mist* to Universal Studios. Fossey, a self-taught authority on the mountain gorilla, had been studying the gorillas in Rwanda, Africa. She was more crusader than scientist, a woman single-minded in her campaign to save the mountain gorillas in danger of extinction because of the indiscriminate slaughter by poachers.

When they bought the book she suggested to the studio executives at the time that her part be played by Brooke Shields as a young woman and Elizabeth Taylor as an adult.

Anna Hamilton Phelan, who had written *Mask* while she was a student of mine, was called by Frank Price, then head of Universal Pictures, and offered the job of writing the screenplay for *Gorillas in the Mist*.

Anna Hamilton Phelan graduated from Emerson College in Boston with a degree in theater arts, then migrated to New York to become an actress. After several auditions, she realized she would never get any-where reading the same monologues that all actors read, so she decided to write her own. Soon, her monologues became so good that other actors began asking her if she would write something for them. She agreed: for $25 she would write a monologue that would be tailored for that specific actor, and for $50 she would write a scene, also specifically designed for the actor. And "if they got the job, they agreed to buy me dinner," she says.

After several seasons of off-Broadway theater and East Coast summer stock, she came to Los Angeles and worked as an actress in TV. She was usually cast as a dumb blonde or a hooker; when they started casting her as a madam, she realized her days as an actress were numbered. So she compiled her writings with those of noted feminists, and came up with a one-woman show called *Corsages and Ketchup,* which she toured with during the early '70s.

For the next ten years she raised her children, and it was during this time that she was trained as a genetic counselor at Harbor General Hospital. One of the patients there was a young man named Rocky Dennis. She was so taken with Rocky and his mother, Rusty Dennis, that she optioned the rights to their story, which eventually became *Mask.*

During one of my special four-session workshops she wrote a screenplay called *Healing,* about a doctor who learns she has cancer. I knew from her execution of that situation that she had a great deal of talent. That script has been optioned several times but as of this writing is still unproduced.

The next year she took a couple of seven-week workshops, during which she wrote *Mask.* The film, starring Cher and Eric Stoltz, made her one of Hollywood's "hottest" writers.

When Phelan read Dian Fossey's book, she found it to be "really a scientific study, a textbook, with charts and graphs, and while there were incidents that were interesting, I passed on the project. 'I write dialogue,' I said, 'and there's no story here.'

"About a year and a half later," she recalls, "I opened a national magazine and saw a news article about the murder of Dian Fossey. I read the article, and one thing grabbed me immediately: in the closet of her little cabin high in the Virunga Mountain Range, in the deepest, darkest part of Africa, this woman had several ball gowns and a green satin dress. There was also caviar, expensive Scotch, and other things you wouldn't expect to find. I thought to myself, What's going on here? There was nothing like that in the *Gorillas in the Mist* book. So I started thinking, maybe there really is something here, a real story, a real character.

"So I asked my agent what happened to the Dian Fossey project. And my agent replied, 'It's funny you should mention it because a producer is now attached to it, and he came to us and asked if you would write it, and we said no, you had already passed on it about a year and a half ago.'

"I said, 'I better talk to this man now because this is a whole different ballgame and I'd like to know a little bit more about this woman.'

"So I met with Arnold Glimcher, the producer who had obtained the rights to the Fossey book, and owner of the Pace Gallery in New York, and we talked and he asked if I would write the script. At that time I was interested, and that's about all. There was no way I was going to do this project unless I could really find out who she was. So I said let me think about it, which I did, and then Universal said they'd send me to Africa to do research if that would help me.

"So I said yes.

"It was really interesting. The studio happened to have the rights to a book that nobody was doing anything about. In fact, it was described by a studio executive as being like 'manna from heaven.' Here you have this book that's languishing on your shelf, and the woman dies a very bizarre death, so all of a sudden you have this very hot property that wasn't hot before her death. Which was true. Because I felt that way too.

"I went to Africa in June and researched Dian Fossey through the eyes of other people, speaking to students who had worked with her and friends who had known her. I was able to spend a week at Karisoke, her campsite. It was very bizarre, because I was sleeping about a hundred yards from where she had been murdered. I slept fully clothed with my rosary wrapped around my hand.

"During the day I sat for hours next to her grave. She's buried with one of her gorillas in a cemetery a few yards from her cabin.

"I was really confused, because I couldn't find anyone who said anything positive about this woman, and I had to find something redeeming about her as a character, not only as a person who saved the gorillas.

"Everyone except Roz Carr [later portrayed by Julie Harris] hated this woman. She was a tough cookie. She had lived for about fifteen years in this incredibly isolated place which was like a haunted forest. It's on the equator with big volcanic cones around it and the weather is cold, humid and rainy, and totally isolated. She was a heavy smoker and drinker, and over those fifteen years her physical and mental health gradually declined.

"But I loved her. She had an intensity I was drawn to. When I interviewed people I'd say, 'What's the one word you remember about her?' and they would say, 'Her passion.' She was extremely passionate. And she had many lovers.

"But the big love of her life was Bob Campbell [played by Bryan Brown].

"When I returned from Africa, I started writing the first draft. I knew the story well, and I structured it on the paradigm [see *The Screenwriter's Workbook*] when I was flying home. I did my index cards, then sat down and wrote a very fast draft in about five weeks.

"I gave it to Arnold Glimcher; he read it, liked it, had one suggestion which I agreed with; then he took it to Universal. A few weeks later I get a call from the head of the studio saying, 'This is a home run. I'll see you at the premiere.' I was very pleased.

"At this time a trade paper ad came out from Peter Guber and Jon Peters of Guber-Peters Production Company at Warner Bros., saying they had just hired Bob Rafelson [who directed *Five Easy Pieces,* written by Carole Eastman a.k.a. Adrien Joyce, one of best films of the '70s,] to direct their picture called *Heaven and Earth,* a script also based on the life of Dian Fossey.''

So began the period of infighting known in Hollywood as the "gorilla wars." Warners donated a large sum of money to the African Wildlife Foundation to secure its assistance in filming the gorillas, while Universal hired Rick Baker, the famous makeup expert, to build radio-controlled "gorillas" for the two scenes where the animals are slaughtered by poachers. Both studios spent about $4 million before one frame of film was shot.

At the same time Skip Steloff, who owns Heritage Entertainment, an independent production company, bought the rights to Fossey's story from her parents and Cornell University, which financed much of her research. They also bought the rights to the book about Fossey called *Woman in the Mists,* by Farley Mowat, for a proposed CBS miniseries.

Heritage sued Universal, and they both ended up in court fighting for the rights to Fossey's diaries and other objects. (The court case was finally won by Heritage after *Gorillas in the Mist* was made.)

"Now two major studios and one independent company are all going for the same story,'' Phelan continues. ''The studios decided rather than make two separate pictures, they should join forces and make the picture together.

''That meant two studios and three producers: Arnold Glimcher, Peter Guber, and Jon Peters. They decided to work together on the project, with Guber-Peters being the executive producers and Arnold Glimcher the producer. And they would use my screenplay, but since I had already delivered my contractual draft along with a set of revisions, I knew I could be 'terminated' by the new producers, whom I'd never met. I didn't want that to happen.

''So I called Peter Guber's office, introduced myself, and told his secretary I was going to be on the lot next Tuesday, and I'd love to stop in and say hello to him. I was not really going to be on the lot, but I needed to get in to see him to make sure I stayed on the project. So I called a friend who got me a studio pass, and I went into Guber's office, waited until he could see me, walked in, and said, 'If you don't continue to use me on this project, you're crazy. I know it's your decision, but I really know this character.'

''Peter Guber looked at me, smiled, and said, 'You've got balls, coming in here like this. I like that, that shows me a lot. Let's go with this.'

''It sounds crazy now, but I really don't know what would have happened if I hadn't made this little visit to Peter's office. He may have brought on another writer, someone he knew.

''I was determined that nobody was going to get rid of me on this script. I was willing to sneak onto a studio lot and tell a producer like Peter Guber that he's crazy if he doesn't use me, that I was going to write this script no matter what they did to me. If they wanted to fire me they couldn't, because they'd have to get somebody to pick me up and throw me out the door. I was going to stay on this project no matter what.

''That's when I really got on it. I became just like Dian Fossey. During this time my friends told me I started walking like her; I literally became her, stubborn and ornery and steadfast as hell.''

Actors do this all the time. If you talk to an actor's wife, husband, lover, or friend, you'll hear how impossible they are to be with when they're preparing for a role, or in their character. Writers go through this general metamorphosis as well, searching and probing their creative self for the characters who are struggling for life.

When the character finally "clicks" into place, it's the most wonderful feeling in the world. Everything slides into place with almost no effort; you're literally in a state of grace.

Of course, that depends on your point of view. "A short time later," Phelan continues, "Michael Apted was hired to direct the piece. All the way through development Warner Bros. kept very tight reins on us. The three of us—Apted, Glimcher, and I—met to discuss changes for another draft of the script, but at the same time I was having story meetings with Peter Guber for almost seventeen hours at his house, and wrote yet another draft based on his suggestions. This is now the fourth draft of the script I'm doing.

"Universal's notes on the script were always positive: 'We think the script is fine. Maybe you need a little tension here, and there,' and that would be it.

"It was much different with Warners. They gave me a lot of notes, ten to twelve pages long, single-spaced, detailing little things, like don't have her cough so much. I had no idea who wrote these notes. They came from a source called the 'Creative Group.' As a matter of fact, I had one particular story meeting where nine executives were in attendance."

This raises a very interesting question. When a writer is commissioned to write a screenplay, that is, the project is placed in development, what is the relationship between the studio executives and the writer?

Jean Renoir, my mentor, the late great French film director, once remarked that a movie could never be considered an art, in the classical sense, because too many people are involved with it; it becomes a collaborative process. Art, Renoir believed, springs from the individual's view of the world, and can never be achieved by collaboration. The filmmaker is not like a novelist, composer, or painter, because he's dependent upon too many other people, either to contribute ideas or execute his own. Compromise is the only way to get things done. The film may be successful, Renoir believed, even commercial, but it should not be considered art.

That was his point of view. I wanted to see what it looked like from the studio's perspective, so I did some research.

I contacted a former student of mine who worked at Warners and asked him to get me copies of the executives' script notes on *Gorillas in the Mist*.

About a week later he got me the notes. As I read them, I was impressed with their grasp of detail; their grasp of story and context was something else.

I thought it would be the useful to include some of the comments at various stages of Anna Hamilton Phelan's scripts. (She had written fifteen different drafts, she told me.) There were three sets of memos, between ten and thirteen pages of single-spaced notes, with seventy-two specific comments. I sorted through them and selected a few for purposes of illustration.

After Phelan wrote her fourth draft, the "Creative Group" made their first comments, dated November 19, 1986:

1) We like the scene in *Gorillas in the Mist* where Dian chooses Sembagare. We like the humor of his making the sign of the cross when she says "Christ!"

2) We do not understand what motivated Dian. Why was she so driven to study gorillas? We like that she takes the job to escape her marriage once again. However, did she have any more serious academic inclinations than are shown in this draft? Does she have something to prove? Maybe Leakey can ask her directly what her motivations are.

3) We object to the ease with which Dian first makes contact with the gorillas. We prefer the suspense in the "Heaven" draft as Dian makes several journeys into the bush before she even spots the animals. We should have a rooting interest for Dian so that when she succeeds, we should experience her thrill.

4) The first meeting with the gorillas should be highly emotional. But we do not believe that Digit would immediately be interested in her. [page 25. Plot Point I.] We prefer that while experiencing contact with them, we should also experience her disappointment at being unable to get closer to them.

5) We like the treatment of Dian's scientific method in *Gorillas in the Mist*. There are strong scenes with her taking notes on the gorillas' behavior, which validates her study to the audience.

6) Small point - the many references to gorilla packs by *number* in *Gorillas in the Mist* are too confusing. We don't know the packs that well.

7) The relationship between Dian and Campbell should be better developed. It should be a cross between *The Way We Were* [Arthur Laurents] and *The African Queen* [James Agee].

8) Leakey should be better integrated into the story. In neither draft is his influence on Dian clear. What should Dian's response to the idea of tourism be? We like the fact that Dian writes letters to attract attention to her cause.

9) What is the character of the poachers and who are they? They must not be caricatures.

10) The death of Digit is very strong and horrific in *Gorillas in the Mist*. We like the clear-cut effect of Digit's death on Dian. This is where she loses all objectivity and goes on the warpath against the poachers. This is the final straw to culminate a general movement by her pushing people away in favor of the gorillas.

"What the executives at Warners were saying, in effect, was that my first draft was a character study, and they wanted more of an action piece," says Phelan. "So I wrote another draft and finished it in England, working at Shepperton Studios with Michael Apted and Arne Glimcher."

The second memo is dated January 27, 1987. Also from the "Creative Group," it is ten pages, single-spaced, with seventy-one individual comments.

1) This is much improved, but the main thrust will still be Dian and her loves - Digit, Sembagare, and Campbell - and Dian and her adversaries, Deltour, the black poachers, the Rwanda government official.

2) Use shorter opening and try to include some humor.

3) What is her exact mission when she begins? What is its supposed duration?

4) We'd like to add a scene where David, Dian's fiancé, comes to visit her in Africa, just as she has made contact with Digit.

5) Since we will be unable to age Dian, it is crucial that we have a clearer sense of the passage of time. We should see some physical change in the other characters and/or the landscape and/or the camp.

6) Dian's adjustment to jungle life is good - how she rigged up a makeshift shower and struggled to find a hairdo that minimized tangles. This could be an even greater source of humor and can perhaps be interspersed with escalating action.

7) Campbell's departure should be a bigger moment. Dian might even express that his departure signifies the loss of the last thread of her connection to reality, to humankind, so how is she affected by his departure?

8) We like the idea of Dian seeking consolation from Digit after her romance doesn't work.

9) We need to increase the sense of gorillas as an endangered and rare species. We must understand what is so worth preserving about them; and what is worth saving about our own species has to be related to that.

10) We need to establish both Dian's effectiveness as a scientist and that later she passed her time, and had outlived her usefulness, i.e., that she was a pioneer who opened the door for more normal scientists to follow.

11) Dian's death feels tagged on. It needs to be better integrated into the story.

"At this point in the project, Sigourney Weaver came on the film. She had wanted it so badly, she had been turning things down for a year because of it. At this point she became part of the writing process.

"Sigourney wanted to play Dian like she really was; Dian went over there with her guns out and that's the way Sigourney wanted to play it, and that's exactly the way it came through when I saw the dailies. This is the way the part was written, because she's not really a sympathetic character. I heard that Oliver Stone said that he had never read a female character with all the warts out as much as in this script. Sigourney wanted more of that.

"She was wonderful. She had good ideas and I welcomed them. She gave me about six pages of typewritten notes, some of which I tried to incorporate and some of which I had to refuse.

"We're supposed to start production in London in three weeks, and just as I finished this new draft for Sigourney, Arne and I are driving back to the hotel, when he gets a phone call. Suddenly, he goes white. He looks at me, unbelievingly, and says 'Warner Bros. just pulled out.' We were in shock.

"Later we found out why Warners pulled out: the studio thought the budget was too high, and they weren't going to make the picture because of it. I was stunned. Arne was trying to get this thing back on track. He said, all right now, this is what I can do. If I call this person, I can do this, if I call that person I can do that, and so on. And I remember thinking Arne's doing just what Dian Fossey would do. No one was going to tell him he couldn't make this picture.

"So there was a money meeting in New York. I stayed in London and kept writing. All the producers and executives from both studios were there, as well as Michael Apted.

"The budget had to be trimmed. So most of the creative people involved were asked to defer their salaries. Warners owed me about $30,000 when I completed the shooting script. I told them, 'Keep my money, just make the picture.'

"They did both. And when everyone said they would do that, Warners said okay, the picture's a go again.

"After that I got another set of notes from the last draft I had written." Dated May 22, 1987, this memo is eight pages long, single-spaced:

We are very pleased with the improvements made in this draft. They have succeeded in further clarifying the dramatic structure of the story and in heightening the sense of urgency about Dian's mission. We now need to concentrate on the *characters* - in particular, the relationship between Dian and Campbell - the *transitions* from scene to scene (so that the film feels less episodic), and the *ending*. Additionally, we need to see where we can make cuts and trims for *length*.

DIAN/CAMPBELL RELATIONSHIP

We would like more drama and romance between Dian and Campbell. As is, theirs is still not a satisfying, bittersweet love story.

They come together too quickly, and break up too abruptly, and their scenes together are too expository.

When Campbell departs, we should sense that Dian has lost her last chance at meaningful human contact.

Also, there are too many scenes in which Campbell is seen filming Dian. It feels like a device and distances the audience from the action.

TRANSITION/CONNECTION BETWEEN THE SCENES

The transition from one scene to the next often seems to diminish, rather than maximize, the emotional impact. For example, the scene in which the silverback first charges Dian not only feels abrupt and unconnected with the scenes before and after, but the emotions carried forward from the previous scene (in which Sembagare talks about how his family has been killed) distract from the emotional impact of the charge.

ENDING

As the rest of the script has improved, it has become clearer that we have neglected to address the ending sufficiently. As written, it feels anticlimactic and unresolved. We do not want the audience leaving the theater having enjoyed the film, but being disappointed by the ending. Consequently, Dian's murder has to provide a resolution, and a sense of finality, on various levels.

We would like to heighten the sense of destiny and inevitability about Dian's death. Sembagare and Dian seem to foreshadow her death at the Batwa cemetery, but this prophetic theme seems to fade away.

We would like to heighten the sense of Dian's life having come full circle. Just as she was a nonconformist in life, so too in death. And just as she achieved great things through her nonconformist behavior while alive, the unconventional nature of her death will enable great things to be accomplished thereafter.

A FEW SPECIFIC NOTES

1) All the scenes with Dr. Leakey feel too expository.

2) Should Leakey call her the "Gorilla Girl"?

3) There could be more fun with Dian having to choose her bag. There could be a moment when she pauses to make the decision, and then decides that her cosmetic bag is most important to her.

4) Dian's escape needs to be reworked. As written, the escapes are a little too convenient, and contrived, and feel like a grade "B" Zulu movie.

4) "Mt. Karisimbi!", "Mt. Visoke!", "Karisoke Research Center." This dialogue feels a little corny. [As we will see, this was put in at the specific request of the Rwandan government.]

5) It seems strange that Dian and Bob make love straight after she has discovered that he is married.

6) The dynamics of Campbell's departure are not yet clear. We need to understand that when he leaves, she has lost the last thread of her life with human beings. It should be clearer that she is reaching out to him and he cannot help but reject her.

7) Let's be careful that Dian doesn't cough too much - i.e., how irritating it was when Jane Fonda coughed throughout *Julia*.

8) The script is timing out too long (2 hours, 20 minutes). We need to take approximately 10 pages (25–30 minutes) out.

"Very early on the Rwandan government had specified that they wanted approval of the script," Phelan continues, "and after they read it a four-page letter came back saying, in effect, that if the screenwriter didn't stop making fun of the Rwandan people she was going to get her feathers clipped! I had described some of the Rwandans as short and compactly built, which they are. But they wanted to be described as tall.

"I had described the Sembagare character as a Watusi, with kingly blood lines, and they would not tolerate that. So a week before shooting I had to write another draft specifically for the Rwandan government."

The script notes from the Rwandan government covered four pages, single-spaced. Here are some of the remarks:

1) Three conflicts are shown in this film. Dian Fossey and the Belgium poacher. Dian Fossey and the Batwa poachers. Dian Fossey and the research students. The three conflicts could lead to her murder. If the screenwriter cannot be democratic enough nor be above preconceived ideas to accept the Rwandan judgment that the conflict between Dian and the researchers had led to her murder, then he should stay neutral. It was agreed during our first contact [a meeting which had taken place in Paris a few months earlier] that the murdering shadow could be gloved and could use an instrument that we cannot assign to the whites (guns), or to the Negroes (machete). Keeping the mystery of Dian Fossey's death would honor the screenwriter, and the director.

2) Under the pretext of historical authenticity, the screenwriter looks at Rwanda with an obstinate colonialist eye. Clichés give an old vision of Africa and the Africans. It is scandalous that at the end of this century an educated man gives the impression we are on a primitive foreign planet, Central Africa, where dancers are primitive, savage and barbaric, and where women cluster around the abandoned luggage of the white woman while the white walks around as the big dominator with more experience than a troop of soldiers, the rapist of white women, and a shady drunk incompetent. Even if the price is a lack of obvious serious intent with no respect for the American public (they don't know anything about these regions, we can tell them whatever we want). If the screenwriter makes fun of the people, he'll lose his feathers!

3) In order to keep good relations with Zaire, maybe we could try not to denigrate its army, not to have Dian taken by the soldiers and raped by rebels.

4) An effort has to be made to visualize Rwanda. The public must realize that the film happens in Rwanda. For example, a few signs and a few words could indicate this: For example, Dian says: ''Look at that, Rwanda is like a mystical, magical kingdom. I love being here.''

5) Did we notice that Dian Fossey after so many years in Rwanda never touched local food? Is it necessary that she stays like a bad graft refusing to integrate? Why give an antipathic meaning to this film?

"After I finished the draft for the Rwandan government," Phelan goes on, "Arne Glimcher gets on a plane and flies to Kigali for approval. It passed, but a few days later we got a wire saying that Kenya had held up the sets at the Rwandan border because they didn't like the Congolese being portrayed in a bad way, because it reflected on all Africans. So I had to do some rewriting to fix that.

"Then, of course, after writing fourteen different drafts of the screenplay, Warners finally says that maybe we should go back to the original draft. It had always been my favorite anyway."

That happens all the time. When there have been six, eight, or ten drafts of a screenplay written, from one writer or several writers, everyone seems to lose sight of what they originally responded to in the beginning. This is what Frances Doel refers to in Chapter 7. What's true in most cases is that the first draft is usually always better than the others. But people in Hollywood believe they are larger than the original material and want to make their contribution to the film. And of course, with so many fingers in the pie, they inevitably end up losing the original integrity of the screenplay, which is what they responded to in the first place. That's just the way it is.

"There were no script problems while shooting in Africa," says Phelan. "But after they finished shooting in Africa and began shooting the interiors in London, they told me the scene where Dian and Sembagare are trimming the Christmas tree did not feel right. Arne Glimcher called me from London saying, 'Get your pencil, we need a new scene. And you only have an hour to do it.'

"I protested and said, 'Arne, I don't know if I can do it in an hour.' He listened politely, then read me the scene as Sigourney Weaver had rewritten it and said, 'What do you think of this?'

"So I said, 'Give me an hour.'

"It was arranged that a secretary from CAA would call me in an hour. I wrote the scene. When the secretary called, I dictated the new scene to her on the phone. She faxed it to London, where the director and actors were waiting. And that's how the tree-trimming scene was done.

"In real life Dian was very worried before she was killed. She knew her life was in danger so she carried a gun with her at all times. The night she was murdered, she got the gun, tried to put a clip in, and couldn't do it. We didn't show that because we didn't want to dwell on her death. We dwelled on her life.

"No one really knows who killed her. The Rwandan government accused and convicted one of her research assistants, but it was a setup and he was able to leave the country before anything happened to him.

"All in all, fifteen drafts of the screenplay were written. The secretaries had them all labeled: the first draft was called the Home Run draft; there was Regency draft, because I did it at the Regency Hotel; we had the Guber draft, the London draft, the Norwalk State Mental Institution draft (because the secretaries were sure that particular draft would put me in the Norwalk State Hospital). We had Sigourney's draft, the Rwandan draft, and finally, the shooting draft. And I did two or three drafts on all those.

"Now, after it's all done, people ask me how I'm still able to stand. It was a tremendous ordeal. The truth is that the Dian Fossey character had gotten so far under my skin that she held me up. I was ornery and stubborn as hell."

Was it worth it? Of course. The story of Dian Fossey has illuminated the plight of these magnificent silverback gorillas and inspired the formation of the Digit Fund dedicated to save and protect these animals from their indiscriminate slaughter and possible demise.

But for the screenwriter it's just another story in the process of development.

18

Douglas Day Stewart

On creating a market: *"There's got to be a better way to
live your life than to take
those special ideas of yours
and smash your head
against a brick wall with them."*

Douglas Day Stewart and I are both members of the Council of Advisors at the University of Southern California Filmic Writing Program. It is the only program in the United States that awards an undergraduate degree, a BFA, in screenwriting.

I had seen *An Officer and a Gentleman* and was impressed by the emotion and depth of the main character, Zack Mayo (Richard Gere); there was also a gritty emotional honesty in his relationship with Paula (Debra Winger), and a very tough no-holds-barred relationship with the drill instructor (Lou Gossett). Certain scenes in that film stayed with me long after I left the theater.

When I first met Douglas Day Stewart at our advisory board meeting, I was impressed with his candor and political savvy. Over the course of the next few meetings, I got to know him a little better, and one day he told me it had taken him seven years to sell the screenplay of *An Officer and a Gentleman*.

I was astonished. Why had it taken so long? I wondered. Made in 1982, the film was extremely successful; Stewart was nominated for an

Academy Award for his screenplay, and Lou Gossett received an Academy Award for his performance as the drill instructor.

When I asked him about it, Stewart said he had written the script in the mid-seventies, and because it dealt with the military it received the same response as Oliver Stone's *Platoon*. Nobody was interested.

If there's one thing I've learned about Douglas Day Stewart, it's that he's as strong and persistent as a bulldog; he trusts his own instincts and will do whatever's necessary to get the job done.

Born in Oklahoma, he received his undergraduate degree at Claremont Men's College and when he graduated, he joined the navy, serving as an officer for three years. After his discharge he went to Northwestern University to receive a master's degree in film. While there, he won the Shubert Playwriting Fellowship, then left for Los Angeles in 1968, seeking fame and fortune. "The only thing those degrees taught me," he says in retrospect, "is all that bad information had to be unlearned."

Once in L.A., he started writing screenplays, and during the next four or five years he wrote nine feature-length scripts that "never saw the light of day." One was a first draft of *Jeremiah Johnson*, which finally ended up with seven different writers doing seven different versions; the final draft is credited to John Milius and Edward Anhalt. Another was a script for a film financed by the Mafia, and yet another was commissioned by a name actor which made the rounds and never got made. During this period, he says, he lived a hand-to-mouth existence, and "I was so tragic economically that my agent wouldn't even take a commission from what I earned as a writer."

After several years of disappointment, a friend advised him to write for television, so he wrote some episodic half-hours, then turned his skills to writing movies of the week; one was called *The Man Who Could Talk to Kids*, starring Peter Boyle; another was *The Boy in the Plastic Bubble*, starring John Travolta, for which he was nominated for an Emmy and a Writers Guild award.

He was dissatisfied with television because "television doesn't go into the character's point of view the way features or novels go into a point of view," he says. "TV has a way of showing you everything through everyone's eyes; basically, it's an omniscient point of view.

"What television taught me," Stewart says, "is specific genres; it taught me the detective genre, the Western genre, the love story genre. And once I learned the particular genre, I was able to take that knowledge into features.

The last thing he did for television was an eight-hour miniseries called *Voices of Guns,* about the life and times of the Symbionese Liberation Army (SLA), which kidnapped Patty Hearst and whose members were killed in a shootout in Los Angeles in the '70s. "It was," he says, "the story of how your next-door neighbor could evolve into a full-blown terrorist. But the show never got off the ground because the networks were afraid of the subject matter.

"Television, for all its talk about truth, is the least truthful medium of all," he says. "They have truth teams at the networks [called Standards and Practices] and their job is to stop anything truly truthful from happening. You have to conform to all the possible legalities inherent in the stories. In the end, the writer's main job is to protect the network from being sued, so you end up with a whitewashed show that only has the lamp of 'safe' reality hanging over it and no passionate truth flowing in its veins."

Is that why he decided to go back to writing features? Yes, he replied. "One night, when I was talking to my agent, I was reminiscing about my navy officer days and these bizarre girls, the 'debs' who date you and make love to you right away, then try and trap you into marriage because you're their ticket out. That's how *An Officer and a Gentleman* surfaced," he says. "He got very excited about the idea, and encouraged me to pitch it to some people around town.

"So we set up several meetings and I tried to develop the story during those pitch sessions. I ran into a lot of problems immediately because of the military aspect. Even though this was the 70s, there was such a negative reaction to the military that no one really thought there was anything commercial in a military story. Just about that time *Private Benjamin* (Nancy Meyers and Charles Shryer) came out, and that opened everyone's eyes to the fact that the military wasn't a forbidden subject. That gave us some hope, but still nobody was really buying.

"I pitched it to Universal, and they didn't want it. I pitched it to a couple of other studios and they didn't want it either, and then I realized I was going to pitch myself right out of a market if I wasn't careful.

"So I went back to Frank Brill, a friend who had gotten me my first television job, and asked him what I should do. I told him the story; he liked it and set up a meeting for me to pitch the story to Jerry Weintraub, at that time the business manager for several top music stars, now head of Weintraub Entertainment.

"I convinced him that *An Officer and a Gentleman* would be a great vehicle for John Denver, whom he represented. Of course, I was lying through my teeth when I said it because I knew I was going to write a very profane, edgy kind of story about a loser who wants to be a navy officer, and it just didn't fit John Denver's white-bread image. But I'd gotten turned down by three studios already, and I didn't know who was going to buy it. I was convinced this was the screenplay I had to write. Weintraub liked it and ended up financing the script.

"Before I could begin writing, I had to do some research; I felt it was imperative to go to Pensacola and spend time with the drill instructors and the candidates. It had been a long time since I'd gone through the program, and I needed to update my perspective.

"When I came back I started writing. It took me a year to finish the screenplay because I only did about five drafts of the script; usually I do more. When I completed it, I knew and they knew it wasn't a John Denver script at all; after Weintraub and his people read it, it was a dead project.

"For me," he continues, "*An Officer and a Gentleman* was much harder to sell than it was to write. There was just no market for it; Weintraub put it into turnaround and the rights reverted back to me so my agent and I had to try and create some kind of a market for it.

"Nobody wanted it. Every single studio in town passed on it. People liked it; they liked the writing, but they had a variety of reasons why they weren't interested in buying it. Most of them said the military's a turnoff; some said we don't like the characters, they were too real, or too pretty, or they have sex on the first date. It was a joke. But the worst was when someone said it was a TV movie. Either it was too much of a gritty yarn, or it was a TV movie. I couldn't believe it. It just really goes to show you that no one knows what in the hell is going on.

"Finally, after going from place to place, only one person showed some interest in the story, and that was Don Simpson at Paramount. We had a meeting and we saw eye to eye on the story; Don especially understood that macho, *mano a mano* side of the story between the drill instructor and the Richard Gere character.

"He liked it, but when it came to making a deal, that was another story. Because *An Officer and a Gentleman* was taking so long to get off the ground, I was doing other projects at the same time. One of those was *The Blue Lagoon* for Randal Kleiser [*Grease*.] We had done *The Boy in the Plastic Bubble* together, and we liked each other, so he asked me to do *The Blue Lagoon*. We went around trying to sell this old book that Randal was so in love with; I had to sit there in meeting after meeting, trying to romance it and breathe some sexuality into it. We went everywhere with it. Randal and I used to joke about how many bottles of Dom Perignon we opened to celebrate getting the movie made, only to find out a few weeks later that the studio had dropped the project and we were out on the street again. It seems every project I've been associated with has required the kind of salesmanship that would make my life insurance salesman father proud!

"In the end, it was my agent, Martin Caan, at the William Morris Agency, who was instrumental in getting *An Officer and a Gentleman* made. He wouldn't let anyone at the Morris office forget about it; he got the script to everyone and insisted they read it. He was so in love with the project and had such a strong belief in it that he just wasn't going to let it die.

"Randal Kleiser finally managed to get *The Blue Lagoon* made, and I was with him in Fiji, shooting, when I got a call from my agent in L.A. I'm on this old hand-crank, wind-up telephone, and he tells me he can't make a deal for *An Officer and a Gentleman;* because it was in turnaround, Jerry Weintraub had to be paid off, and the deal Paramount wanted to make required me to give up some of my points to Weintraub. He told me in no uncertain terms that Paramount liked the project but they weren't about to give up any of *their* points to make this movie. If anyone's going to give up points, it's got to be me. And since I've only got basic writer's points, five percent of the producer's net, I didn't know what to do. I wanted to make the deal but I didn't want to give up my points.

"My agent says there's only one other nibble and that's from Lorimar. He told me he doesn't think they'll make the movie because they weren't set up to do any feature films at that time. But a producer there, Marty Elfand, liked the script very much, and he thinks we should sell it to Lorimar.

"Even though I knew Lorimar would not be able to make the movie, I knew selling it to them would make Paramount want it even more. That's what makes this town function; if you say no, they want what you've got even more.

"So we sold it to Lorimar, and Marty Elfand became the producer. He was a major help, a stabilizing force on the project, everything a good producer should be. That move forced Paramount to make a deal with Lorimar.

"What was so important for me was the fact that an agent and a writer could sit down and create a market for a script even though there wasn't a market!

"The deal was made, and the film became a go project, with Taylor Hackford [*Against All Odds*] signed to direct. I knew I had to protect what I'd written, so I signed on as associate producer. Marty Elfand and I both knew that I could be an asset to the production.

"Since I had been in the military it allowed me an opportunity to set up the technical side of it. As associate producer, it was my job to hire the people who would bring in the realism. So I brought in a drill instructor from Pensacola to show us how to make the officer candidate training exactly what it was. I don't think anyone else would have known the importance of that military accuracy if they hadn't gone through the military. That was important from a producing standpoint, and essential in terms of protecting the screenplay.

"During the shooting of the movie, everybody seemed to lose sight of the fact that *An Officer and a Gentleman* is a love story. What everyone liked about it was the tough edge between the Lou Gossett character and Zack Mayo; but I knew the whole movie revolved around that one scene at the end when Richard Gere carries Debra Winger out of the factory.

"I understood it on a romantic level because I'm *the* most romantic human being on the face of the planet, and a lot of people think I'm corny because of that, but it works. It works because the audiences are just as starved for romance as I am. And I'm the first to admit it isn't reality. We're tapping into a prettier sunset here, and I don't want any other person's point of view to interfere with my ability to deliver that sunset. That's what I had to protect.

"When they first started shooting they wanted to do it without the ending, without him carrying her out of the factory. The studio said, 'No, no, that's too corny.' In reality, they had a point, because it looked corny; all those women applauding. They didn't even want to shoot it. I walked on the set the day they were going to shoot, and they were not going to have Zack carry her out. The women were not going to applaud. They were just going to walk out; low key.

"I literally begged them to do just one take. Have those flashes of uniform seen moving through the equipment; have at least one chance at romance.

"When they tested the film they tried it two ways; one screening had Zack driving off on his motorcycle, and in the other he went to the factory and carried her out. It was obvious the audiences preferred Richard Gere carrying her out. So we kept it in.

"That wasn't the only battle we engaged in. The studio didn't want us to film the opening Philippine sequence; even though Taylor Hackford believed in it, he was powerless to get it. To film the opening would have cost a quarter of a million dollars, and everyone said, 'We don't need it, we've got a great movie; we'll just open with him coming to school on his motorcycle.'

"And I said, 'Yeah, Clint Eastwood, the man with no name?'

"But that's not what I write about; I write about character, and I portray an understanding of military brats, and the men who sired them. When I was in the navy, the enlisted men who worked for me were the craziest, wildest human beings I'd ever encountered. They had children in every port.

"That's what Zack Mayo's father was all about. And you had to see that, you had to *see* his life among the Filipino prostitutes, because that's what this kid was raised on, what he was suckled on. That's how his vision of women emerged, and all that had to be seen.

"I don't think anyone really understood that until I walked into Don Simpson's office and explained that this was a movie about the evolution of Zack Mayo. It was not the *mano a mano* struggle with the drill instructor. This boy had to become an officer *and* a gentleman. And to do that he's got to come out of the slime. So we've got to see the slime.

"To his credit, Simpson backed that quarter-of-a-million-dollar decision. He put his career on the line because he was getting a lot of flack not to do it.

"It's those day-to-day decisions that the writer is usually not privy to that can ultimately shape the style and tone of a film. I've often asked myself what would have happened if I had not been on the set. For example, one night Richard Gere mentioned that he thought Lou Gossett was altering the balance of conflict between the two characters. There was supposed to be a big confrontation scene between them the next day that led to the fight in the old gymnasium. And Lou Gossett wanted his character to fall into a nicer pattern; he wanted to say, 'Well, son, tell me what the problem is. What's on your mind?' But the line in the script was 'Looky, looky what we got here.'

"The way Lou wanted to do it was good, but it wasn't right within the context of the character or the story. This guy's supposed to be crazy, he wants the fight as bad as Zack does. He misses wartime. This is as close as he's ever going to get to war, and he wants to kick Zack's ass.

"So with that bloody lip he says 'Looky, looky what we got here'; it's a whole different movie from 'Tell me your problems, son.'

"So we were able to keep those character lines right on course." He paused for a moment, then recalled, "When I was writing *An Officer and a Gentleman,* I made the decision that if this movie doesn't get made, I was going to leave the business. And during the seven years it took I reached this point where I said to myself that maybe I missed the bus; I began to think that movies are not for people like me, not for someone who has an individualistic voice.

"I felt I had done something that was as commercial as I knew how to be, and at the same time it was a personal story based on things I really knew and cared about. There's got to be a better way to live your life than to take those special ideas of yours and smash your head against a brick wall with them, against people who want you to fit a certain format all the time.''

What Doug Stewart was saying is applicable to everyone. All the way through this book, the people who buy and sell in Hollywood are saying the same thing. What moves you, as a writer, is what moves them. And when you have the faith and belief in who you are and what you're doing, you will attract success.

What it takes is simple: patience, persistence, and determination.

After the success of *An Officer and a Gentleman* Stewart wrote and directed an original screenplay titled *Thief of Hearts,* starring Stephen Bauer and Barbara Williams. The story, about a thief who breaks into a woman's apartment and steals her secret diary, then sets out to steal her heart, is an extraordinary premise for a screenplay.

"From the beginning everyone fell in love with the premise," Stewart says, "but it was hard for me as a writer to live up to the challenge of the premise. From the very beginning it was a story in search of a point of view. It took almost twenty-two drafts to figure out how to approach it. Is it the wife's story? The husband's story? Or the thief's story? I didn't know, and I needed all those drafts to figure out what I was really trying to say.

"Everything in storytelling is a point of view. That's why a television story, with its omniscient point of view, washes out. What makes good storytelling is what novelists learned a long time ago: you have to get right into that very, very specific vision of the main character.

"Whose story is it? Whose eyes should it be seen through? That's the question that has to be answered, because that's what makes it fresh and different and unique.

"But point of view doesn't come out of a vacuum. You have to work your way around the story, trying to analyze it from a different point of view each time. That's why it took me twenty-two drafts on *Thief of Hearts*. I thought it was the wife's story through seven of those drafts. It looked like the thief's story through seven of those drafts, and it looked like the husband's story through seven of those drafts.''

I paused, wondering if I heard him correctly. Did he say he wrote different drafts of the screenplay through the eyes of different characters?

I had never heard that before. I know writers do it with specific scenes, to find the thread, or purpose, of the scene. But Stewart was saying something else: he wrote entire drafts of his screenplay, from start to finish, through the eyes of different characters. That means in the first words-on-paper draft he wrote it from beginning to end through the eyes of one main character. Then he went and wrote another draft through the eyes of another character. Then he went through and wrote it again, through the eyes of a third character.

Point of view is defined as "the way a character sees, or views, the world." It is usually a belief system: believing in God is a point of view; not believing in God is a point of view. Being a vegetarian is a point of view; believing, like the Native Americans, that the earth is a living being, and all the living things on it are part of it, is a point of view. Believing that what we do to the earth will not injure it is a point of view. And believing that we must start to protect our earth from global warming, the destruction of the Amazon rain forests, and the destruction of the ozone layer are also points of view.

I wondered if I had ever done that in any of the scripts I had written. Then I remembered an original script I had been commissioned to write, a western about Cole Younger and Jesse James, called *Legend at Dead-End Junction*. Originally it had been Cole Younger's story, but as Jesse and Frank James became more and more involved in the story line, I began to see that I had to go deeper into the relationship between Cole Younger and Frank James.

So I wrote one draft through the eyes of Frank James, Jesse's older brother, a freewheeling, spirited, Bible-spouting idealist, and that "exercise" provided me with the insight I needed to deal with their relationship: they were like brothers. If I had not done the "Frank James" draft, I would not have discovered the binding friendship between the two men.

In my seven-week screenwriting workshops, people come in with the idea of writing a love story, or a relationship story, or a story about a failing marriage, and the first question I ask them is, Whose story is it? And most of the time they don't know.

One of my students, a twin, was writing a screenplay about twins. And she was writing it through their point of view. But I kept asking her, Whose story is it? She kept saying it's the twins' story. And I kept pressing her, saying it can't be both their stories, otherwise why write about twins?

Translating this into the point of view of character requires the same process. *Big Business,* with Bette Midler and Lily Tomlin, focuses on one of the Bette Midler twins as the main character. *Dead Ringer* (David Cronenberg) expresses the point of view of one of the brothers (both played by Jeremy Irons).

In *Twins* (William Davies & William Osborne and Timothy Harris & Herschel Weingrod), in which the twins (Danny DeVito and Arnold Schwarzenegger) are ill matched both physically and mentally, the point of view is easy to distinguish. But if you're writing a story about twins who look, act, and think alike, there's no conflict; without conflict you have no character; without character you have no action; without action you have no story; and without story you have no screenplay. So whose story is it?

One of the reasons *Thief of Hearts* didn't work for me is that I didn't know whose story it was. Like Larry Kasdan's *Silverado,* it lacked a definite and specific point of view.

Stewart's new film is called *Listen to Me.* "It was a script I worked on for two years," he says. "The inspiration was a personal background in debating, coupled with the memory of something that happened when I was in college. The campus superstar had been killed in an automobile accident, and I started thinking about what that meant to the lives of the people who were tied in with him. So I created this story about freshman debaters who hook up with a senior who's very much like a James Dean character; he's perfect, their idol, everything they dream of being. Yet when the superstar meets them, and sees their real down-to-earth values, he realizes they represent everything he's missed in his own life, and he wishes, in a way, that he could be them. That creates a symbiosis of these three main characters going through a debating season."

Since Douglas Day Stewart and I are both involved with college writers, I asked him what he thought new writers could learn from his experience. He thought about that for a few moments. Then he said, "It's important to remember that there are people who can make your dreams possible in Hollywood. But you have to find them, and then you have to be willing to be a lot of things that other writers are not. Sometimes you'll hear stories about writers who are suddenly 'discovered,' and it seems their whole future is laid out in front of them. And deep down in your heart you may think they're the lucky ones, because they had someone to sell their material and promoted them, whereas you might have to promote yourself, sell yourself, either pulling tricks or using Machiavellian wile in order to realize your goals. But the opportunity is there; all you need is faith, discipline, and the willingness to work hard and learn your craft.

"To imagine that at some distant point in your career you'll hit some level of success when things will start to go smoothly is the biggest joke of all. Because it's just as hard, or even harder, every time you go out into the marketplace as it was when you were unknown and struggling."

"Being is intelligible only in terms of becoming," says the poet T. S. Eliot.

19

William Kelley,
Earl Wallace

On the art of screenwriting: *"Finding places where silence
serves better than words."*

Witness is one of my favorite teaching films; I use it in seminars and
workshops everywhere, from L.A. to New York, Oslo to Toronto, Rio de
Janeiro to Berlin, Copenhagen to San Francisco; it is an excellent screenplay, a study of interesting characters in difficult situations, a strong
sense of action and great visuals.

Written by William Kelley and Earl Wallace, from a story by William
Kelley, Earl Wallace, and Pamela Wallace, *Witness* won an Academy
award for best original screenplay.

The film, directed by the Australian Peter Weir (*The Last Wave,
Picnic at Hanging Rock, Gallipoli*), stars Harrison Ford and Kelly
McGillis. The story, about a young Amish boy who witnesses the murder
of an undercover cop, is a study in contrasts; when the detective in
charge learns the killers are crooked cops, he must flee for his life,
and returns the boy and his mother to their Amish home. While recup-
erating from his wounds, he falls in love with the boy's mother, and
when the killer cops come to get him, there is a shootout and he brings
them to justice.

What drives this film forward from beginning to end is what I term a
"contradiction of image." The movie opens with a lyrical sequence of
rolling fields as we see a few Amish men and women on their way to a

farmhouse. We feel we are in another place, another time; then we see the title "1984; Lancaster County."

Already there is a "contradiction of image." We cut inside the farmhouse, and a funeral is taking place. The young widow (Kelly McGillis), her young son (Lukas Haas), and Eli, the grandfather (Jan Rubes) are mourning, the relationships are established immediately, in silence and only a few words of dialogue. It is screenwriting at its best.

By page 8, Rachel (Kelly McGillis) and her son are on the train for Baltimore, but there's a three-hour wait in Philadelphia, and we enter the twentieth century through the eyes of the Amish.

When I first started teaching *Witness,* I thought the screenplay *should* have opened with them in Philadelphia at the train station. I thought the death and funeral of Rachel's husband should have been the backstory (an incident, episode, or event that occurs just prior to the story beginning).

As I thought about it, I remembered the opening of Aleksandr Solzhenitsyn's great book *Cancer Ward*. In the first chapter we learn the character has been diagnosed as having cancer and is leaving his job in Moscow to enter the hospital. In the second chapter he is admitted to the hospital and we see what he sees, experiences what he experiences. In the third chapter we meet the other characters: patients, family, and doctors. At the time I read it, I couldn't understand why Solzhenitsyn began the novel with the main character in Moscow. If I were writing it, I said to myself, I would have opened it when he was already in the cancer ward.

Only when I finished the book did I understand why he began it the way he did; we had to enter the hospital through the eyes of the main character; we had to go from his life in Moscow as a government official to his life as a patient. That means we experience his entrance to a new life crisis at the same time he does; reader and character move together through the point of view and emotional parameters of the story line.

Isn't that what happens to us if *we* get sick? *We* have to go to the doctors, undergo the grueling, humiliating tests, wait for the results, accept the diagnosis, then undergo therapy and rehabilitation.

In *Witness* we have to enter the twentieth century through the eyes of the Amish in order to meet John Book (Harrison Ford) the way Rachel does. We end with a clash of cultures and a reevaluation of values, much as in *Cancer Ward*.

On page 10 the murder occurs in the bathroom at the Philadelphia train station; John Book arrives, and the story gets under way. He explains to the young boy that the man who was murdered was an undercover policeman and "it's my job to find out what happened." That's where the story kicks in.

William Kelley and Earl Wallace were established television writers on *Gunsmoke* and *How the West Was Won* and I conducted my interviews with each of them several months apart.

William Kelley went to Villanova University, received his degree from Brown, then went to the Harvard Law School and the Harvard Grad School. Before becoming a writer he served in both the marines and the air force. He has more than 175 credits on TV shows and movies of the week. While writing for *Gunsmoke* he met Earl Wallace, then the story editor.

Earl Wallace worked for UPI as a reporter before he got a break writing for *Gunsmoke*. He has written for several television shows and recently worked on the prestigious *War and Remembrance* miniseries.

It was hard pinning Bill Kelley down because he'd been traveling so much. We finally met one day in the conference room at the USC Film School where we were both attending a meeting of the Filmic Writing Program. I asked him how the story of *Witness* came into being.

"When I was writing for *Gunsmoke*," he began, "I came up with a 'get Matt out of town' story, about a man who has been impressed [drafted] into duty in the Confederate Army, deserts, goes west, and gets involved with an Amish type community. I had researched the Amish for a two-hour television movie for ABC by going back to Lancaster, Pennsylvania, a few years earlier, and when I came back, I wrote the script; it never got made because the producer, Steve Gentry [then Barry Diller's assistant at ABC] crashed his airplane into a mountain near Santa Barbara and was killed.

"*Gunsmoke* was canceled before they could do the story, but Earl Wallace, the story editor at *Gunsmoke* at the time, had gone over to *How the West Was Won,* and he took the story with him. They filmed it, and it bears a remarkable similarity to *Witness*.

"During the Writers Guild strike in the early '80s, Earl called me from

Fresno, where he was living with his then wife, Pamela, and he told me they had taken my story and were modernizing it. They had a Philadelphia cop getting involved with an Amish woman.

"I liked what I heard and Earl mailed the first ten pages to me. I loved them. He asked if I would collaborate in writing the screenplay, and I said yes, and we roared into it and did the first draft together."

"Before that," explains Earl Wallace, "we had taken a house in Pacific Palisades for the summer, and Pamela, a romance novelist, found some books in the library about the Amish. She started thumbing through them, found them interesting, and then started asking, 'What would happen if a tough cop fell in love with an Amish woman?' I saw that Pamela had hit upon something; I didn't know exactly what it was, but I knew that simple idea carried a lot of freight with it: it was the clash of cultures, the clash of urban versus rural, the clash of contemporary life versus our traditional Western heritage. I knew if you could make that work, the subtext would be implicit.

"I always knew this should be a classic gunfighter love story," Wallace continues. "Picture Gary Cooper riding into a corrupt town, or Alan Ladd in *Shane* riding into a situation where everything's going to hell, and he cleans it up, but can't stay. If you can make that work, that's a good story.

"When you're talking about the classic Western gunfighter, you're talking about a man with a profound set of ethics, of right and wrong. I perceived the John Book character [Harrison Ford] as experiencing moral outrage when his undercover protégé is killed. His rage was so powerful, he could pick up this Amish woman and throw her and her son into the car and say, 'You're going to come with me and we're going to find that son of a bitch.' Nothing's going to stand in his way; he is ultimately the moral man.

"But if you go back to the premise, you say to yourself a city cop falls in love with an Amish woman. Okay, so what? There's a lot of different cops. What kind of cop are we going to pick here? Is he a beat cop? A vice detective? Is he in administration? What kind of a cop is he? Where could we place him in the cop structure that would enhance the impulses and actions of this ultimately moral man?

"Internal affairs," says Wallace, answering his own question, "because if you want an ethical world, you have to keep the people enforcing those ethical standards absolutely straight. And if a man is betrayed by the people he trusts, his underpinnings would be knocked out from under him. He would lose his anchor.

"Basically, I perceived John Book functioning in the Philadelphia police department as having all the impulses of an Amish man. He could fit into that world. That's what anchored him. On that level, he had the values that connected him with that place. If you look at it that way, when he goes to the Amish it's like he's really come home; he doesn't realize it, of course; everything's strange, they milk cows, they don't have phones or refrigerators, but there's something else there for him, something spiritual, an ethical environment he's perfectly in tune with, even though it takes a while for him to realize it.

"That's why the original title was *Called Home*. It's the phrase the Amish use for dying; the notion that you're in this world to get to the other world; so when you're 'called home,' that's a happy experience.

"Of course, everyone hated the title. You can see why. Suppose you want to go to a movie tonight; you call up a friend and say 'Let's go to the movies.' 'What do you want to see?' he says. 'Let's go see the movie *Called Home*.' 'It's called *Home*?' 'No, the movie is *Called Home*.' You can see the problems; it's like who's on first. They finally changed it to *Witness*."

It was the perfect choice.

How do two writers who have worked so long on their own collaborate? After Kelley and Wallace agreed on the story line, "I'd take a chunk," says Kelley, "and go off and do it, and then Earl would take a big chunk and do it, then each would edit what the other had written. We finally got to a point where we sat down and did a whole draft at Earl's house over one long, long weekend."

The way *Witness* evolved, with one writer knowing the Amish and the other knowing the cop, poses another question: How did they manage to work together to make the screenplay a unified whole, in terms of vision, point of view, style, character, and dialogue? So I asked Bill Kelley how he approached creating the character of John Book.

"I could tell early on that Earl just saw the character and that was that," says Bill Kelley. "Because I wrote most of the Amish stuff, and

Earl wrote the Philadelphia stuff, I had to know a lot about John Book. 'Who was John Book?' That's a question I had to ask myself all the time. Who was his father? Where did he come from? I had to know the character to write that. So I made up cards on all the characters while I was working on my part of the screenplay, but John Book really came right out of Earl's psyche, and when I'd ask him a specific question like how long he'd been a cop, he'd say, 'How the hell do I know?' But I had to know; I even knew his birth sign: Leo.''

From beginning to end it is a film that works on all levels. ''The toughest thing was finding the right ending,'' says Wallace, ''because the story was moving along and driving in a particular direction. We went through any number of endings, and it wasn't until much later, after we had a start date, that Peter Weir did his own action ending.''

The ending of *Witness* is an action-filled, dramatic shootout that resolves the story line. The shootout is the entire Third Act, from the time John Book and Rachel embrace the night before he's going to leave (plot point II) to the point where Book leaves in his sister's blue car as Daniel walks into frame heading toward the farm. It is effective both dramatically and cinematically. Though changed slightly from the ending as originally written, it still resolves all the major story points.

The lyrical opening also came about in an interesting manner. Superbly directed by Weir, photographed beautifully by John Seal, the sequence establishes a mood and a feeling that grabs you immediately.

When I asked Kelley about the opening, he replied that he ''was driving in Lancaster County, and there was a slight rain falling, and I saw an Amish cemetery on a hill; an Amish man was standing at the foot of a new grave. He knelt, then stretched himself out full-length, belly-down on the grave, and stayed quite a while in that prone position. Then he got up, brushed off the mud—not too carefully—got back into his buggy, and drove off.

''So I went to the grave, and written on the headstone was 'To my darling Susanna,' who had apparently died six months earlier at the age of thirty-six.

''The Amish are a passionate people; they've got nothing against sex within marriage, and they truly love. The scene was so touching, but we couldn't use it; I don't even know if I would have used it because it was so different, so sentimental.''

That scene did become part of the opening, however. Kelley and Wallace wanted to open with a funeral, and Wallace recalls that ''when I was back there, I was watching buggies come up the road and the people all dressed in black, and an image started to form in my head; I saw these snow fields in wintertime, and a buggy going up a snow field, followed by two buggies, then three, and then you discover there's a funeral going on. I don't know why it seemed right to me, but it seemed a good way to open the script.

''It was that notion of a stark beginning in the dead of winter that would turn into spring during the course of the picture. That, of course, went by the boards when they finally started shooting, but that was the intention of that sequence. You're always looking for the true beginning of a movie, and there's a point when you're establishing things and then all of a sudden the movie begins; and that happens when John Book arrives in Amishland.''

Kelley and Wallace finished their first draft in about three months, then sent it to director Mark Rydell (*The Rose, On Golden Pond*). Rydell loved it, but because he was finishing *The River* it would be almost nine months before he managed to set up a meeting with the two writers at United Artists. They passed.

Then they sent the script to John Avildsen (*Rocky, Serpico, Saturday Night Fever*) in New York, and he liked it, but wanted certain changes done before he committed; after the rewrite was complete, both writers knew he was not the director for the project. Seven months had passed.

At that point they sent the script to Ed Feldman, the producer of *Save the Tiger, Golden Child, The Other Side of the Mountain,* and *Wired,* to name a few, and president of Filmways (now Orion) during the '70s. ''Ed is a moviemaker,'' says Kelley. (Feldman plays a small part in the film, as the tour guide who tells the tourists to be careful about taking pictures of the Amish because they're touchy. When a tourist lady approaches Book and asks if he minds having a photograph taken of him, he says, ''Lady, you take a picture of me and I'll rip your brassiere off and strangle you with it.'' Feldman is the man in the background, wearing bermuda shorts and blue hat.)

Feldman loved the script, and to show them his ''good faith'' in the project, he put up $20,000 of his own money to option the screenplay. At this point it had been almost two years since they finished their first draft and sent it to director Mark Rydell.

Because Feldman had a deal at Fox, he was obliged to give them the right of first refusal. They liked it but suggested some changes, which Kelley and Wallace reluctantly made. Then he resubmitted it to Fox, and they passed. Twice.

Feldman then sent the script to Paramount. Jeffrey Katzenberg (now head of production at Disney), and David Kirkpatrick (now head of production at Touchtone Pictures at Disney), were both enthusiastic about it, and wanted to bring in a director. They talked to several directors, but both writers and producer knew they weren't right for the project.

They waited. After a couple of months Bill Kelley received a call from Ed Feldman, who asked what he thought of Peter Weir, the Australian director. He explained that the production of *Mosquito Coast* had just collapsed, and there was a possibility he could get both Peter Weir and Harrison Ford for *Witness*. When Feldman presented the script to them, both Weir and Ford committed immediately. ''So we had a deal with Paramount in nothing flat,'' says Kelley.

How long did it actually take to get the deal on *Witness*? From inception of the script to start date for the movie? ''Four years,'' Bill Kelley replied. ''And if you look at it another way,'' he continues, ''from the time of my original idea for *Gunsmoke* until the film actually got made, it took almost twenty years.''

William Goldman, in his book *Adventures in the Screen Trade,* talks about writing two drafts of the screenplay; the selling draft and the shooting script. It's one thing to sell the screenplay. But when you get a director and stars, things change: dialogue, scenes, and ego all come into play and the script has to be modified to accommodate everybody.

When Weir and Harrison Ford got together it was only natural that they talked about some changes; and once those changes were set, it was Weir who sat down and rewrote the script. The writers heard about it, and when Weir called Feldman he told him he was just renumbering it. "When we met Peter in L.A.," says Kelley, "he wanted some things changed, some of them for the better as far as I was concerned.

"So it was changed. Then, when we were supposed to be on location for a couple of weeks to do the changes that were needed, Weir called Feldman and said, 'Don't send the writers back, we don't need them.' As soon as the producer heard that, he said, 'I'm sorry, they're already on their way.' Then he called me and said, 'Can you get on a plane right away?' I said, 'Hell, yes.'

"So we got the next plane out; it was rather the underhanded way that Weir did it that annoyed us. [After Kelley, Wallace, and his ex-wife Pamela received the Academy Award, they publicly chastised the director because "he doesn't know how to work with writers." It caused quite a stir in the community.] We didn't speak to him when we arrived; we just checked into the hotel and set right to work putting the script right back where it was.

"Finally, after we had been there about five days, I ran into Peter in the production office and he said, 'Bill, I think its time we had a talk, don't you?'

"And I said yes. So we argued all day Good Friday, half a day Holy Saturday, and we won eight or nine points, major points. Because Earl had to leave early, I had to finish the barn scene."

The raising-of-the-barn sequence is one of the most lyrically beautiful sequences in American film. It ranks right along with the start of the cattle drive in *Red River,* the shower scene in *Psycho,* and the opening of *Raiders of the Lost Ark.* In tempo, rhythm, and style, the raising of the barn literally builds the relationship between Kelly McGillis and Harrison Ford, and it does it with hardly any dialogue at all. It's great screenwriting.

"I'd seen a barn raising," says Kelley. "It's an inspiring sight, and I learned there are two things an Amish man allows himself to be proud of: his horses, and his ability to walk around on those crossbeams some fifty-five feet in the air, just as if he were an Iroquois on high steel. It's amazing to see them hop around like monkeys up there.

"I saw that sequence as the centerpiece of the idyll, and Earl said, 'Once they move to the barn and start to raise it, let's try to do it without any dialogue at all. Not even a grunt.' Well, we had some grunts, but I knew we had to put a note in the script for the man who scores it that this particular sequence would have to be a virtual symphonette. And Maurice Jarre just did a wonderful job.''

Harrison Ford, before he started working steadily as an actor, was a carpenter. In fact, there are garages built around Beverly Hills that have brass plaques stating, ''This garage was built by Harrison Ford.'' I asked Kelley if they changed that to accommodate Ford, and he replied that the fact that John Book was a carpenter ''was purely a coincidence.''

This ''coincidence'' all comes together in the barn-raising sequence. A sequence, remember, is a series of scenes connected by one single idea with a beginning, middle, and end. Like a wedding, funeral, race, chase, or heist. The barn-raising sequence begins at dawn with the Amish arriving to build the barn. There is a brief interchange between Daniel (Alexander Godunov) and Book, still recovering from his wound; Daniel asks how his gunshot wound is, and Book replies, ''Good.'' ''Ah,'' replies Daniel, ''then maybe you'll be leaving soon,'' and walks away. In that one line, we see Daniel feels threatened in his efforts to court Rachel.

As the barn rises, Book and Daniel work side by side. No matter what their feelings are toward Rachel, both of them enjoy the work and are quick to acknowledge each other's skill. Daniel takes a glass of lemonade, drinks, then looks up at Book and offers him some.

Not one word of dialogue is said, nor is it needed. It is behavior; and that's what good screenwriting is all about: manifesting behavior.

The middle of the sequence occurs when they're having lunch. The men are seated at long tables, with the women serving. Rachel takes a pitcher of lemonade, and despite the glances of Eli, her father-in-law, and some of the women, defiantly pours it in Book's glass. The men stare, especially Daniel, and Rachel stares right back at them. Rachel pours Daniel's glass, then pours for the rest of the table. In that one gesture, that one action, she has deliberately shown her preference for the ''Englishman,'' John Book.

Those few looks, all written in the script, serve to let us know the subtext of the scene. (The subtext of a scene is what is *not* said.) When one of the women mentions it to Rachel, she shrugs if off haughtily.

The end of the sequence is the conclusion of building the barn. At the end of the day, when the men are finished, Rachel takes John Book by the arm and introduces him to two of her friends, a recently married couple. The man extends his hand and tells Book he is "a hotshot." "And when they use the word *hotshot,* they truly mean it," says Bill Kelley.

The scene that follows is one of the most memorable in the movie. Again, it's handled mainly in silence. After the barn raising, Book is sitting on the front porch staring at jolts of lightning crackling through the night sky. Rachel is across the way, bathing herself with a sponge. We see her wash her upper body, her feet. She looks up, sees John Book staring at her, hunger and desire etched across his face. She pauses a moment, then turns, bare-breasted, offering herself to him. He looks at her for a long moment before he finally turns away and leaves.

The next morning he looks for Rachel and finds her collecting eggs in the chicken coop. "Rachel," he says, "if we had made love last night, I would have had to stay. Or you would have had to go." And "that's a Gary Cooper line," says Bill Kelley. It fits right in with the classic Western character. What it does for John Book is to bring home the truth of why he's there; he has a job to do, and for the moment he's been distracted from his dramatic need—to bring the killers to justice.

"Yet if he wanted to stay, this is the one man out of a million who might have been able to make it," says Earl Wallace. "But there's just been too much blood under the bridge and he knows he can't stay."

Bill Kelley told me that when "we were writing this scene, I one time referred to Book as being puritanical, and Earl said no, he's not puritanical. If a hooker comes along he'd take advantage of her like anybody else. And I saw what he meant; Book wasn't puritanical in the sense of fighting against the blue laws, or anything like that. He was an idealist, really, believing that cops should be good people. And I think that's what drives him, and it almost carries over to the sex part as well. He has this high regard for Rachel, and it's hard for him to imagine that he would be acceptable to her.

"Before that scene was written, I asked Earl if John Book had a girlfriend. If he did, how many times has he been in love? And Earl replied that he'd only been in love two or three times in his life."

Which goes back to the scene where Rachel, the boy, and Book are eating a hot dog, and she tells him that his sister (marvelously played by Patti LuPone) says he should have a family of his own, rather than try to be a father to her children, and he's slightly taken back.

This is the first recognition we have of her being the kind of woman who just might leave; later, we pay this off when the two of them are in the barn, and he's trying to get the car started. Suddenly, the radio comes on, playing an "oldie but goody"—"What a Wonderful World This Would Be." Book can't restrain himself. He takes Rachel by the hand and they start dancing. As they dance, we see two things: one, she likes it, and two, they are attracted to each other. As they dance, Book stops, looks intently at her; he leans forward to kiss her, then stops himself, pulls back, and resumes dancing as if nothing had happened. (This is the midpoint of Act II.)

Something has happened. At that point, Eli (Josef Sommer) enters the scene and angrily tells Rachel to get back in the house. "You should be ashamed," he tells her.

"What people saw in *Witness*," Kelley explains, "was really two different cultures, and two different people trying to bridge the gap. It's almost like a synapse, where an electrical current bridges the gap between two nerve cells; there's a coming together, and that's the way it had to be with them. Like sparks jumping between two nerve endings."

That's what it's all about.

Ingmar Bergman, the great Swedish director, when asked why he thinks film is such a powerful medium, replied that film seems to be like poetry because it "strikes you in the heart before it hits you in the head."

In other words, it bypasses the mind, so we respond on an emotional, subconscious level before we analyze it and figure out why it works, or affects us the way it does.

That's what art is. And that's what good screenwriting is all about.

Finding places where silence serves better than words.

20

The Future

The ancient Egyptians were the only civilization, other than our own, to study the giraffe. No other culture has felt that the animal warranted any special scientific or religious significance.

The Egyptians had an involved relationship with the species. Ancient hieroglyphs reveal that the Egyptians used the symbol of the giraffe—the tallest animal in the world, almost two stories high—to communicate the meaning of "the future." Why? Because they were so tall, they could "see into the future."

At a time when the shifting winds of economic pressures sweep through the marketplace, what is the future for today's screenwriter? Never better.

The way we communicate visually is expanding every time we turn on the TV. When asked in an interview what he likes about American television, Stanley Kubrick (who lives in London) replied, "The commercials."

It makes sense. Take a look at the Michelob commercials, some of the Levi 501 ads, or the Pepsi spots, and you see a new visual language evolving. Each cut tells a story, and when you put them together you get a chunk of information to act upon; see this, try that, buy this, whatever. "Make sense out of nonsense," Alvin Sargent says. It's the image that counts.

When we start exploring the possibilities of film and the future of the screenwriter, we have to begin with two basic foundations: craft and technology. Change one and you change the other.

The evolution of film revolves around these two functions. If we expand the technology, like we did in the twenties with the introduction of sound, screenwriters will have to test the limits of the technology to see what it can do; they'll have to write *up* to the medium. When we expand the technology, we have to adapt and elevate our level of craft to meet the new demands.

If you expand the craft and write something that requires new film effects, you're expanding the parameters of technology. That's what *Star Wars* did: computer camera tracking data systems, new special effects, microchip technology, high digital resolution, all have created techniques and applications of special effects undreamed of fifteen years earlier.

If we take a look at the history of the motion picture business we find it's a study in cannibalism. The movie audience was devoured by television, then the network audience for prime-time screenings of feature films was chewed up by cable TV, which in turn has fallen prey to the VCR revolution and the home video market.

In 1988, the videotape rental market grossed more than $5 billion. Within ten years, they expect rentals alone to be anywhere from $15 to $20 billion. Sales of videocassettes last year reached $1.3 billion, and within the next decade will probably leap to $5 or $6 billion.

Now there is pay-per-view, the home entertainment technology that allows you to choose a movie at home at the spur of the moment and be billed later. And it is here, in the home entertainment market, that the future of the screenwriter resides.

The cost of making movies is skyrocketing, and like the cost of real estate, it is not going to come down, it's going to go up. Studios may have to cut their production schedules in half; either that or make movies that cost less, which they can't do.

To survive, the studios will have to make different kinds of films: some low-budget, some high-budget, some spectacles, some controversial, some lighthearted entertainment. There will always be a special kind of movie for the theaters and a special kind of movie for home entertainment.

Stanley Kubrick has switched to making movies on tape, not film; in other words, he's making them for the home entertainment market. If you want to see them you're going to have to rent or buy them. They will not be shown theatrically anywhere in the world.

Stanley Kubrick knows what he's doing.

Steven Spielberg is reported to have received some $75 million from the sale of *E.T.* on video. Even if that figure is exaggerated, it's still a lot of money. Suppose a new Stanley Kubrick film attracts an audience of 4 million homes at $10 a pop. That's $40 million for one screening.

The market for home entertainment, pay-per-view, is just beginning; right now there are only a few sporting events and that's about it. But with the state of technology expanding as rapidly as it is, it's not too difficult to see films playing the home entertainment market. The technology is there; just look at the new microchip computer technology, the High Digital Resolution systems currently in development; add in the modified and expanded use of the Cray computer (the finest computer conceived, specializing in computer graphics and possibly hologram imagery), and you have the foundation of a home entertainment system that is as good as, if not better than, a movie theater.

For some kinds of films, the home entertainment pay-per-view market seems a better alternative than standing in line at a movie theater and paying anywhere from $5 to $7.50 for the privilege of seeing a movie you'll forget as soon as you walk out.

It's not too hard to imagine "a wall" in every home that will be the focus of the home entertainment system. That means you'll have to design the room around *it* and place the technological components in specially concealed places to receive the maxium audio and visual effects.

And what a system it will be: a wall with depth and resolution that is "more real" than reality itself. Sound will be strategically placed to achieve "surround around" sound. There might even be interactive films, where you push a button on a small remote control and create alternative versions of the movie you're viewing. What happens if the main character doesn't go in the house? What if he turns around and gets back in the car and drives away? What happens then? What if he doesn't make the phone call to his friend?

Then there are signs of the imminent prospects of three-dimensional holographic films, or films that are "touchy feelies." It will all be part of the home entertainment center.

If that's the screening facility, then movie producers will have to supply that particular marketplace with product. That means the studios will have produce the movies as well as supply the electronic transmission used to transmit the image for viewing.

That means satellites. It's not inconceivable that the motion picture studios of the future will have their own satellite networks, uplinks, downlinks, and whatever portable hardware they need to supervise their pay-per-view audience. The revenues from this type of programing will probably outgross any normal distribution and exhibition operation now in effect in a much shorter time.

If that's the case, the studios still in existence will not want to spend their operating costs on satellite hardware; it's too expensive and too inefficient. Which means those remaining studios just might pool their resources, like Universal and Warner Bros. did on *Gorillas in the Mist*.

"Fifty percent of something is better than a hundred percent of nothing," is what Fast Eddie Felson (Paul Newman) says in *The Hustler*.

To capture that market they're going to need screenwriters. Because you can't do anything without a script.

The situation facing the studios today seems to be the same as it was in the theater at the turn of the century. New stage productions were at a standstill; there was vaudeville, and the same old one-dimensional comedies, and those stark melodramas that were a holdover from the nineteenth century, all out of step with the emerging times. The first movies came in, "peep shows," but they were nothing but a novelty. The theater did what movies did when TV first came in—created spectacles (3-D, Smellorama, Cinemascope, Panavision, all were created to lure customers away from the TV set and bring them back into the theater).

Theatrical entrepreneur David Belasco in the 1900s knew he had to revitalize the theater and bring something different to the stage. So he created the spectacle, large theatrical productions with animals and clowns and dancing girls performing with the most illustrious theatrical names of the time accompanied by a hundred-piece orchestra.

And what happened? Most plays were thin and one-dimensional, but it was precisely at this time that the American theater spawned its greatest genius, Eugene O'Neill (heavily influenced by Ibsen and Strindberg, of course). And it was O'Neill's plays that led to the theater of revolt, to Odets, Miller, the Group Theater, and all those dynamic plays and players of the twenties and thirties.

Most of the movies produced today are very much like the plays at the turn of the century: slick, comedic, shallow films, forgotten by the time you reach the parking lot. There's no brain food.

But there is hope. As I crisscross the country each year giving lectures and seminars on screenwriting, I see new and interesting screenwriters, along with qualified film technicians, studios, and labs in cities like San Francisco, Seattle, Dallas, Atlanta, Chicago, New York, Vancouver, Toronto, all with high-tech facilities that can make commercially viable films. That means regional filmmakers like the Coen Brothers in Minneapolis (*Blood Simple* and *Raising Arizona*) can make their films at home and only come to Hollywood for financing and distribution.

In the next decade, regional filmmaking centers will be on the rise; that means we're going to see smaller, more personal films. Screenwriters working in the Midwest, the South, the East, can write stories and make their films against local backgrounds and issues, and then come to Hollywood for distribution. Hollywood has already done that for several domestic and international productions; they're called "pickups," and one of the most successful was *Crocodile Dundee*. There will be more.

What about the craft of the screenwriter? How will that be affected by future computer technology? The state of the computer is expanding so rapidly that it might be possible to program your PC with special software that writes in pictures. Remember, a screenplay is a story told in pictures. Suppose you could press ALT L, for example, and a lake comes up on the screen. Press ALT M, and a mountain appears, with a highway in foreground or background, take your pick. Press ALT A, and an automobile comes up, driving next to the lake and mountain. Press CTRL B, and your main character—Bob, Bruce, Barbara, or Belinda—comes up, and as you start writing your scene you can *see* what you're writing. You are writing a story told in pictures. You can change, add, modify, and delete, all at the stroke of a single key. It's not that far away.

But what you write, and how you write it, is another story. For that, you need your own vision, your own point of view, your own feeling, your own passion.

A great being, Swami Muktananda, a Siddha master, once said, "Whatever understanding you have of yourself, that is what you become. You can become anything, because this world exists through the power of feelings. There is nothing fixed about a human being. He is whatever feeling he has about himself. He is what he thinks. A person acts according to his feelings and according to his own understanding."

In other words, whatever you put your mind to, whatever you focus on, whatever you believe, that is what you will become.

Because the future is as you see it.

Index

Guildford College
Learning Resource Centre

Please return on or before the last date shown.
No further issues or renewals if any items are overdue.
"7 Day" loans are **NOT** renewable.

Class: 808. 23 FIE

Title: Selling a Screenplay

Author: FIELD, Syd